D1527452

HISTORICAL DICTIONARIES OF RELIGIONS, PHILOSOPHIES, AND MOVEMENTS
Jon Woronoff, Series Editor

1. *Buddhism,* by Charles S. Prebish, 1993
2. *Mormonism,* by Davis Bitton, 1994. *Out of print. See No. 32.*
3. *Ecumenical Christianity,* by Ans Joachim van der Bent, 1994
4. *Terrorism,* by Sean Anderson and Stephen Sloan, 1995. *Out of print. See No. 41.*
5. *Sikhism,* by W. H. McLeod, 1995. *Out of print. See No. 59.*
6. *Feminism,* by Janet K. Boles and Diane Long Hoeveler, 1995. *Out of print. See No. 52.*
7. *Olympic Movement,* by Ian Buchanan and Bill Mallon, 1995. *Out of print. See No. 39.*
8. *Methodism,* by Charles Yrigoyen Jr. and Susan E. Warrick, 1996. *Out of Print. See No. 57.*
9. *Orthodox Church,* by Michael Prokurat, Alexander Golitzin, and Michael D. Peterson, 1996
10. *Organized Labor,* by James C. Docherty, 1996. *Out of print. See No. 50.*
11. *Civil Rights Movement,* by Ralph E. Luker, 1997
12. *Catholicism,* by William J. Collinge, 1997
13. *Hinduism,* by Bruce M. Sullivan, 1997
14. *North American Environmentalism,* by Edward R. Wells and Alan M. Schwartz, 1997
15. *Welfare State,* by Bent Greve, 1998. *Out of print. See No. 63.*
16. *Socialism,* by James C. Docherty, 1997
17. *Bahá'í Faith,* by Hugh C. Adamson and Philip Hainsworth, 1998
18. *Taoism,* by Julian F. Pas in cooperation with Man Kam Leung, 1998
19. *Judaism,* by Norman Solomon, 1998
20. *Green Movement,* by Elim Papadakis, 1998
21. *Nietzscheanism,* by Carol Diethe, 1999
22. *Gay Liberation Movement,* by Ronald J. Hunt, 1999
23. *Islamic Fundamentalist Movements in the Arab World, Iran, and Turkey,* by Ahmad S. Moussalli, 1999
24. *Reformed Churches,* by Robert Benedetto, Darrell L. Guder, and Donald K. McKim, 1999
25. *Baptists,* by William H. Brackney, 1999
26. *Cooperative Movement,* by Jack Shaffer, 1999
27. *Reformation and Counter-Reformation,* by Hans J. Hillerbrand, 2000
28. *Shakers,* by Holley Gene Duffield, 2000
29. *United States Political Parties,* by Harold F. Bass Jr., 2000
30. *Heidegger's Philosophy,* by Alfred Denker, 2000

31. *Zionism,* by Rafael Medoff and Chaim I. Waxman, 2000
32. *Mormonism,* 2nd ed., by Davis Bitton, 2000
33. *Kierkegaard's Philosophy,* by Julia Watkin, 2001
34. *Hegelian Philosophy,* by John W. Burbidge, 2001
35. *Lutheranism,* by Günther Gassmann in cooperation with Duane H. Larson and Mark W. Oldenburg, 2001
36. *Holiness Movement,* by William Kostlevy, 2001
37. *Islam,* by Ludwig W. Adamec, 2001
38. *Shinto,* by Stuart D. B. Picken, 2002
39. *Olympic Movement,* 2nd ed., by Ian Buchanan and Bill Mallon, 2001. *Out of Print. See No. 61.*
40. *Slavery and Abolition,* by Martin A. Klein, 2002
41. *Terrorism,* 2nd ed., by Sean Anderson and Stephen Sloan, 2002
42. *New Religious Movements,* by George D. Chryssides, 2001
43. *Prophets in Islam and Judaism,* by Scott B. Noegel and Brannon M. Wheeler, 2002
44. *The Friends (Quakers),* by Margery Post Abbott, Mary Ellen Chijioke, Pink Dandelion, and John William Oliver, Jr., 2003
45. *Lesbian Liberation Movement: Still the Rage,* JoAnne Myers, 2003
46. *Descartes and Cartesian Philosophy,* by Roger Ariew, Dennis Des Chene, Douglas M. Jesseph, Tad M. Schmaltz, and Theo Verbeek, 2003
47. *Witchcraft,* by Michael D. Bailey, 2003
48. *Unitarian Universalism,* by Mark W. Harris, 2004
49. *New Age Movements,* by Michael York, 2004
50. *Organized Labor,* 2nd ed., by James C. Docherty, 2004
51. *Utopianism,* by James M. Morris and Andrea L. Kross, 2004
52. *Feminism,* 2nd ed., by Janet K. Boles and Diane Long Hoeveler, 2004
53. *Jainism,* by Kristi L. Wiley, 2004
54. *Wittgenstein's Philosophy,* by Duncan Richter, 2004
55. *Schopenhauer's Philosophy,* by David E. Cartwright, 2005
56. *Seventh-day Adventists,* by Gary Land, 2005
57. *Methodism,* 2nd ed., by Charles Yrigoyen, Jr. and Susan Warrick, 2005
58. *Sufism,* by John Renard, 2005
59. *Sikhism,* 2nd ed., by W. H. McLeod, 2005
60. *Kant and Kantianism,* by Helmut Holzhey and Vilem Mudroch, 2005
61. *Olympic Movement,* 3rd ed., by Bill Mallon with Ian Buchanan, 2006
62. *Anglicanism,* by Colin Buchanan, 2006
63. *Welfare State,* 2nd ed., by Bent Greve, 2006
64. *Feminist Philosophy,* by Catherine Villanueva Gardner, 2006
65. *Logic,* by Harry J. Gensler, 2006

Historical Dictionary of Feminist Philosophy

Catherine Villanueva Gardner

Historical Dictionaries of Religions, Philosophies, and Movements, No. 64

The Scarecrow Press, Inc.
Lanham, Maryland • Toronto • Oxford
2006

SCARECROW PRESS, INC.

Published in the United States of America
by Scarecrow Press, Inc.
A wholly owned subsidiary of
The Rowman & Littlefield Publishing Group, Inc.
4501 Forbes Boulevard, Suite 200, Lanham, Maryland 20706
www.scarecrowpress.com

PO Box 317
Oxford
OX2 9RU, UK

British Library Cataloguing in Publication Information Available

Library of Congress Cataloging-in-Publication Data

Gardner, Catherine Villanueva.
  Historical dictionary of feminist philosophy / Catherine Villanueva Gardner.
    p. cm.— (Historical dictionaries of religions, philosophies, and
  movements; no. 64) Includes bibliographical references.
    ISBN 0-8108-5346-9 (hardcover : alk. paper)
    1. Feminist theory—Dictionaries. 2. Feminist theory—History—
  Dictionaries. I. Title. II. Series.

HQ1190.G36   2006
108.2′03—dc22   2005026561

To L.V.

Contents

Editor's Foreword   *Jon Woronoff*   ix

Preface   xi

Acknowledgments   xv

Chronology   xvii

Introduction   xxiii

THE DICTIONARY   1

Bibliography   235

About the Author   275

Editor's Foreword

Although outsiders may sometimes think that philosophy is one of the less dynamic fields, solidly rooted in the thought of philosophers of earlier days, that is far from the case. Nothing proves this more emphatically than feminist philosophy, a sector which barely existed a few short decades ago and which is steadily growing. Unlike other sectors, it is in some ways narrower, focusing on the situation of women but not by any means restricted to women philosophers. For the moment, most of the activity is limited to North America and Europe, but the boundaries are gradually expanding. In other ways, it is much broader, having something to say about works of many of the canonical philosophers, sometimes approving, sometimes criticizing, and occasionally appropriating. By now feminist philosophy is busy contributing to virtually every other branch of philosophy, whether ethics, epistemology, logic, or language, and also to Marxism, environmentalism, and obviously feminism.

Historical Dictionary of Feminist Philosophy covers a much longer span than merely the past few decades. Indeed, the chronology stretches back to those ancient Greek philosophers who dealt with the relevant issues tangentially, and on to modern philosophers for whom this is the primary concern. The dictionary entries therefore include Aristotle and Plato, and also Descartes and Kant, along with Wollstonecraft, Beauvoir, and Daly among the persons; care, ecofeminism, and racism among the topics; and dualism, femininity, and universalism among the concepts. Since this is still a young field, the introduction is particularly helpful for understanding its origins, progress, and future agenda. Finally, the rather extensive bibliography will be most useful for those who want to know more of the details.

This volume was written by Catherine Villanueva Gardner, whose earlier education was in the United Kingdom at the University of Leicester and University College of Swansea and who received her Ph.D. from the University of Virginia. Since then she has taught at the Department of Philosophy of the University of Michigan, Flint, and then the University of Massachusetts, Dartmouth, where she is presently associate professor. Dr. Gardner's areas of specialization, along with feminist philosophy, include ethics (especially bioethics) and environmental ethics (especially ecofeminism). Among her writings are several articles and the book *Rediscovering Women Philosophers: Philosophical Genre and the Boundaries of Philosophy*. This spread of interests and experiences on both sides of the Atlantic have allowed her to become familiar with many different aspects and activities in two major centers of feminist philosophy, while her experience as a teacher and writer enables her to pass this knowledge along to the expanding circles of potential readers.

Jon Woronoff
Series Editor

Preface

There is no one reader for the *Historical Dictionary of Feminist Philosophy*. The intended audience is broad, ranging from the casual reader who may simply want a specific term explained, to students wanting an introduction to the main ideas and roots of feminist philosophy, to professional philosophers exploring the history and subject matter of feminist philosophy.

The *Historical Dictionary of Feminist Philosophy* covers both the central figures and ideas from the historical tradition of philosophy and the central ideas and theories from contemporary feminist philosophy. The latter area includes topics that have their roots in critical reactions to, and developments of, the mainstream tradition, such as epistemology or the philosophy of science; it also includes topics that have been introduced into the philosophical arena through the feminist movement itself, such as abortion and sexuality. In addition to an account of their subject matter, the entries on contemporary topics often contain a discussion of the origins and development of these topics.

In deciding which figures and topics would fall under the admittedly broad umbrella of feminist philosophy, the aim was to remain as flexible as possible. It would be a mistake to identify feminist philosophy solely with the intellectual activities that go on within the academic departments of institutions of higher learning. Moreover, given that the notions of feminism and feminist philosophy have changed over time, it is important to allow this to be reflected in the selection of entries.

The purpose, however, is not to introduce controversial areas of feminist philosophy, nor to overemphasize areas that are not particularly well established. Moreover, while the feminist political movement played an important role in directing the goals and subject matter of the discipline of feminist philosophy, entries related to feminist theory, and the feminist movement itself, have not dominated the dictionary.

In terms of the entries on particular philosophical figures, the dictionary includes specifically feminist philosophers or proto-feminist philosophers as well as canonical philosophers who have been of interest to feminist philosophy. It leaves out philosophers of either sex who have simply discussed the role of women. Basic biographical background on these individual philosophers is provided, and the commonly used titles for their works are given. There is enough information to introduce a figure to students or readers new to philosophy and to guide them to find further information in other reference works.

Many of the central figures of the philosophical canon—both male and female—have been given separate entries because of the amount of feminist critical work on them. The central male figures from the canon have not been included simply because of their apparent sexism. The series of entries of canonical male philosophers is not a list of history's greatest misogynists; rather, it is a discussion of those who have been given feminist rereadings. Thus this dictionary does not contain an exhaustive list of figures from the philosophical tradition. This approach is reflected in the bibliography, which gives only the secondary feminist work on figures from the philosophical tradition; it does not contain a listing of the primary works of these figures.

In a similar vein, the women philosophers from the history of philosophy who have been given separate entries are either those whose own work qualifies on some level as feminist, or whose work has been the subject of present-day feminist rereading. The retrieval of forgotten women philosophers for present-day examination is a feminist project in itself, but this does not necessarily mean that any female philosopher—by virtue of her sex—is a part of the enterprise of feminist philosophy.

This emphasis on women philosophers means that the chronology varies from more standard chronologies of historical philosophers. Fewer male canonical philosophers are included than is usual; instead, women philosophers, and their major works, are given a prominent place. This format is intended to reflect one of the elements of the feminist philosophical enterprise: canon revision. The criterion for the inclusion of canonical philosophers is whether they are discussed in a particular entry or entries. The central works of these philosophers are listed in the chronology; the commonly used title for each of these works is given.

The omission of dates and places of birth for philosophers in the chronology is due to the fact that, given the relative obscurity of women philosophers, there are sometimes no records of the dates of their birth or death. If these facts are available, they are included in the dictionary itself. The main goal of the chronology is—through the emphasis on pivotal philosophical works—to reflect the intellectual milieux within which feminist philosophers were writing.

There are relatively few full entries covering contemporary individuals. The few who are included, such as Luce Irigaray and Mary Daly, were chosen based on the influence they have had not only on the work of others, but on the developments of feminist philosophy itself. In order to enhance the use of the dictionary as a reference tool, there are also cross-references or brief explanatory entries for contemporary individuals whose work is discussed at length in other entries. The omission of the work of any one individual was not an attempt to judge the inherent value of that work, nor should it be read as such.

Thus the majority of entries on current feminist philosophy tend to be on issues, concepts, and arguments, rather than specific figures or their works. An individual's work that is significant or important in some way has typically become part of the general discourse. Thus the contribution of this work is usually discussed under a particular topic area. Many of the entries on particular ideas and issues include a sense of their changes and developments over time. When these changes and developments can be clearly linked to the work of a specific philosopher, she or he has been identified by name. Even if a philosopher is not identified explicitly by name, it should be noted that the separation of the Bibliography into different subject areas allows for a mode of citation, and thus allows the reader an ease in identifying and locating source materials for each entry.

The issue of whether or not to acknowledge explicitly these specific contributions of individuals by name is a troubling one for a feminist philosopher. On the one hand, there has been a history of the philosophical contributions of women being co-opted or unrecognized. On the other hand, there is a sense that feminist scholarship is a collective enterprise. The contributions of each individual are subsumed into the larger political and intellectual whole. This is not only appropriate for the end of achieving feminist philosophy's political and intellectual goals, but as a means to that end.

Given that much of contemporary feminist philosophy comes out of the Western tradition in some way, the orientation of the dictionary is Western. However, where there is identifiable feminist work being done in other traditions and regions, there are entries covering this work. Also, more weight is given to feminist work coming out of the analytic tradition, rather than the Continental tradition. This is due to the amount of work that has been produced in the former area; the role of the dictionary is to report, rather than to make a case for a particular way of doing philosophy. In the interests of balance, however, the contributions from the Continental tradition have been recognized both as separate entries and within general topic entries.

Feminist philosophical work has been done within all the major subject areas of philosophy, but to varying degrees. There is little feminist work, for example, in logic, whereas the field of feminist ethics has grown to the point where it has generated its own academic societies and conferences. Given the relative newness of feminist philosophy as an academic discipline, it is hard to identify the causes of these variations. It may be that some subject areas are more open to feminist critique and reconstruction, or it may be that some subject areas have been the focus of feminist philosophical study for a longer time than others. Thus there is no standard length for the entries. Some entries may seem relatively short compared to others on perhaps similar or related topics; this simply reflects the different amounts of work produced on these topics.

The last point to note is that there is a certain amount of overlap between some of the entries, usually in entries on subfields within philosophy such as epistemology or philosophy of science. This reflects the integrated nature of feminist philosophy. Despite the variety of approaches, there are some important cohesive aspects. Moreover, it is often typical that feminist philosophical criticism within its subfields follows a common pattern. This reflects a certain commonality of political and philosophical goals among the different feminist philosophical approaches and perspectives: it reflects the feminist philosophical enterprise itself.

Acknowledgments

I would like to thank all of those people who encouraged me while I was working on this project: Luis Villanueva, Mike Bennett, Diane Barense, and Rick Hogan.

I would also like to thank Jon Woronoff, series editor, for his help and patience throughout the process.

Chronology

ca. 500–400 BCE   Early women Pythagoreans: Themistoclea, Theano, Arignote, Myia, and Damo.

399 BCE   Death of Socrates.

ca. 300–100 BCE   Late women Pythagoreans: Aesara of Lucania, Phintys of Sparta, Perictione I, Theano II, and Perictione II.

347 BCE   Death of Plato.

322 BCE   Death of Aristotle.

413–427   Augustine of Hippo writes *On the City of God.*

430   28 August: Death of Augustine of Hippo.

ca. 1141–1151   Hildegard of Bingen works on *Scivias.*

1179   17 September: Death of Hildegard of Bingen.

1259–1264   Thomas Aquinas writes *Summa contra Gentiles.*

1265–1273   Thomas Aquinas writes *Summa Theologica.*

1274   7 March: Death of Thomas Aquinas.

1405   Christine de Pizan writes *The Book of the City of Ladies.*

ca. 1430   Death of Christine de Pizan.

1620   Francis Bacon publishes *Novum Organum.*

1622   Marie le Jars de Gournay publishes *The Equality of Men and Women.*

1626   Marie le Jars de Gournay publishes *Complaints of Women.* **9 April:** Death of Francis Bacon.

1641 René Descartes publishes *Meditations on First Philosophy*.

1645 **13 July:** Death of Marie le Jars de Gournay.

1650 **11 February:** Death of René Descartes.

1651 Thomas Hobbes publishes *Leviathan*.

1659 Anna Maria van Schurman publishes *The Learned Maid; or, Whether a Maid May Be a Scholar* in English.

1666 Margaret Cavendish publishes *Observations upon Experimental Philosophy*.

1670 Benedict (Baruch) de Spinoza publishes *Tractatus Theologico-Politicus*.

1673 Bathsua Pell Makin writes *An Essay to Revive the Antient Education of Gentlewomen, In Religion, Manners, Arts & Tongues*. **15 December:** Death of Margaret Cavendish.

ca. 1675 Death of Bathsua Pell Makin.

1677 **21 February:** Death of Benedict de Spinoza.

1678 Death of Anna Maria van Schurman.

1679 **23 February:** Death of Anne Finch Conway. **4 December**: Death of Thomas Hobbes.

1680 **8 February:** Death of Elisabeth of Bohemia, Princess Palatine.

1690 Anne Finch Conway's *The Principles of the Most Ancient and Modern Philosophy* published posthumously. John Locke publishes *Two Treatises of Government*.

1691 Sor Juana Inés de la Cruz writes *Respuesta*.

1694 Mary Astell publishes part one of *A Serious Proposal to the Ladies for the Advancement of Their True and Greatest Interest*.

1695 Gottfried Leibniz publishes *The New System*. **17 April:** Death of Sor Juana Inés de la Cruz.

1696 Damaris Cudworth Masham publishes *A Discourse Concerning the Love of God*.

1697 Mary Astell publishes part two of *A Serious Proposal to the Ladies for the Advancement of Their True and Greatest Interest.*

1704 **28 October:** Death of John Locke.

1705 Damaris Cudworth Masham publishes *Occasional Thoughts in Reference to a Virtuous or Christian Life.*

1708 **20 April:** Death of Damaris Cudworth Masham.

1716 **14 November:** Death of Gottfried Wilhelm Leibniz.

1731 **9 May:** Death of Mary Astell.

1739 Sophia publishes *Woman Not Inferior to Man or, A Short and Modest Vindication of the Natural Right of the Fair Sex to a Perfect Equality of Power, Dignity, and Esteem.*

1739–1740 David Hume publishes *A Treatise of Human Nature.*

1762 Jean-Jacques Rousseau publishes *The Social Contract.*

1776 **25 August:** Death of David Hume.

1778 **2 July:** Death of Jean-Jacques Rousseau.

1785 Immanuel Kant publishes *The Groundwork of the Metaphysics of Morals.*

1790 Catharine Macaulay publishes *Letters on Education with Observations on Religious and Metaphysical Subjects.* Judith Sargent Murray publishes *On the Equality of the Sexes.*

1791 **22 June:** Death of Catharine Macaulay. Olympe de Gouges writes *Declaration of the Rights of Woman and the Female Citizen.*

1792 Mary Wollstonecraft publishes *A Vindication of the Rights of Woman.*

1793 **4 November:** Olympe de Gouges executed.

1797 **10 September:** Death of Mary Wollstonecraft.

1804 **12 February:** Death of Immanuel Kant.

1807 G. W. F. Hegel publishes *Phenomenology of Mind.*

1820 **6 July:** Death of Judith Sargent Murray.

1825 Anna Doyle Wheeler co-authors *The Appeal of One Half the Human Race, Women, Against the Pretensions of the Other Half, Men* *to Restrain Them in Political and Thence in Civil and Domestic Slavery* with William Thompson.

1831 **14 November:** Death of G. W. F. Hegel.

1848 Death of Anna Doyle Wheeler.

1851 Harriet Taylor writes *The Enfranchisement of Women*.

1858 Death of Harriet Taylor.

1863 John Stuart Mill publishes *Utilitarianism*.

1867 Karl Marx publishes *Das Kapital* (vol. 1).

1869 John Stuart Mill publishes *The Subjection of Women*.

1873 **8 May:** Death of John Stuart Mill.

1875 Antoinette Brown Blackwell publishes *The Sexes Throughout Nature*.

1883 **14 March:** Death of Karl Marx.

1883–1884 Friedrich Nietzsche publishes *Thus Spoke Zarathustra* (parts 1–3).

1884 Friedrich Engels publishes *The Origin of the Family, Private Property, and the State*.

1892 Anna Julia Cooper publishes *A Voice from the South by a Black Woman of the South*.

1895 **5 August:** Death of Friedrich Engels.

1900 **25 August:** Death of Friedrich Nietzsche.

1905 Sigmund Freud publishes *Three Essays on the Theory of Sexuality*.

1911 Charlotte Perkins Gilman publishes *The Man-Made World; or, Our Androcentric Culture*. Emma Goldman publishes *Anarchism and Other Essays*.

1921 **5 November:** Death of Antoinette Brown Blackwell.

1935 **17 August:** Death of Charlotte Perkins Gilman.

1939 **23 September:** Death of Sigmund Freud.

1940 **14 May:** Death of Emma Goldman.

1943 Jean-Paul Sartre publishes *Being and Nothingness.*

1949 Simone de Beauvoir publishes *The Second Sex.*

1951 **29 April:** Death of Ludwig Wittgenstein.

1953 Ludwig Wittgenstein's *Philosophical Investigations* published.

1957 Ayn Rand publishes *Atlas Shrugged.*

1964 **27 February:** Death of Anna Julia Cooper.

1965 Hannah Arendt publishes *Eichmann in Jerusalem: A Report on the Banality of Evil.*

1972 The first academic society for women philosophers, the Society for Women in Philosophy (SWIP), founded in the United States.

1975 **4 December:** Death of Hannah Arendt.

1976 Michel Foucault publishes *The History of Sexuality* (vol. 1).

1980 **15 April:** Death of Jean-Paul Sartre.

1982 **6 March:** Death of Ayn Rand.

1984 **25 June:** Death of Michel Foucault.

1986 **14 April:** Death of Simone de Beauvoir. First issue of *Hypatia: A Journal of Feminist Philosophy* published in the United States.

1988 First formal gathering of Latin American feminist philosophers—the International Conference in Feminism and Philosophy in Latin America—held in Mexico.

2001 The first conference of the Feminist Ethics and Social Theory (FEAST) association held in the United States.

Introduction

The fundamental distinction between feminist philosophy and mainstream philosophy is that feminist philosophy does not claim to search for knowledge for its own sake, but rather for the sake of a political goal: resistance to, and elimination of, the subordination of women. Feminist philosophy is no one thing; it covers a wide variety of perspectives and approaches. It is possible, however, to characterize the approach of many feminist philosophers to this political goal as one that uses gender as a lens of analysis, both to create a new, distinctly feminist philosophy and to expose the "maleness" of the Western intellectual tradition. The fact that philosophical work is done by a female philosopher, or that it focuses on the presence or absence of women in philosophical thought in some way, is not enough for that work to be identified as feminist.

Feminist philosophy as an overall project has a twofold commitment that is both intellectual and political. First, it is committed to the uncovering and elimination of gender biases in philosophy. It is also, by extension, committed to the identification and removal of the androcentric thought in society more generally, as this thought has been bolstered by the philosophical tradition. It is here that the mutual relationship between feminist philosophy and the feminist movement is at its most evident: feminist philosophy is both generated by and adds to the knowledge produced by the feminist movement of the situation of women. The second commitment of feminist philosophy is—through the use of the philosophical perspectives and insights that have come from this initial critique—to inform and reconstruct the discipline of philosophy itself.

A surprisingly long history of philosophical work can be categorized as feminist, but it was not until the 1970s that feminist philosophy developed into a distinct subject field. The earliest publications of this work in mainstream philosophical journals were in the United States: *The Monist* (1973) and *The Philosophical Forum* (1973–1974). Feminist philosophy, since then, has developed rapidly.

The original sources of feminist philosophy have been central to its different stages of development, and remain central to an understanding of its scope and aims. These original sources are the philosophical tradition and the feminist movement; indeed, the trends and changes within feminist philosophy have often paralleled the developments of the feminist movement itself.

Generated by the feminist movement's critique of the androcentrism in society, feminist philosophy began as a critical reaction to the gender biases within the mainstream philosophy tradition. This critique does not necessarily mean that the tradition has been rejected wholesale, nor does it mean that feminist philosophy is merely a negative or destructive enterprise. The emphasis in the feminist movement on the revaluing of the experiences of women has played out in the construction of feminist philosophy as an identifiable field of study in its own right. Feminist philosophers, for example, have reconceived traditional subject fields, such as ethics and epistemology, to include gendered perspectives, or they have introduced new areas of study, such as the issues surrounding sexuality.

The original sources of feminist philosophical thought are evident in the way that its subject matter includes both a feminist examination of different subject areas of philosophy and also a philosophical examination of feminist theory and practice. It is worthwhile examining these two sources, as this can give a better understanding both of the subject matter of feminist philosophy itself and of the changes within this subject matter over the decades.

THE FEMINIST MOVEMENT
AND FEMINIST PHILOSOPHY

The feminist movement of the United States and Western Europe is typically divided into three periods or waves. Essentially, the feminist movement has as its goal the elimination of the social, political, economic, and cultural oppression of women, although the emphasis placed on these different elements has varied during the history of the movement. While there has been feminist activism in other countries, the Western feminist movement is taken to define the boundaries of the theories and goals of feminism.

The first wave of feminism is the period of challenges to the legal and social inequalities from the mid-1800s to 1920 in the United States and the United Kingdom. Intellectually and theoretically, this period of feminist political activity began earlier, with the publication of feminist philosopher Mary Wollstonecraft's clarion call for female equality in her 1792 work *A Vindication of the Rights of Woman*. Wollstonecraft's achievement was to crystallize the concerns of her predecessors into a systematic philosophical and political argument. She exposed not only the oppression of her contemporaries, but identified the need for a wholesale social reform to remove that oppression.

The work of this first wave of feminism was directed at the social and economic barriers faced by women of the time. Women during this era received little formal education. They were also prevented from being economically independent, either through social attitudes toward women working, or through laws that, for example, did not allow women to control their own property and earnings. Instead, marriage was considered the appropriate destination and goal of a woman's energies.

The philosophical writings of this era reflected these concerns. Harriet Taylor Mill in the late 1800s, for example, argued for economic opportunities for women, and against the oppressive institution of marriage. Feminist writings of this era also challenged the negative images of women—and the faulty assumptions about their capacities—that were often invoked by anti-feminists as the reasons women should not be properly educated nor be allowed independence (economic or otherwise) from men.

While the era of this first wave was a significant period of legislative and social reform, there is some hesitation, on the part of modern feminist thinkers, to define this era as truly feminist. Reformers of this first wave did not necessarily see themselves as working on behalf of women per se; rather they often focused on reforming different aspects of women's lives, such as marital laws and education. Moreover, reformers often directed their energies only toward the needs and interests of middle-class women.

The second wave of feminism covers the period of intense feminist activity in the 1960s and 1970s in both Europe and the United States. Betty Friedan's 1963 work *The Feminine Mystique*, in which she describes the frustration experienced by women trapped in a domestic role, is often seen as the start of this era. Friedan's work can be seen as capturing the motivating insight of the second wave: the legal and civil equalities previously granted to women had not been enough to eliminate the oppression of women.

Friedan founded the National Organization for Women (NOW) in 1966 in order to campaign for the equal rights of women in all areas of society, such as education and the workplace. The feminism of NOW, with its emphasis on civil rights, was grounded in the theory of political liberalism; this emphasis played out in feminist philosophy of the 1970s in the way that discussions of equality and rights were important issues of that time.

However, the liberal feminism of NOW was not the only way that feminists of this period responded to the recognition that women continued to be oppressed. The women's liberation movement was a more radical umbrella movement, containing a variety of loosely connected groups. Typically, these groups were formed by women who had worked within other protest movements of the 1960s, such as the civil rights movement, but who had become discouraged by the sexism within these male-dominated movements.

It was within this latter, more radical movement that the process of "consciousness raising" became a central strategy for women's liberation. Grounded in the view that "the personal is political," small groups of women would meet to share their individual personal experiences. In discussing these experiences, it was believed that the participants would come to see the common themes in these experiences: there was a structure or institution of female oppression. The participants would then work toward strategies for social and political change. Unsurprisingly, many of the central feminist issues of this period were those of the "personal," such as abortion or the family. These interests were frequently reflected in the philosophical work of the 1970s.

Consciousness raising was not only a driving force for the political aims of the women's liberation movement; it was also important because it allowed for a connection to be made between the generation of knowledge and the experiences of women. No longer were men privileged as the sole "knowers," creators, or subjects of knowledge (or men loosely disguised as the supposedly gender-neutral "man"). Women wrote about themselves and against male-biased knowledge. This critique of androcentric knowledge, and the possibilities of knowledge generated by the experiences of women, can be seen as connected to the development of feminist epistemology in the 1980s.

The second wave of feminism as a movement also brought to the fore the need for the development of feminist theorizing, both to interlink the movement's political goals and agendas and to organize and analyze the experiences of women. Philosopher Simone de Beauvoir's 1949 work *The Second Sex* is often credited as providing the genesis for much of the feminist theorizing of the 1970s in the United States and France. Her work was influential on some of the feminist theorizing in the United Kingdom during this time, but socialist feminism was also a dominant force. Beauvoir can be credited with offering the first analysis of the phenomenon of gender oppression, its effects, and its causes. Beauvoir claims, in essence, that woman is not born: woman has been culturally constructed as the negative, inferior "Other" to masculinity, the latter being identified as the positive norm within patriarchal society. Beauvoir argues that this construction is the source of women's oppression.

There is no one unified or defining feminist theoretical perspective; rather, a variety of theoretical perspectives are employed to analyze the oppression of women and to offer strategies for its elimination. Some of these perspectives are explicitly rooted in traditional Western political theory: liberalism and Marxism. Others are seen as products of the liberation movement itself: radical feminism, lesbian feminism, socialist feminism, anarchist feminism, black feminism, and Third World feminism.

By the mid-1980s, changes in the feminist movement were taking place. Much of the original activist energy of the political feminist movement had dissipated. In contrast, the theoretical side of feminism had grown and had become established as a distinctive subject within academia. Indeed, it is this point that marks the expansion of feminist philosophy into new areas such as epistemology, ontology, metaphysics, and the philosophy of science.

Feminist theorizing, from the 1980s onward, became more pluralistic. There was no one cause of this shift; however, it is possible to identify two central causal elements. One cause was the fact that the work of black feminist theorists had become increasingly available at this time. This work challenged mainstream, predominantly white feminism in a variety of ways. Black feminists critiqued mainstream feminism for its exclusion of the voices of women from marginalized groups and for not recognizing that this exclusion contributes to the continued oppression of these groups. Black feminists also criticized mainstream feminists for their failure to realize that their proposals for gender equality may rest on the exploitation of others.

The other central cause in the shift in recent feminist theorizing was the growth of postmodernist thought. The precise effects of postmodernism on feminist thought are hard to pin down, as postmodernist thought itself is composed of a plurality of views. Moreover, because of postmodernism's opposition to Enlightenment thought, it has a contested relationship with feminism because of feminism's historical roots in Enlightenment thinking. It is reasonable to say, however, that the postmodernism rejection of essentialism, its emphasis on pluralistic knowledge, and its rejection of the Enlightenment notion of the self have been important influences on recent feminist thought.

While the political strength of the second wave feminist movement lay in its apparent unity, it would appear in retrospect that the movement was defined by the experiences and goals of heterosexual, white, middle-class women. What is often called the third wave of feminism is, in part, a conscious movement away from these difficulties of the second wave. Third wave feminists recognize that sexual oppression cannot be eliminated without also addressing racial and economic oppressions. Because of the emphasis of third wave feminists on a plurality of viewpoints, and their rejection of the assumption that there is one identifiable experience of sexist oppression, the third wave has been hard to define as a political movement.

Feminist philosophy owes its initial impetus to the feminist movement, and—in many ways—the subsequent progress of feminist philosophy reflects the changes within the movement. Despite the variety of approaches within feminist philosophy, its dominant characteristics illustrate this connection to the feminist movement: an emphasis on analysis using the lens of gender; a recognition of the need to ground theory on, and make it accountable to, real-life experience; and a sense of collaboration typified by its openness to work from other disciplines. Above all, feminist philosophy continues the political work of the feminist movement: the analysis and elimination of the oppression of women.

THE EARLY STAGES OF THE FEMINIST PHILOSOPHICAL PROJECT: FEMINIST EXAMINATION OF THE PHILOSOPHICAL TRADITION

Even for those philosophers who self-identify as feminist philosophers, the relationship of feminist philosophy to "mainstream" philosophy can be a contentious one. In its essence, feminist philosophy aims to uncover and critique male bias in the philosophical tradition. For some philosophers this does not mean that they need to argue for a complete rejection of the tradition; they ground their thought in this tradition in some way, often adapting it to fit feminist goals.

This relationship is further complicated by the fact that potential tensions can exist between someone's feminist commitments—political commitments to social and political change—and her or his commitments as a philosopher, for the latter can often include a commitment to the particular issues and methods of the very tradition under criticism. Given this relationship, some prefer to frame feminist philosophy as a separate subject area from, or as an alternative to, mainstream philosophy; others want to frame feminist philosophy as being within this mainstream philosophy.

This dual nature of feminist philosophy—of its criticism of the philosophical tradition and its adaptation of this tradition—is present even in the earliest of feminist philosophical work. Mary Wollstonecraft, for example, in her 1792 work *A Vindication of the Rights of Woman*, was critical of the inequalities produced by Rousseau's sex-complementarian views of the role of women. However, her own philosophical view of the relationship of reason and passion owed much to the work of Rousseau.

Even though the work of the earliest feminist philosophers did contain criticism of the sexism inherent in some mainstream philosophy, it is best seen as a series of isolated criticisms, rather than as forming a pattern of identifiable feminist philosophical work. Indeed, it was not until the 1970s that a clearly identifiable pattern of work began to emerge, in particular in the United States. It was during this period that feminist philosophy started as an academic discipline, specifically as a subject area within women's studies.

Feminist philosophy in France also began to develop during this time. There were similarities in the initial subject areas of American and French feminist philosophy, with work being done mainly in ethics and political philosophy. The theorizing of French philosophers, however, was consciously less abstract, and it drew on, for example, Marxist and existentialist thought. In the United Kingdom, feminist philosophy as a critical force did not surface until the 1980s.

During the 1970s, the most dominant theme was canon critique, a theme that can be seen to parallel similar feminist critiques in literature and the arts at this time. The focus of this project was to uncover gender biases inherent in the philosophical tradition, and to question whether these biases were separable from the tradition. This canon critique was practiced in both France and the United States, albeit utilizing different approaches.

Within Anglo-American philosophy, early examinations of these biases tended to focus on what canonical male philosophers had to say about women, and how these accounts of women might affect our reading of their work. Other approaches examined the way that women themselves—or areas of life closely associated with women, such as the family—were excluded, implicitly or explicitly, from philosophical discussion. Reflecting the knowledge that had been generated by the feminist movement, it became clear that—despite the apparent neutrality of Western philosophy and its supposedly universal accounts of "mankind"—the Western canon contained only the perspective of its central proponents: white, bourgeois men.

Canon critique in non-Anglophone Europe during this period has come to be identified with the work of Luce Irigaray and Michèle Le Doeuff. Essentially, Irigaray argues that Western philosophy is masculinist, and she illuminates the ways in which the feminine has been suppressed in the history of philosophy. Le Doeuff's focus is the exploration of the ways that Western philosophy is grounded in the negation of women. By the late 1980s, these deconstructive readings of texts by French feminist theorists began to influence Anglo-American philosophers, and the latter began to pay attention to the way that the male-female distinction plays out symbolically within texts as well as in conceptualizations of reason and its opposites (such as passion).

The other dominant strand, besides canon critique, in Anglo-American feminist philosophy during the 1970s and early 1980s was the exploration of issues in political philosophy and ethics, such as equal rights and the family. These issues were not only connected to the practical concerns of the feminist movement of that time, but also to its political ancestry. Liberal democratic theory, such as that of the seventeenth-century English philosopher John Locke, had supplied the foundations for the liberal feminism of the 1960s and 1970s. Some feminist philosophers, however, began to question these foundations, because the rights and freedoms promoted by traditional liberalism are not gender neutral but can exclude women or issues associated with women.

Once canon critique got under way, several things became evident. It became clear that the male biases of Western philosophy could not simply be redressed by somehow just adding women or their experiences, interests, and concerns into philosophical theorizing. Feminist philosophers began to see that the biases in philosophy were deeply ingrained within philosophical thought itself: in its concepts, its ideals, and even its methodology. They began to explore the ways that the concepts of reason, objectivity, and impartiality are culturally associated with masculinity, while their opposites are culturally associated with femininity—and devalued accordingly. Moreover, feminist philosophers came to see that the biases of the Western canon stretched beyond the realm of philosophy. The canon had had a part to play in the creation of the system of gender relations and ideals, and it continued to have the potential to be used as a tool of oppression.

This recognition of the biases deep within philosophical thought is seen by some as marking the development of feminist philosophy as its own distinct project.

THE CONTEMPORARY FEMINIST PHILOSOPHICAL PROJECT: CENTRAL ASPECTS OF THE REVISION AND EXPANSION OF THE PHILOSOPHICAL ENTERPRISE

The most recent work in feminist philosophy can be grouped roughly into three categories that cannot be separated completely: Anglo-American analytic feminism, French feminism, and postmodern feminism.

Analytic feminist philosophy is typically aimed at the preservation, albeit with a feminist revision, of the traditional ideals and goals of Western philosophy. This is antithetical to the postmodern feminist enterprise, as it does not contain a sweeping rejection of modernism. Because of this, postmodern feminists consider analytic feminists to be engaged in theorizing about a shared truth, reality, and knowledge: to be repeating the mistakes of the Enlightenment project. French feminist philosophers are frequently categorized as postmodernist; however, their thought is distinctive in the way that it resists, and subverts, the Western philosophical tradition through the development of a female language and writing that produces new meaning and knowledge.

Although some feminist philosophical thought comes from non-Western countries, little of this work at present can be identified as a distinct feminist philosophy, for a variety of reasons. Third World feminists in particular, because of their specific economic, social, and political situations, are frequently more occupied with the practical, rather than the theoretical, dimensions of feminist thought. Intellectual work being done by feminists from the Third World may also not fit into the definition of feminist philosophy in the North American and Western European model. Feminist philosophy, in this model, is partly defined by its commitment to uncovering and eliminating male bias in both current and canonical philosophy.

For Anglo-American analytic feminist philosophers, gender analysis exposes as false the claims to neutrality and universality of the traditional philosophical project. Philosophical inquiry, they argue, must begin with an understanding that embodiment, emotions, relationships with others, and social status all affect inquiry, knowledge, and moral decision-making and perspectives. This concept of the "socialized"—or "situated"—self is a central hallmark of the analytic approach.

It is in the field of ethics, more than any other, that Anglo-American analytic feminist philosophy has pressed on the ideals and concepts of mainstream philosophy. The best known proponent of a feminist approach to ethics is Carol Gilligan, whose work is usually seen as initiating this area of study. Although work by feminists of color is increasing, thus far most feminist ethicists have been white Western women.

In essence, the traditional goal of ethics is to identify a single principle or set of rules that, on rational reflection, will be recognized by all moral agents as a guide for moral choice. Thus the central moral ideals are objectivity and universality, ideals which can allow little place for the emotional and concrete life of the agent. Gilligan argues that, in the traditional model, the moral "voice" and the experiences of women become neglected or devalued. She challenges dominant moral philosophy by claiming that a different moral framework, an "ethics of care," comes out of women's moral thinking; this ethics understands morality in terms of responsibility, relationships, and a contextualized answering of moral problems.

The majority of analytic feminist philosophers agree that some form of this alternative moral framework exists, and thus that it provides a central criticism of mainstream moral philosophy. However, there is distinctively less agreement over what this entails. One of the two central debates is over the importance of this alternative moral thinking for the dominant framework. The overarching question here is whether this alternative moral framework should replace the dominant framework or whether it should inform and improve this framework. The other central debate is over the importance of the identification of a women's moral voice for the feminist philosophical project. The promotion of this moral voice, as it stands, may defeat the purpose of this project by reaffirming the potentially oppressive stereotypes of women as emotional and nurturing and as less capable of abstract thought. For some feminist philosophers, the recognition of gender differences in moral thinking and experience can only be valuable if it contributes to the analysis and removal of the subordination of women.

The feminist charge that traditional moral philosophy has ignored the experience and situation of women has also led to new perspectives in the field of "applied" ethics. For example, feminist ethicists focus on power relations within abortion decisions, as opposed to the mainstream focus on the rights of freely choosing, autonomous women. These new perspectives have also led to the development of new subject areas within this field, such as cosmetic surgery and its interrelation with oppressive ideals of female beauty.

Feminist philosophers do not focus solely on moral philosophy. Feminist work in the "core" Anglo-American analytic fields of epistemology, philosophy of science, metaphysics, philosophy of language, and logic is growing. All of these fields have been subject to the feminist project of critique and revision of traditional philosophy. It is only, however, in the fields of epistemology and philosophy of science that a distinct project can be identified, a project that is directed at exploring the question of whether the sex of the knower is epistemologically significant: the concept of situated knowledge.

Within this overall project there have been a variety of approaches to this notion of the situated knower: in particular, the approaches of feminist empiricism, standpoint theory, and postmodernism. In essence, feminist empiricism questions the ideal of a pure objective knowledge, and asks whether the political values and historical particulars of the knower can, and should, inform empirical inquiry. Feminist standpoint theorists ask whether the particular social and political situation of the knower provides an epistemic privilege. Postmodern feminists critique these other two approaches for their reliance on the essentializing notion of "woman," used either as an object of knowledge or as a knowing subject. Postmodern feminists form this critique out of an understanding that there are multiple situations of women, and thus multiple epistemic perspectives.

Within traditional social and political philosophy, the family, sex, and reproduction have historically been seen as part of the private sphere. Thus these elements of human social and political life have not been seen as within the realm of justice, as a component of the good society, or as subject to laws or government intervention. The earlier Anglo-American feminist theorizing in the fields of social and political philosophy tended to accept this distinction. Feminist philosophers typically concentrated on allowing women equality within, and entry into, public arenas such as the workplace and educational institutions. Or they argued for the removal of laws that restricted women's freedom of choice within the private lives.

Current feminist work in social and political philosophy is primarily focused on breaking down, in various ways, the traditional distinction between the public and private spheres, and on examining the implications for women's social and political lives that will come out of this. Feminist philosophers argue, for example, that the political subject, the subject of the public sphere, is individualistic and abstract. They claim that this notion is conceptually incoherent and antithetical to the lived experience of women. Because of their family ties, for example, women do not have a true freedom of choice over their lives, which is a characteristic of the traditional political subject. Those feminist philosophers who aim to develop a distinctly feminist theory of justice agree that a just society is one that is free of oppressive social hierarchies. Beyond this, there is little agreement on what a feminist theory of justice would comprise.

Feminist social and political philosophy can be credited with bringing to the fore issues that are of particular concern to women, or that have been culturally associated with women, such as sexuality and the domestic life. It has also introduced new subject areas into philosophical discussion, such as lesbian philosophy, which do not have correlating subfields in mainstream philosophy.

Anglo-American analytic philosophy is being increasingly influenced by the work of both postmodernist philosophers and French feminist philosophers, in particular, for theorizing about gender, the body, and sexuality. Some Anglophone feminist philosophers categorize as postmodernist the work of the prominent French feminists Luce Irigaray and Hélène Cixous. Certainly, their work shares much with postmodernism, but it is perhaps more usefully seen as an identifiable way of writing that has some central shared perspectives on femininity, sexual difference, and language. The label "French feminist" is not necessarily accepted by the actual thinkers living in France, as they see their work as having more differences than similarities. However, it is the shared elements of these thinkers that have had the greatest impact on feminist philosophy in the rest of Europe, Australia, the United States, and the United Kingdom. Their influence is also beginning to extend into Latin American feminist philosophy.

Whereas Anglophone feminist philosophers discuss whether the liberation of women can be achieved through equality, or through the recognition and revaluing of their sexual difference, the specific characteristic of what is known as French feminism is to challenge the actual framework of discourse that gives these terms meaning. Thus, for French feminists, sexual difference is produced through the operation of discourse, not biology.

Of the three central figures in French feminism, only Irigaray is considered a philosopher. Thus her work has had the greatest impact on feminist philosophy in general, especially her contribution to the more general discussion of the possibility of a critique of the Western intellectual tradition that does not replay the problematic "male" elements of this tradition. Irigaray's challenge to the traditional frameworks of language and knowledge, her questioning of the concepts of sex and gender, as well as her approach to reading philosophical texts, have all been influential on Anglophone feminist philosophy. For Irigaray, women are represented in the patriarchal symbolic order as the negative "Other." Thus femininity or the female is male defined and has no meaning outside of patriarchal discourse. Moreover, as female sexuality has no cultural representation, it does not have an existence. Irigaray offers a critique that aims to make visible the effects of this symbolism both on texts and, because it is mistaken as real, on the lives of actual women. For Irigaray, the central effect of this symbolism is to place women outside the philosophical tradition; thus, she argues, the knowledge generated by the Western intellectual tradition is not neutral or objective, but gendered.

Irigaray aims to create a different structure of thought and speaking, a "feminine" writing—*écriture féminine*—that operates outside the male symbolic order. This writing symbolically represents women's bodies and sexuality. This speaking position is one of critique, but like female sexuality, it is no one thing: it is multiple and fluid. Thus, as this new language comes from a position that is consciously not neutral or fixed, it has no one meaning or truth. This disrupts the "male" discourse of the Western philosophical tradition, a discourse premised on the existence of an objective truth discoverable by reason alone. Irigaray's language that is spoken by women is not just one of critique; it is also meaning-making. Thus it also leads to the exploration of the new ways of knowledge that come from the (metaphorical) female body.

Postmodern feminist thought has been a central influence on feminist philosophy in both Europe and the United States, due in particular to its questioning of the categories of sex, gender, and sexuality. Postmodern feminism disrupts these categories, rejecting them because they are unitary and essentializing concepts that are creations of networks of political power. Instead, for postmodernists, these categories are unstable, not fixed.

Postmodern critique undercuts the terms of the sex/gender debate, for this framework is grounded in the assumption that there is some unitary and essentialist notion of woman. While this was the motivating concept of the feminist political movement, many feminist philosophers— influenced by postmodernism—now criticize as false any claim that there is a universal notion of woman. According to postmodern feminists, the view that there is an essential meaning of "woman" results in the enforced production of certain behaviors and practices that reflect and sustain that meaning. They argue, furthermore, that the essentialist category of "woman" is exclusionary, for this separates gender identity from, for example, racial identity. This means that, for women of color, their racial identity is external and secondary, and thus their specific experiences and oppressions as women of color become marginalized or invisible. This recognition of difference has been a central influence on non-postmodern feminist philosophy, to the point where a recognition of difference is almost automatic in theorizing in any of the fields of feminist philosophy.

Despite the increasing influence of postmodernist thought on feminist philosophy, there is no agreement among feminist philosophers over whether a postmodernist feminist philosophy itself is possible. Some feminist philosophers aim to uncover connections of postmodernism and feminism, but for others there is an irresolvable tension between the two.

Both postmodern philosophers and non-postmodern feminist philosophers agree that the neutrality, rationality, and objectivity of the traditional philosophical subject (the unsituated knower using reason alone), and the knowledge or truths acquired by that subject, are a mythology. The ideal of the objective knower in search of the truth is not in itself objective or true but is, instead, the ideal of a particular historical and cultural context.

The tensions between the two approaches lie in the next step of the feminist philosophical project. Feminist philosophers resist offering an alternative overarching narrative of truth and knowledge; however, they maintain that the feminist philosophical project is aimed at the production of a generally applicable theory of political philosophy, one that requires some kind of stable, and identifiable, category of women. Without this, they claim, feminist politics would be nothing other than multiple subjectivities, and feminism would have no real explanatory or political power; it would be simply one mode of discourse among others.

In their turn, postmodernist feminists reject the legitimacy of the feminist philosophical project, because it aims to offer a unified, or overarching "grand narrative" of political philosophy that is grounded in essentialist notions of women. Some postmodern feminists, however, question this tension, as they hold that postmodernism need not require the rejection of all theorizing itself, but only the rejection of essentializing and universalizing theory.

Feminist philosophy, in all its different global forms, continues to evolve. The feminist philosophical enterprise has never been static; it is always in the process of change and development. Indeed, part of the goal of the feminist philosophical enterprise is the generation of new philosophical theories and perspectives, such as ecofeminism, as well as new subject fields, such as philosophy of film.

THE INFLUENCE OF FEMINIST PHILOSOPHY ON MAINSTREAM PHILOSOPHY

It is clear that mainstream philosophy is expanding in its scope as it becomes increasingly influenced by the discoveries and critiques of feminist philosophy. This influence is often below the surface; thus it can be hard to discern. However, two clearly identifiable aspects of this influence are the trends toward virtue theory and more contextualized theorizing in mainstream ethics, and the loosening of disciplinary boundaries between philosophy and, for example, literature.

Feminist philosophers have begun to ask new questions of the relationship between mainstream philosophy and feminist philosophy. They no longer simply ask whether the ideals and commitments of traditional philosophy, as well as the work of canonical philosophers, could perform important work for feminism. They now also ask what feminist philosophy can offer philosophy itself. In this way, feminist philosophy can be seen as not simply destructive, or even reconstructive, but as the next level in the evolution of philosophy.

The Dictionary

– A –

ABORTION. Abortion became a topic of particular interest for professional philosophers in the early 1970s, as changes in its criminal status occurred in many Western countries. There is no unified feminist philosophical view of abortion, but a variety of perspectives. While feminism is often linked with an abortion **rights** stance, there is no necessary connection between the two. Some feminists are not committed to abortion rights because they believe that such rights may increase women's subordination through, for example, the possibility that women can be pressured into abortions by their male partners. Some feminists of color, while not necessarily arguing against abortion rights in theory, point to the differences in meanings and **experiences** of abortion between white women and women of color; they refer, specifically, to the history of **reproductive** control over women of color, and the history of abortion rights as primarily benefiting white middle-class women.

Mainstream (i.e., non-feminist) debate over the issue of abortion typically takes place within a framework of rights: whether the fetus has personhood and is thus the bearer of rights, and if so, whether the right to life of the fetus outweighs the rights of the woman to **privacy** or ownership of her **body**. Some contemporary feminist philosophers have argued that this rights framework is male-biased, in that it deals with people as abstract individuals, not as members of a social community. Others have argued for a **care**-based perspective, claiming that the moral focus must be on responsibilities and relationships, rather than rights. Feminist perspectives on abortion tend to emphasize the role and existence of the **mother** and her **moral agency**, while also situating the abortion debate within the wider social and political context of how abortion access may serve to liberate women. Accordingly, these perspectives on abortion often move beyond the specifics of the debate itself to discussions of accessibility, contraception, child care, and employment. *See also* FAMILY; POLITICAL AND SOCIAL PHILOSOPHY.

ABSTRACT INDIVIDUALISM. *See* INDIVIDUALISM, ABSTRACT.

ADVERSARY METHOD. *See* METHODOLOGY.

AESTHETICS. Feminist aesthetics covers the same two areas of study as mainstream aesthetic philosophy: the philosophy of art and the philosophy of the aesthetic **experience**. A pivotal difference, however, makes feminist aesthetics a distinct subject field. Underlying the feminist project is the belief that these two areas of study are not **value neutral**; specifically, they are not **gender** neutral. Thus, for feminist philosophers, the central aesthetic questions concerning the nature and function of art, and the relation of art to society, are ultimately questions of gender and **justice**.

Feminist work in aesthetics began in the 1970s with a questioning of the Western tradition, both for the way that definitions of art and creativity exclude women, and also for the gender bias in the ideals of, and the theorizing about, the aesthetic experience.

Feminist philosophers hold that the distinction in Western aesthetics made between fine art (which is produced for aesthetic pleasure) and craft (which is produced for a specific practical use) functions to exclude forms of art, such as quilt-making, that are traditionally done by women. This critique has been accompanied by work aimed at both the recovery of forgotten women artists for the **canon**, and the inclusion of aesthetic traditions that have been marginalized because they have been dismissed as not "real" art.

Feminist philosophers argue, moreover, that women are excluded not just by definitions of artistic work but also by notions of the artist and creativity. Although the conception of the artistic genius has not been static, there is a dominant notion that crystallized in the eighteenth century of the genius as a solitary individual who combines a powerful intellect with a fine-grained sensibility. Furthermore, the

autonomy of this individual was a requirement for a free creative process. While the possession of "womanly" **emotions** was seen as part of the make-up of the genius, the actual emotions he possessed were often seen as distinct from those of the actual emotional life of women. Women's emotional life was supposedly dominated by mundane and non-transcendent feelings that were part of their biological roles of bearing and rearing children. Moreover, the ability to distance oneself from daily life is viewed by feminist philosophers as one aspect of male privilege, as it contrasts with the reality of many women's lives.

This questioning of the Western tradition of art for its exclusion of women led to discussions among feminist theorists from philosophy, literary theory, and art history about the possibility of a "**feminine** aesthetic." The specific question is whether there is such a thing as "women's" art or art criticism. In the 1980s, feminist philosophers began to criticize this notion for its underlying **essentialism**, and for its foundation on the traditional "feminine" characteristics, such as intuitiveness and empathy, created by **patriarchy**.

The examination of the marginalization of women in the arts led to a consideration of whether this marginalization was a simple case of sexism, or whether there was a deeper cause that came from the ideals of traditional aesthetics. Feminist philosophers claim that the ideals of the traditional account, which come primarily from the philosophical work of the eighteenth century, are gendered. Traditionally, aesthetic pleasure is "disinterested" and contemplative, and is not supposed to be affected by the individual's own desires or situation. The fact that aesthetic experience is freed of context then means that **universal** value judgments can be made about the beauty of a work of art.

It is argued that this traditional conception of the aesthetic experience is gendered for two main reasons. First, this capacity to take a disinterested stance was not attributed to women, as they were thought to lack the necessary intellectual capacity for "taste": the faculty for judgments about art and beauty. Second, artistic representations of women typically treated them as passive **objects** for the aesthetic experience of the spectator. The distanced contemplating **subject**, and this subject's aesthetic pleasure, are then framed as the privilege of men. This "male gaze" on representations of women is an activity of power: it transforms the female **body** into an object of desire. Thus women, as object not subject, cannot return the gaze. This notion of the "male gaze" originated with art criticism, but it is a central notion in feminist aesthetics as it challenges the possibility of an objective aesthetic response: the ideal of traditional aesthetics. Specific interests of feminist philosophers in this notion include the origins of the gendering of the gaze and the way that perception functions as an act of power.

One central theme in the most current work in feminist aesthetics is the examination of the roles the body, and the beautification of the body, play in women's lives. There is work, for example, on the differences in representations of black and white women's bodies within a **racist** culture, and how these representations function to reinforce power relations between groups, as well as to affirm the value placed on members of these groups. The examination of the beautification of women's bodies shifts the discussion of beauty from the traditional discussions of abstract beauty in the arts to the creation of personal beauty. There is disagreement as to whether the attainment of beauty can be understood as a means to self-expression and pleasure for the individual or whether it is solely a required characteristic of femininity: for the pleasure of men.

Another central theme in the most current work in feminist aesthetics, particularly in the developing subfield of philosophy of film, is the examination of theories of interpretation. Feminist philosophers discuss, for example, whether a totalizing theory, such as psychoanalytic theory (which is grounded in the assumption that there are universal psychological responses), can produce a full analysis of the playing out of gender ideologies in a film, or whether a better analysis can come from a particularist examination: a focus on specific genres and individual films.

AFFIRMATIVE ACTION. The term affirmative action originated in a U.S. government policy that came from President Lyndon Johnson's 1965 Executive Order 11246. This order stated that any institution that was connected to federal government was required not only to avoid explicit discrimination, but to "take affirmative action to ensure that applicants are employed, and that employees are treated during employment, without regard to their race, creed, color, or national origin." In 1967, Johnson expanded the order to cover women. In the first decades following the order, the focus of affirmative action in the United States was on both **gender** and **race** in a variety of institutional settings. In the early 1970s, the full implementation of the executive order started to affect American universities. At this time there were few people of color with Ph.D.'s, so debate within academic institutions crystallized around the hiring of female Ph.D.'s. The debate soon spilled over into philosophical discussions (both feminist and non-feminist), especially because there was a growing trend at that time toward a more applied philosophy in **political and social philosophy**. Affirmative action policies are now prevalent in many Western countries besides the United States; since the 1990s, the focus of these policies is usually on the admission of racial minorities to higher **education**.

Affirmative action is intended as a temporary measure to bring about **equality** of opportunity in society. The goal is equality of results, rather than equality of treatment. The argument is that policies based on equality of treatment may only perpetuate inequality, as they fail to recognize how gender, race, and other factors may serve to disadvantage people.

Affirmative action policies typically fall into one of two categories that can be labeled "weak" and "strong" preference policies. In the case of the former, preference is given to a member of a targeted group whose qualifications are equal to other applicants. In the case of "strong" preference, a member of the targeted group with appropriate qualifications is chosen over other candidates with better qualifications. A variety of different arguments have been given for this latter, more controversial approach: for example, that it provides role models, it provides reparations for past injustices, and it does not penalize a candidate for lacking the social and economic privileges that tend to lead to better qualifications.

Although affirmative action is a component of the politics of **liberal feminism**, it has wide support from feminist philosophers of all types, who have considered a variety of issues. Among them are discussions of equality itself, what it means to be qualified, and how to defend particular practices and policies.

However, affirmative action has not been without its critics among feminist philosophers. For some, it is merely tokenism that does little to change the causes of inequality. Others claim that affirmative action requires an overly simplistic categorization of its beneficiaries into set groups; this cannot allow for policies flexible enough to deal with individuals who **experience** multiple disadvantages produced by membership in more than one of these groups. *See also* RACE AND RACISM.

AFRICA, FEMINIST PHILOSOPHY IN. While there has been a lot of feminist intellectual work and activism in Africa, there has not been much that can be categorized, strictly speaking, as work in feminist philosophy as it now is defined. Feminist philosophy, as understood on the North American and Western European model, is partly defined by its commitment to uncovering and eliminating male bias in both current and **canonical** philosophy. Scholars are presently engaged, through a variety of approaches, in identifying an African tradition or traditions of philosophy, ones with specific philosophical worldviews, theories, and positions; but African philosophy, as a whole, remains fragmented. There is not a sufficiently cohesive African tradition of philosophy that can be the subject of a feminist philosophical examination (as feminist philosophy is currently understood). Thus, at present, there appears little room for the development of an African feminist philosophy. However, African feminist philosopher Helen Oduk argues that there is the potential to develop an African feminist philosophy if it is informed by traditional disciplines such as philosophy. *See also* BLACK FEMINIST PHILOSOPHY.

AFRICAN AMERICAN FEMINIST PHILOSOPHY. *See* BLACK FEMINIST ETHICS; BLACK FEMINIST PHILOSOPHY.

AGE/AGEISM. Ageism refers to systematic discrimination against the elderly. This discrimination occurs in a variety of ways: for example, through harmful stereotyping or economic restrictions. Thus far, there have been few contemporary philosophical discussions of age and ageism; the one central exception is the twentieth-century French philosopher **Simone de Beauvoir**. In her 1960 work *La Force de l'Age* (*The Coming of Age*), Beauvoir examines what she calls society's "secret shame." By this she means the systematic marginalization of the aged; this marginalization has been implicitly justified by degrading stereotypes of this section of society, and reinforced by their lack of economic and political power to defend themselves. Beauvoir's analysis is sweeping, examining everything from the biological process of aging to the condition of the aged, both historically and in different contemporary societies.

AGENCY. *See* MORAL AGENCY.

ALIENATION. The concept of alienation can be traced back to the Judeo-Christian tradition; it was first used in the Western philosophical tradition by the German philosopher G. W. F. Hegel for the state of human estrangement from **nature**. The term was used in Karl Marx's earlier works to describe the human fragmentation and isolation that is a distinctive feature of capitalist society. This latter conceptualization of alienation, once it has been extended to include specifically feminist philosophical concerns, provides a useful lens through which to examine the subordination of women. Viewed in terms of traditional **Marxist** theory, women are alienated in the same way as men: as wage laborers. The majority of feminist philosophers reject this account of women's alienation as overly simplistic, arguing that women's alienation takes a variety of forms, such as alienation from cultural production and from their own intellectual capacities. The two most evident forms of women's alienation come from **sexuality** and from **motherhood**.

In the case of sexuality, as male economic support is women's best economic security, women have little choice but to direct their sexuality and their **bodies** toward this end. Women labor to transform their bodies for the approval and attention of men, and define their sexuality in terms of what is pleasing to men. Like wage labor, not only does this alienate women from themselves, but it forms a barrier toward genuine female friendships, as women are potentially in competition with each other for economic "rewards": men.

Motherhood is also alienating for women in ways similar to the alienation of the wage laborer. The increased medicalization of childbirth alienates the mother both from the child, who is the "product" of her **reproductive** labor, and from the "process" of reproductive labor itself. Furthermore, the work of child-rearing has increased for Western women; the isolated suburban mother, for example, works a double shift as both a wage earner and a chauffeur/tutor/baby-sitter. This alienation is further increased by the perception of children as commodities produced for the satisfaction of the **emotional** needs of the mother.

Some feminist philosophers have argued that it is not just the different elements of women's lives that are alienating, but **femininity** itself. The feminine and the **masculine** are conceptualized as both opposite and opposing; conformity to **gender** stereotypes thus means that men and women are alienated from each other. Moreover, this also leads to alienation from one's own self, as the free productive activity that leads to the development of human capacities is drastically limited.

The notion of alienation in general has been an influential one, even for feminist thinkers who do not accept wholesale the possibility that alienation can provide a complete theoretical framework for the analysis of women's **oppression**. Alienation was a prominent concept from the late 1960s to the mid-1980s in discussions of the damage produced by **patriarchal** norms of female beauty and bodies. More recently, however, the notion has come under criticism from **postmodern feminists** who claim that it implies the existence of an *unalienated* self: an **essentialized** self. *See also* SUBJECTIVITY.

AMERICAN FEMINIST PHILOSOPHY. *See* PRAGMATISM.

ANALYTIC FEMINIST PHILOSOPHY (ANALYTIC FEMINISM). Since the earliest beginnings of feminist philosophy as an academic discipline in the 1970s, most anglophone feminist philosophers have worked within the analytic tradition. At this time, however, the analytic tradition itself was typically the subject of feminist critique for the male bias in its goals, ideals, and methods. It was not until the early 1990s that feminist philosophers began the comprehensive project of examining the use of the analytic tradition as a resource. At this point analytic feminist philosophy developed as an identifiable field and the term analytic feminist was coined. This development happened primarily because these philosophers believed in the importance of locating feminism within mainstream philosophy, rather than seeing it as separate or alternative.

Just as there is no one thing that is analytic philosophy, so there is no one thing that can be called analytic feminism; however, it is possible to offer a working definition of both. Historically, the ancestry of analytic philosophy is the **canon** up until the nineteenth century—marking the split from Continental Europe—and then the philosophy of, for example, Gottlob Frege, Bertrand Russell, and the Logical Positivists. The primary values of the analytic project are **reason, objectivity**, and truth; its central areas of study are the core areas of **epistemology**, philosophy of **science**, **logic**, and philosophy of **language**. The typical methods for philosophical study are logical and linguistic analyses of arguments, claims, and concepts. Analytic philosophers often start from a particular argument, claim, or concept with the aim to demolish, clarify, or improve upon it. These processes and results of philosophical investigation are evaluated in terms of their clarity, rigor, and precision. The ideal or standard for analytic philosophy is thus, in its essence, the discipline of science.

These are the shared elements of mainstream analytic philosophy and analytic feminism; however, there are some central distinctions between the two. Analytic feminists recognize that even purportedly **value-neutral** and abstract analytic philosophy is political in some way, for even a deliberately non-political stance is still a political choice. Analytic feminists do not see the goals and methods of analytic philosophy simply as valuable in themselves; rather they are also valuable because they can be pressed into the service of feminism's political goals. These political goals are typically those of **liberal feminist** politics, which is the least radical of the different types of feminist theory; indeed, it is sometimes the case that analytic feminism is criticized for being too conservative.

While analytic feminism values the central goals, ideals, and methods of mainstream analytic philosophy, it also acknowledges their male bias. The knower and the **moral agent** of the analytic tradition have been criticized as overly abstract, and as devoid of the historical particulars that are part of the reality of human knowers and agents. In addition, the **methodological** paradigm of the analytic tradition, the adversarial method, has also been criticized for its **masculinist** nature. The combative nature of this method is antithetical to the way women are **socialized** to behave. Moreover, the method itself excludes other valuable philosophical styles, approaches, and histories, and is thus non-feminist.

Ultimately, however, analytic feminists have embraced the analytic tradition, arguing that reason and objectivity are valuable for the feminist project. They claim, for example, that these notions are required to demolish the irrational and subjective arguments of antifeminists. While questions still remain about the **gendering** of the ideals and tools of analytic philosophy, analytic feminists claim that the analytic tradition is not fixed or permanent, and thus can become gender neutral. Analytic feminists have worked within a wide variety of philosophical fields, but they have tended to concentrate on the core field of epistemology. Central to this work is the naturalization of epistemology: that empirical data about knowers and their particular situation (the concept of the situated knower), as well as theories from the social sciences, are an important source of information.

The proponents of analytic feminism hold that their approach, because of its rigor, precision, and clarity, is a useful tool for uncovering and analyzing **oppression**, and thus it can promote social reform. It has been maintained, for example, that analytic feminism can help clarify what exactly are the categories of **sex** and gender, and how they can be defined. Analytic philosophy can show that there is no set of criteria (i.e., characteristics) that can provide the necessary and sufficient conditions for someone to be called "female" or "**feminine**." Thus analytic philosophy can, for example, undermine arguments—either liberating or oppressive—that are grounded in the existence of identifiable sexes or genders.

Questions have been asked, however, about the inclusivity of analytic feminism, an issue that is especially pertinent in light of the history of exclusion of women and the feminine from science. A properly feminist philosophy not only must offer possibilities for social reform but must also be inclusive. Yet analytic philosophy, by its very nature, struggles to allow for different **experiences** and ways of thinking. Part of the way of ensuring inclusivity is attention to difference, yet the logical and linguistic analyses characteristic of analytic philosophy function best when they are free from actual context. This difficulty of incorporating the political goal of inclusivity remains a stumbling block for analytic feminism. *See also* CONTINENTAL PHILOSOPHY.

ANARCHIST FEMINISM (ANARCHA-FEMINISM). A variety of feminist views are covered by this umbrella term, which can be characterized as a political resistance to social hierarchy and the authority of the state. Modern anarcha-feminists are heirs to the thought of anarchist feminist philosophers **Emma Goldman** and Voltairine de Cleyre, both of whom wrote at the turn of the twentieth century. Goldman and de Cleyre can be credited with making the first connections between the anarchist goal of individual freedom and the freedom of women. They made these connections through their claims that dominance, and the corresponding need for freedom, were as much a part of the private sphere (the **family** and **marriage**) as of the public sphere.

Present-day anarcha-feminists maintain the anarchist ideal of individual freedom but frame it as something that can occur only within a community, specifically a non-hierarchical community. The classical anarchist understanding of the purpose of a society is to produce the good life for its members, and for anarcha-feminists this is understood as one of freedom and room for the growth of the individual. By definition, hierarchical society—and its institutions that reflect and reinforce hierarchy, such as the family, work, and schools—prevent the good life. For anarcha-feminists, organization against social hierarchy must be spontaneous, as more formal or structured groups can have the potential to replay social hierarchies and systems of dominance. *See also* PUBLIC/PRIVATE DISTINCTION.

ANCIENT GREEK PHILOSOPHY. Given that Western philosophy owes its foundation—the idea of the capacity of human **reason** to discover truth—to the thought of classical Greece, there has been a significant amount of analysis of the philosophy of the ancient Greek world. The feminist project in this area is typical of other work in the feminist **history of philosophy** in that it is threefold: the identification and reclamation of **women philosophers**, the examination of texts for sexist bias, and the consideration of these texts as potential resources. Given the status of **Plato** and **Aristotle** in the **canon**, most of the work in this project has focused on their philosophy; since the

1970s, there has been a variety of different approaches to the critique and recovery of their thought. In the case of the rediscovery of women philosophers, this is not in fact an original project. In 1690, Gilles Ménage wrote *History of Women Philosophers*, in which he undertook a similar project of examining ancient texts for evidence of the existence of women philosophers, identifying about twenty Greek women thinkers. Some of these Greek thinkers have been known by name only. In the case of Pythagorean and Neo-Pythagorean women philosophers, however, some fragments of their work have survived, and there is a strong case for their authenticity. Only at a stretch could any of these Pythagorean thinkers be called feminist; their interest for feminist philosophers is mainly because they attest to the existence of early female philosophers.

With recent developments in **feminine ethics** exploring the existence and potential of **gendered** morality, there has been an increased interest in the thought of these ancient Greek women. There are some central themes in the writings of these Pythagorean and Neo-Pythagorean women philosophers, although these themes are not common to all thinkers, nor is there agreement in their views. One of these central themes is the encouragement of women to develop their capacity for philosophy. The other is the elaboration of the differences in virtues between the **sexes**; the virtues specific to women are moderation and obedience, both of which are needed to achieve harmony in the household. On the surface this might seem nothing more than a reinforcement of standard sexist attitudes; however, these thinkers hold that women's virtues are, though different, **equal** to those of men. Indeed, there does seem to be the implication in some of the texts that female virtues are in fact the superior ones. This practical use of virtue and philosophy is of interest to those feminist philosophers who wish to confront traditional **dualist** notions of philosophy as purely intellectual and separate from material life. Furthermore, it also provides a prototype for those feminist philosophers who wish to consider ways in which a women's philosophy will reflect women's concerns and possibilities, in contrast to the ways that traditional philosophical thinking has reflected the concerns of men.

The earliest indication of the sometimes ambiguous nature of women's connection to wisdom throughout the history of philosophy can be found in ancient Greek thought. Parmenides (ca. 539–500 BCE) provides the first instance of a female figure who leads men to wisdom through her own reasoning and arguing. Despite the dominant view that women lack the capacity (for a variety of reasons) for philosophical thinking, this competing, more minor imagery of women as providers of wisdom is a recurring one. A central example is the figure of **Diotima**, who supposedly taught Socrates his philosophy of love.

The first manifestations of those elements of traditional philosophical thinking that are of concern for contemporary feminist philosophy can be found in ancient Greek thought: normative dualism, gendered morality, and the gendering of wisdom and reason. There is evidence of gendered dualist thinking that can be traced as far back as the poet Hesiod (ca. 700 BCE). For Hesiod, there was an antagonistic relationship between the opposites of female earth and male sky, as well as between the male and female gods. Indeed, he depicts women as a punishment for or a danger to men.

Based on reports of his philosophy, it is apparently Pythagoras (ca. 570–497 BCE) who introduced the normative framing of these pairs of opposites as binary opposites. Thus male was framed as superior to female, as light was to dark, good to evil, and so forth. Moreover, by association, the superior of each pair became linked to each other, and the same happened for the inferior of each pair. Thus female became associated with dark, evil, and so on.

The ways in which this dualist thinking play out in human life for Pythagoras are more complex. Pythagoras offers the earliest philosophical thinking about what is now labeled by feminist philosophers as the gendering of reason and morality. The moral ideal for all humans is harmony both of the soul and in society, and both sexes are equally capable of achieving harmony through chaste behavior. However, the route to harmony between husband and wife is different for each sex: women are to practice the virtue of obedience, while men show virtue in ruling. Pythagoras's view of women is ambiguous, for he holds that, outside of the realm of material life, the sexes are equal. He views reason as gender neutral, and thus holds that both sexes are capable of philosophy. This explains the distinct presence of Pythagorean women philosophers and may also explain their philosophical interests.

Early signs of the gendering of **language** can also be traced back to the thought of ancient Greece. It was apparently the Sophist Protagoras (490–420 BCE) who introduced the notion of nouns being male, female, or neuter. Even though this framework was not dualist, what is problematic is that the choice of gender for each word was not random; rather the gender of the word supposedly reflected the gendered nature of the object. In this way, language reinforces gender divisions—specifically, divisions that were not **value neutral**.

It is Aristotle, however, who is credited with offering the first comprehensive theoretical account of the superiority of men and their correlating superiority in virtues, capacity for reason, and social status. In Aristotle's account, the inferior virtue and reason of women potentially exclude them from the good life. This account not only restricts women to the life of the household but also makes it plausible to claim that their role in maintaining the household is required in order to give men the freedom and comfort they need to pursue the good life for themselves. Because of this, and given Aristotle's status in the canon, his work has been a central target for feminist philosophers working on ancient Greek philosophy.

ANDROCENTRISM. The term androcentrism was first used by **Charlotte Perkins Gilman** in her 1911 work *The Man-Made World; or, Our Androcentric Culture* to describe a male-centered culture or system of thought in which the male is identified and valued as the norm and the female as deviant from that norm. Gilman states in this work that "all our human scheme of things rests on the same tacit assumption; man being held the human type; woman a sort of accompaniment and subordinate assistant, merely essential to the making of people. . . . Nevertheless, . . . what we have all this time called '**human nature**' . . . was in great part only male nature. . . . Our androcentric culture is so shown to have been, and still to be, a **masculine** culture in excess, and therefore undesirable."

ANDROGYNY. A Greek word that comes from *andro* (male) and *gyn* (female). An androgynous personality is neither stereotypically **masculine** nor **feminine** but displays some kind of combination of both sets of traits. This notion has been of interest for feminist philosophers for its political and ethical dimensions. Androgyny can be seen as a good for an individual, male or female, because it does not limit the freedom of that individual to choose among the spectrum of social roles and characteristics. Moreover, not only does androgyny seem to offer **justice** for the individual, but it would appear to have the potential to benefit society as a whole.

Psychological and behavioral differences between the **sexes**, and thus differences in their subsequently allotted roles and occupations, have traditionally been seen by scientists and philosophers as the product of biological sex. In the 1960s and 1970s, **second wave feminist** thinkers began to argue that these differences in behavior were in fact differences of **gender**: they were not "natural" to either sex, but the result of social convention and conditioning. For some of these early feminists, the elimination of gender through the creation of an androgynous society became the solution to the **oppression** of women. Those who argued for androgyny were careful to emphasize that only "worthy" characteristics would be available for choice; negative gender characteristics, such as "masculine" violence, would not be included.

More recently, androgyny as the route to gender justice has fallen out of favor; the standard notions of masculinity and femininity, from which androgyny is produced, are viewed as unstable and non-unitary notions that are constructed by **patriarchy** and also serve to reinforce it. *See also* BIOLOGICAL DETERMINISM.

ANGER. Examinations of the specific **emotion** of anger are part of a more general feminist philosophical examination of theories of emotion, and the role of emotion in both human life and philosophical thought. Anger is of interest for feminist philosophers because of its potential as a "political" emotion. The recognition by an individual that her personal **experience** of sexism is part of a pattern, or institutionalization, of sexism can function as a prompt for activism, or contribute to knowledge.

ANGLO-AMERICAN FEMINIST PHILOSOPHY. *See* ANALYTIC FEMINIST PHILOSOPHY.

ANIMAL ETHICS. There is a history of feminist concern over the treatment of animals. Although they were not animal **rights** advocates properly speaking, many **first wave feminists** were concerned about the welfare of animals. Typically, this concern was displayed through support for the anti-vivisection movement or criticism of the killing of animals and birds solely for the purpose of women's fashion. The seventeenth-century philosopher and proto-feminist **Margaret Cavendish** offered a critique of cruelty to animals, based on her view that all of **nature** was rational and sensitive. This critique is distinctive because it was one of the earliest to invoke philosophical notions of **justice** in its arguments for animal welfare.

Feminist animal ethics as a specific theoretical stance is a new area of contemporary ecological feminist theory: **ecofeminism**. While many ecofeminists argue that non-human animals must be a part of the moral community, there are differences of opinion over the grounds of or justification for that inclusion. A central problem is whether use can be made of standard non-feminist arguments for animal rights, as the morality of rights is sometimes criticized as fundamentally **masculinist**; for example, the traditional picture of the rights-holder is of an isolated and **individualistic** being, devoid of cultural or historical context. *See also* VEGETARIANISM.

ANTI-MILITARISM. *See* WAR AND PEACE.

AQUINAS, THOMAS (ca. 1224–1274). Thomas Aquinas was born in Roccasecca, not far from Naples. His early education was at a Benedictine monastery. He entered the University of Naples at the age of fourteen. Here he encountered the teachings of the Dominicans, a new monastic order, and in 1244 he became a Dominican. Aquinas was a teacher of theology in Paris and was also part of the papal court. He was a prolific writer; his two major works are the *Summa contra Gentiles* (*Summa de Veritate Catholicae Fidei contra Gentiles*), which he finished in 1264, and the *Summa Theologica* (*Summa Theologiae*), which he began sometime around 1265. Aquinas was canonized in 1323.

While Aquinas saw himself as writing academic theology, he covers many of the fields that are part of current philosophy: **metaphysics**, ethics, and **human nature**. The hallmark of Aquinas's theological philosophy is his synthesis of **Christian** theology with **Aristotelian** philosophy. Given that both of these systems of thought have been criticized by feminist philosophers for their overt misogyny, it is not surprising that feminist interpretive work on Aquinas has been minimal. The little work there is has usually focused on elaborating his problematic philosophy of women, specifically his discussion of women in the *Summa Theologica* (1, 92).

In the *Summa Theologica*, Aquinas takes Aristotle's famous statement that the female is a misbegotten male and considers it in the light of the Christian belief system (specifically Genesis); due to this latter element, Aristotle's original claim undergoes some nuancing. Aquinas argues that the production of a female child is only a defect in the actual process of generation. In terms of her human nature, woman is an intentional creation of God. Moreover, in terms of grace, women are men's spiritual **equals**. Unfortunately, in order to support his view, Aquinas claims that woman was created specifically for the purpose of **reproduction**. This is her sole "operation," whereas man also has the operation of rationality. The reduction of women to their biological function, and the association of men with **reason**, has been seen by feminist philosophers not simply as problematic in itself, but as another example of the symbolic exclusion of women from the realm of reason in the **history of philosophy**.

Some present-day theological philosophers have considered ways to come to terms with Aquinas's troubling philosophy of women. Their interest is not so much in the interpretation of Aquinas as a figure of medieval philosophy, but rather, it is prompted by the continued presence of Thomist thought in academic philosophy. A central aim of such scholars has been to diffuse tensions between Aquinas and modern notions of women's equality and their supposed nature by extracting usable elements from Thomist philosophy. For example, Aquinas is quite clear that the subjection of women to men is not for the benefit of men; individual humans are not "things" in the material world. The symbolism of Eve being made from the rib of Adam is seen by Aquinas to confirm that woman's relationship to man is neither one of authority nor one of servility.

For some modern interpreters of Aquinas, this underpins a recognition that, within the **marriage** relation, women are neither **sexual** objects nor objects of ownership. Interpreters have pointed to the way that the Aquinian marriage is a deeper relation based on the recognition of the spiritual value of both partners: each is the particular creation of God in his image. Thus, it is claimed that Aquinas's philosophy of women is not necessarily antithetical to some present-day feminist views. *See also* CANON, CRITIQUE OF.

ARENDT, HANNAH (1906–1975). Hannah Arendt was born in Germany of Jewish parentage. As an undergraduate, she studied first at the University of Marburg and later at the University of Freiburg. She received her Ph.D. in philosophy from the University of Heidelberg. Arendt left Germany for Paris, where she lived from 1933 to 1941, and then emigrated to the United States. She became a naturalized U.S. citizen in 1951. Arendt's best-known work is *Eichmann in Jerusalem: A Report on the Banality of Evil* (1965).

Arendt's philosophical writings are of increasing interest to **political philosophers** because many of the subjects with which she engaged philosophically, such as identity, **race**, nationalism, and imperialism, have come to the forefront of recent feminist work. Indeed, since September 11, 2001, the importance of Arendt's work on the moral and political nature of violence has been thrown into sharp relief for feminist discussions of **war**, violence, and human evil.

It is important to recognize that feminism did not interest Arendt; in fact, she held that what she called the "Woman Problem" was not an appropriate part of the political sphere. Earlier feminist interpretations of Arendt, those from the 1970s and early 1980s, tend to be more critical than celebratory of her political philosophy. Adrienne Rich, for example, says that Arendt's 1958 work *The Human Condition* "embodies the tragedy of a female mind nourished on male ideology." Often underpinning these earlier interpretations is the assumption that, as a woman, Arendt has a political and moral responsibility to make women, and women's issues, a part of her political theorizing. More recently, with the questioning of identity-based politics, some feminist interpreters are now finding Arendt's work potentially fruitful precisely because of its resistance to **gendered** dichotomizations.

ARISTOTLE (384–322 BCE). Aristotle of Stagira was a member of **Plato**'s Academy for twenty years; eventually he founded a philosophical school of his own, the Lyceum. He is considered the originator of philosophy as a discipline formed of distinct subject areas or fields. Aristotle's contributions to the areas of ethics and politics, the study of **nature**, and what can be called his philosophy of **mind** have been of the most interest to feminist philosophers. His contributions to **logic** and rhetoric have thus far generated little work.

Feminist philosophical critique of Aristotle's work started in the early 1980s; much of this early criticism was focused on the sexist thinking in specific texts or areas of his philosophy. Most famously, Aristotle claimed that woman is a mutilated male (*Generation of Animals*, 737a 27–28). Another particular area of interest at that time was whether Aristotle's discussions of **sex** difference may be at the roots of sexism in the philosophical and scientific traditions; many of Aristotle's ideas have become so incorporated into the tradition that they have set the hidden foundation for philosophical thinking itself.

The central question for feminist philosophers in examining Aristotle's works for sexism has been whether his discussions of the **moral**, physical, intellectual, and **reproductive** nature of women can, and should be, separated from the rest of his thought, or whether they mutually inform and support each other. It is certainly clear that Aristotle considered a study of sex difference an important part of philosophy, and it was a discussion that occurred throughout many of his philosophical works. For these reasons, Aristotle's philosophy of women has been the subject of a fair amount of feminist analysis.

In essence, Aristotle's worldview is functionalist: all aspects of nature contribute in some way to a single good through fulfilling their specific function. Moreover, each aspect of nature has its particular place within a hierarchy of ruler and ruled. For Aristotle the amount of the element of "heat" in an animal is the cause of its relative perfection or development; women were colder than men, and thus inferior or defective. Moreover, Aristotle concludes that, as they are inferior beings, women only provide a passive, and thus subordinate, contribution to generation.

Aristotle holds that the soul is the form of the **body** and that differences in one correspond to differences in the other. Thus the apparent physical inferiority of women is an indicator of inferiority in their souls; Aristotle claims that women are, for example, more **emotional** and less truthful than men. In this way, Aristotle was the first to systematize trends in earlier **ancient Greek** thought that held man was superior or primary to woman. Aristotle's analysis of difference influenced philosophical and scientific thought until the seventeenth century, although his actual explanation was often modified. **Thomas Aquinas**, for example, places women's imperfection within a **Christian** orthodoxy, arguing that God created it specifically for the purpose of generation.

Aristotle's account of the role and status of women is in the *Politics*. Here Aristotle assumes that the male-female relations he observed among his contemporaries are the way they are because each sex is performing its specific function, and thus these unequal relations are natural. The function of women is to reproduce more citizens and to maintain the household. Moreover, the fulfillment of function, and thus one's place in the hierarchy, is understood as a normative good. Aristotle is notoriously unclear about men's specific function within male-female relations in the household. His views are further clouded because he proceeds from his observations of social roles as indicators of proper functioning to a theory about the nature of the sexes that accounts for these roles.

Aristotle holds that the function of **reason** is the human function, yet men are to rule in virtue of their superiority in reason: their capacity for deliberation. Women have this deliberative faculty, but it has no authority, nor can they offer reliable judgments. Thus, Aristotle explains, men rule women just as the intellect naturally rules the appetites; indeed, he takes the latter rule to prove somehow the former. Moreover, women's different function and inferior rationality needs correspondingly different virtues, namely the virtue of obedience. In this way, Aristotle offers a systematization of the notions of sex-differentiated virtue and ethical pluralism, which had been prevalent in earlier Greek thought. Furthermore, he is seen by feminist philosophers as originating the conception that "maleness" is both the norm and a mark of superiority in both the public and private spheres.

Feminist philosophers have not just criticized Aristotle for the blatant sexism contained within his philosophical work. For some, the ultimate problem with Aristotle's view of sex differences in rationality and virtue is that it excludes women from attaining the good life: the life of the person who reasons well, and thus who possesses all the virtues. Given that on Aristotle's own account virtue is not innate, but the result of **education** and habit, this exclusion is not a necessary one. The question then is whether this exclusion is one of expediency: women's roles are a component of the freedom and comfort needed by men to live the good life. If this is the case, then the construction of Aristotle's moral philosophy in the *Nicomachean Ethics* (his central work on ethics) may require the subordination of women.

Despite the inveterate sexism of Aristotle's philosophy, there has been some work on possible feminist reconstructions of his work. Aristotle's moral philosophy has thus far generated the most interest as a possible resource for feminist philosophy; in particular, it has been argued that Aristotelian virtue ethics may provide the necessary theoretical framework to develop an ethics of **care**. Both ethics share an emphasis on moral particulars over **universals** and on the inclusion of emotions in moral thinking.

Care ethics, however, is sometimes criticized by feminist philosophers for its lack of a political or teleological framework, as it builds its theory solely on observations of sex differences in moral thinking. What is significant about Aristotelian ethics is that it is developed within a framework of a political and moral "good life"; thus it could provide a theoretical model for theorizing about care. *See also* CANON, CRITIQUE OF; PUBLIC/PRIVATE DISTINCTION.

ASTELL, MARY (1666–1731). English philosopher Mary Astell came from a merchant family. Little is known about the sources of her **education** and how she supported herself during her adult years. During her lifetime, Astell was a respected contributor to philosophical debates on **metaphysics** and **religion**. Her 1695 work *Letters Concerning the Love of God* was a collection of her correspondence on religious issues with the Malebranchean John Norris.

A Serious Proposal to the Ladies for the Advancement of Their True and Greatest Interest was her first published work and is also her best-known feminist work. The first part, published in 1694, proposes educational communities where women can escape the intellectual restrictions placed on them by social custom and poor education. In these communities women were to study the same subjects as men, rather than being educated only in household management. The women were not to stay there permanently, but to return to the world properly equipped to live in it.

Having argued for **equality** of education for women in the first part of her proposal, Astell focuses in the second part, published in 1697, on a more philosophical discussion of the search for knowledge and the nature of human rationality. In this second work she draws on the views of both the seventeenth-century English philosopher John Locke and **René Descartes**. Most significantly for the equality of women, Astell argues in this work that every individual has the capacity to think rationally and to understand truth, regardless of their opportunities for education.

Some Reflections upon Marriage, published in 1700, is Astell's third and final work of feminist philosophy. Here Astell critiques the **oppressive** nature of **marriage**, for she saw that, once married, her contemporaries were under the power of their husbands according to both law and custom.

AUGUSTINE OF HIPPO (354–430). Augustine of Hippo (Aurelius Augustinus) was born in Thagaste (Algeria), then part of the Roman Empire. During the early part of his life he taught rhetoric. He became a priest in 391. His conversion to **Christianity** in 386 is described in his famous autobiographical *Confessions (Confessiones)*, in which he describes the effect of his reading of books by Platonists that enabled him to understand and accept central doctrines of the church. This melding of the Judeo-Christian tradition with Greek philosophical tradition made Augustine a dominant influence in medieval philosophical thought. Some of his most famous works include *On the Teacher (De Magistro*, 389), *On the Literal Meaning of Genesis (De Genesi ad Litteram*, 401–415), and *On the City of God (De Civitate Dei*, 413–427).

For feminist philosophers Augustine is of some interest because of his transmittal of Neoplatonic **dualism**, specifically for the way that this played out in his philosophy of women. Augustine held that humans are both **body** and soul; however, his accompanying intellectualism meant that (contemplative) **reason** is the way to knowledge; the soul is thus superior to, and the guardian of, the body.

In Augustine's interpretation of Genesis 1:27, Adam and Eve were created in the image of God: they possessed reason. Thus, in relation to God, the two **sexes** are spiritually **equal**. This interpretation was progressive for its time, and Augustine is arguing against those who held that the subordination of women was justified by their supposedly lesser rationality. Moreover, it also meant that Augustine refutes the claim that the Fall was somehow the fault of the nature of woman; rather, he saw it as a failure of the control of reason over the body.

What is problematic for feminist philosophers with Augustine's interpretation of Genesis is that woman represents the body (the subordinate element), whereas man represents reason (the authoritative element). In her relation to man, therefore, the subordination of woman is both justified and natural. Moreover, this may also entail that, even though woman did not cause the Fall, she (as body) comes to symbolize the Fall. *See also* CANON, CRITIQUE OF.

AUSTRALIA, FEMINIST PHILOSOPHY IN. No specific way of philosophizing can be called Australian. However, some feminist philosophers working in Australia have claimed that there are enough similarities in their work, especially in their engagement with both the **history of philosophy** and the history of their country, to form a loose outline of an Australian feminist philosophy. This philosophy does not fit easily into the two categories—**postmodern** and analytic—that are usually applied to feminist philosophy within the United States and the United Kingdom.

The work of Australian feminist philosophers of history has been highly influential on anglophone philosophy, in particular, for the ways these philosophers examine women's exclusion from philosophy using the lenses of historically contextualized metaphors and social practices. Among the significant contributions of Australian philosophers to feminist study of the history of philosophy are their claims that there is no one feminist position from which to engage with history and that feminist philosophers must recognize that their position is not always one of opposition to a politically problematic history; rather, it may also be one of collusion.

One of the most distinctive elements in Australian philosophy is the use of seventeenth-century philosopher Benedict de Spinoza's monism as the framework for philosophical thought. This approach is associated in particular with Genevieve Lloyd and Moira Gatens. The strength of this framework is that it is not grounded in a clear

reason/passion division, and thus provides an alternative to **René Descartes**'s problematic **dualist** division of these two elements of **human nature**. There are two particular strengths of this approach. First, it leads to a different conceptualizing of reason that need not be formed from a rejection of Cartesian dualism; thus this new conception need not even begin from the, albeit rejected, Cartesian framework. Second, it has possibilities for reconceptions of **sex** difference that, like a Spinozistic conception of reason, need not have an initial grounding in dualist categories.

AUTONOMY. The concept of autonomy is a central one for moral, political, and legal philosophy. The term is hard to pin down precisely, and may vary according to the particular field in which it is used, but it can be usefully defined as self-determination. Generally speaking, autonomy has been a double-edged sword for feminist philosophers. Autonomy understood as self-determination seems an important ideal. However, the concept has also historically served to exclude women, as autonomy is conceived as a characteristic of rational beings, and women have not always been accorded full or **equal** rationality by **canonical** philosophers.

In the 1970s, the main focus of feminist philosophical work on autonomy was on identifying the political and social barriers to women's development of autonomy. By the 1980s, there was a shift of emphasis toward examining the concept itself, in particular for its radical **individualism**. Feminist philosophers have pointed to the problematic nature of the character ideal of the autonomous person as an individual: one who is self-sufficient and independent to the point that "he" cannot acknowledge the value of friendship or of caring for others. Indeed, the notion of community or cooperation with others is threatening to this individual. Other feminist philosophers have argued that traditional ideals of autonomy are **masculinist** in that they lead to the valuing of aspects of human moral life that have been traditionally identified as masculine, such as independence, over those aspects traditionally identified as **feminine**, such as nurturing. More radical critiques have been provided by **postmodern feminists** who reject the notion of autonomy—as it requires an untenable notion of a unified coherent self—and by feminist critics who argue that there is a tension between this notion of unified self and the way in which the identities of individuals are constructed from their membership in various groups.

Feminist philosophers have not necessarily argued that the notion of autonomy be abandoned altogether, but they have shown that it needs to be reconceived. The different variations of a reconceived feminist notion of autonomy are often called "relational" or "social" autonomy. All these reconceptions are grounded in the view that the autonomous self is developed within and by its context of interpersonal relationships, as well as by social determinants such as **gender** and **race**. These relational or social approaches to autonomy do not simply aim to offer a reconception of the notion; they may also explore the shift in emphasis on aspects of human life that this reconception brings. These reconceptions may, for example, also provide an analysis of the ways that **oppressive** social relationships and structures hinder the development of autonomy. *See also* SUBJECTIVITY.

– B –

BACKLASH. The term backlash has been used to describe anti-feminist resistance to the women's movement and its achievements, a resistance that has been present throughout the history of the women's movement. The term is usually associated with Susan Faludi's 1991 book *Backlash: The Undeclared War against Women.*

BACON, FRANCIS (1561–1626). English philosopher Francis Bacon was under the patronage of James I and held a variety of court positions. Bacon was at the forefront of the intellectual reform of the sixteenth and seventeenth centuries. Indeed, he is known as a "father of modern science" for his origination of the inductive method and the modern view of technology: rational theorizing is combined with empirical practice to serve humankind. The work of Bacon is significant for feminist philosophers for two reasons: first, because of his historical role in the development of the view of **nature**, **science**, and knowledge that underpins modern Western philosophy; second, for what they see as his particular, foundational contribution to the male bias of this tradition. Bacon's best-known works include *Novum Organum* (1620) and *New Atlantis* (1624).

Bacon offered a new, mechanistic vision of the world as one of rational, ordered, divinely given laws that govern matter, a vision that remains the dominant view in Western thought. His view entailed the rejection of the previous notion of nature, which came from the **ancient Greeks**, as organic matter possessing internal principles of self-directed change and motion. Instead, in Bacon's notion of nature as a machine, change and motion come from external causes. Thus humans could effect change in nature for the good of humankind, and thus science becomes a moral as well as an **epistemological** project.

With this shift in the conceptualization of the subject of scientific study came an accompanying shift in the method of attaining knowledge. Bacon rejected the traditional conception of science, which originated with the Greeks, that scientific knowledge is purely the product of philosophical contemplation and speculation; he held instead that rational theorizing must work in tandem with practical experimentation. However, this new relation of experimentation, and the capacity of the knower to effect change, brought with it a conception of knowledge as achieved through control of nature, and ultimately of knowledge itself as control. Furthermore, this new relation entails a separation of human/knower from nature.

It is Bacon's new conception of scientific knowledge as dominance or control, and its accompanying conception of a separate, passive, and therefore exploitable nature, that is the subject of feminist critique, rather than any one particular work, argument, or theory. Even if the scientific knowledge that is generated can benefit humans, the process is antithetical to feminist goals. This is in part because of the hidden reliance of scientific knowledge on power relations and in part because of the reality of who will be able to wield that power: this power will be more readily available to members of socially privileged groups.

Feminist philosophers have often focused on the problematic **gendered** imagery that is part of Bacon's writings. Throughout Bacon's work, he relies on **sexual** imagery of the control of men over women to elucidate the "proper" control of man over nature. The scientist plays the role of seducer, and (if necessary) rapist, in search of the prize of possession of a female nature who must then give up her secrets. Given that Bacon's actual theory need not entail his vision of scientific knowledge as control, this imagery may work covertly to support this vision by making the domination of man over nature a "natural" or "proper" relation. *See also* CANON, CRITIQUE OF; DUALISM; IMAGINARY, PHILOSOPHICAL.

BAIER, ANNETTE. *See* HUME, DAVID.

BARRE, FRANÇOIS POULLAIN DE LA (1647–1723). The French writer and philosopher François Poullain de la Barre (Poulain de la Barre) wrote three treatises on the **equality** of the **sexes**: *On the Equality of the Two Sexes, A Physical and Moral Discourse Which Shows the Importance of Overcoming Prejudice* (1673) (which was translated in its 1676 English version as *The Woman as Good as the Man, or the Equality of Both Sexes*); *Treatise on the Education of Women, with Regard to the Conduct of the Mind in the Sciences and Morals* (1674); and *Treatise on the Excellence of Men* (1679). This last treatise repeats his earlier arguments, but it takes the form of an ironic self-refutation.

Barre is of particular interest to feminist philosophy because of his use of the philosophical principles of **René Descartes** to argue for the equality of women. Barre was not a philosopher in the sense that he produced systems or theories; rather, he aimed to show how Cartesian principles could be used to produce social reform, in particular the reform of the condition of women. This reform is produced through the way that the Cartesian method dispels the errors of unreasoned thinking that underpin and maintain the inequality of women. Barre uses the method to show that female inequality is simply a case of prejudice based on social custom; it is not a fundamental truth about **human nature**. Furthermore, he argues, if he can show that the Cartesian method could be used to refute what he describes as the oldest and most deeply ingrained prejudice, then it follows that nothing should be taken as true without proper examination. Once the prejudice against women has been refuted, it can be seen that any other prejudice can also be refuted.

Barre claims that the initial establishment of the inequality of women was an arbitrary decision based on women's different **reproductive** capacities. This then became institutionalized through laws and customs, to the point that it appears to be dictated through natural law or directly by God. Barre suggests, moreover, that the custom of the inequality was further reinforced by male desire for dominance, although he also holds that this desire is not natural either. Having established that the inferiority of women has no foundation in human nature, Barre claims that women should be able to assume central roles in the public sphere, such as professor, or in government.

BEAUTY. *See* AESTHETICS; BODY.

BEAUVOIR, SIMONE DE (1908–1986). French philosopher Simone de Beauvoir was born in Paris, France. She studied philosophy at the Sorbonne and the École Normale Supérieure; she completed the *agrégation* in 1923 and began teaching philosophy. Beauvoir began writing full time in 1944 and wrote essays and novels—as well as the autobiographical *Memoirs of a Dutiful Daughter* (1958)—in addition to her philosophical works.

Beauvoir's three central philosophical works are *The Ethics of Ambiguity* (1947), **The Second Sex** (1949), and *The Coming of Age* (1960). This last work is one of the few philosophical analyses of **age** discrimination, but this has remained a neglected field in feminist philosophy. In *The Ethics of Ambiguity*, Beauvoir offers an **existential** ethics grounded in the notion that humans are free. This notion of freedom is one of individual transcendence through action, specifically action that can work for the freedom of others, and the rejection of **oppression**. For Beauvoir, it is our ethical responsibility to take up this freedom. Thus far, there has been little feminist philosophical interest in her work on ethics.

The Second Sex is Beauvoir's only work of feminist philosophy; it is a landmark work offering an existentialist approach to both the historical and the contemporary situation of women. Beauvoir holds that the liberation of women can only be achieved through economic change, individual transcendence, and socialism. Despite the foundational role of her work for feminist thought, Beauvoir, although involved in other political causes of her time, did not initially count herself as a feminist. In 1972, however, she joined the women's liberation movement, as she no longer believed that socialism alone was adequate to change the condition of women.

Beauvoir's work was neglected until the explosion of feminist thought in the 1970s. Despite her role as a foremother of feminism in general, it was not until the 1980s that she became of interest to the specific discipline of feminist philosophy. Her work has been examined both for its philosophical thinking about **gender**, and for its role in the existentialist tradition. She also initiated a philosophical approach that was reproduced by a later more formalized feminist critique of the philosophical **canon**. Even though Beauvoir does not direct criticism at the canon specifically, throughout *The Second Sex* she analyses what has been said about women by canonical philosophers in the context of her main discussion of women's situation.

Beauvoir's well-known life-long friendship with **Jean-Paul Sartre** has affected both the analysis of her existentialist philosophy and its reception. Initially, her philosophical thinking in *The Second Sex* was seen as little more than an application of Sartre's existentialism, specifically the thought of *Being and Nothingness* (1943). This interpretation was reinforced by a few statements made by Beauvoir herself that this was indeed the case. More recently, feminist philosophers have argued that the relationship between Beauvoir and Sartre was more complex, with neither having a fixed role as teacher or originator.

The issue of replication was an important contributing factor to Beauvoir's exclusion from the philosophical canon. By the 1970s, Beauvoir was rarely mentioned in works on existentialism or French philosophy. However, in retrospect, it is also clear that the feminism in her philosophy was the other central factor in the deliberate exclusion of her work from the canon. Even though feminist philosophers have been interested in the introduction of Beauvoir to the canon, the question of her originality remains a problematic issue. This is further compounded by the fact that Sartrean existentialism has sometimes been critiqued for the **masculinist** nature of the ideal of transcendence, a notion that is a foundation of Beauvoir's analysis of women's condition in *The Second Sex*. Sartrean transcendence is, in effect, transcendence from women or the female **body**; thus women can only achieve transcendence through a psychic rejection of their own embodiment. Indeed, Beauvoir problematically holds that women's **reproductive** capacities limit their potential for transcendence.

In *The Second Sex*, Beauvoir utilizes Sartre's concept of the

"Other" as well as his notion of a self that is both a transcending "authentic" self and a fixed immanent self. The former self is free, and here freedom is understood in terms of a continual process of self-realization that characterizes this self. This authentic self is reflective consciousness, but this consciousness is of the unchanging self. Thus, even though the authentic self must transcend the unchanging self, it still requires it. This relation plays out in the relation between self and others. The "looking" subject self defines itself in relation to the "looked at" Other. There is a struggle of "looking" subject and "looked at" object, each resisting the subjugating look of the other, which both limits the being of the object and produces the transcendence of the subject.

Beauvoir extends this notion to gender relations. She claims that, in this unique case, women are permanently object. Furthermore, she argues that women do not genuinely struggle against their position as object. Women have already admitted defeat, accepting instead the privileges of the protection and status they gain from men. In this way, women not only forego transcendence from "objectivity" but fail in their ethical duty as individuals. In this move from an existential analysis of the individual to an existentialist analysis of culture that is also both political and ethical, Beauvoir adds something unique to existentialist philosophy.

Feminist theorists in general have often treated Beauvoir's analysis of the condition of women as something that can be separated from her existentialism. Indeed a criticism often made of Beauvoir is that her existentialist framework is overly intellectual, and thus unworkable. Feminist philosophers, on the other hand, have treated Beauvoir's existentialism as integral to her work on women. However, the central problems in her work that have been found by feminist philosophers are seen as a result of its existentialist framework. For Beauvoir's critics, her conceptualization of freedom, and its location in the individual, is the central cause of the lack of praxis in her work. They argue that her acceptance of the normative **dualist** hierarchy of transcendence over immanence, and its apparently masculine nature, is not only problematic itself but leads to a devaluing of women's capacity for reproduction and a potential rejection of the body. Moreover, this self/other dialectic leads to a false **universalism** of women/ the Other. This is further compounded by the fact that Beauvoir identifies the **experience** of women with the experience of the white bourgeoisie. In contrast, some feminist philosophers have argued for the potential of Beauvoir's work for their theorizing. Some philosophers, for example, have pointed to the way that Beauvoir's account of the female body does not in fact attribute its passivity, or its role in preventing women from achieving individual transcendence, to biology; rather, she holds that these characteristics are the result of its social construction. Beauvoir thus can provide a resource for some of the current feminist work in body politics. *See also* SUBJECTIVITY.

BINARY OPPOSITION. *See* DUALISM.

BIOETHICS. Bioethics was established as a subfield of **feminist ethics** by the early 1990s; many of the concerns of feminist ethics are relevant for feminist bioethics, such as questions of **autonomy** and the ethical importance of **care**. Feminist bioethics provides both a critique of, and an alternative to, mainstream bioethics: the study of moral issues raised by health and health care. It provides a feminist perspective on standard bioethical issues such as **abortion**; it also allows for the introduction of new concerns into the field of bioethics, such as eating disorders. The vast majority of work in this area has been done within the **analytic** tradition (broadly conceived), but there have been a few **postmodernist** approaches to the development of a feminist bioethics.

Feminist bioethics is committed to an examination of the moral issues of health and health care through the multiple lenses of **race**, **gender**, class, **disability**, **sexual** orientation, and **age**. However, gender usually functions as its pivotal element, given such facts as that the largest number of health care workers are women; the majority of patients are women; women are disproportionately represented among the poor; research has focused on men or male health issues; and women often provide the invisible care provider services at home that support the health care system.

While proponents of mainstream bioethics recognize the existence of inequalities between patients and health care providers, and the importance of contextual decision-making, feminist bioethics is based on a commitment to the removal of such inequalities and to an analysis of the social and political contexts of bioethical concerns.

Moreover, unlike mainstream bioethics, which tends toward framing bioethical concerns in terms of individuals and often focuses on the moral dilemmas of those in power (doctors, health care administrators), feminist bioethics emphasizes the inclusion of the moral, political, and health care needs and perspectives of groups, particularly those with the least power.

BIOLOGICAL DETERMINISM. Biological determinism is the concept that physiological differences between the **sexes** determine the different social and cultural roles of men and women as well as the relations between men and women. Most feminists dismiss biological determinism, typically claiming that psychological, social, and cultural differences between the sexes are the product of **socialization**. Some feminists, however, hold that there are valuable characteristics, such as a lack of aggressiveness, which are the product of female physiology in some way.

Historically, the notion of biological determinism has been an important one for feminist philosophy. Deterministic arguments have often been employed by those who wish to preserve male social and cultural dominance as well as traditional female roles. The first sustained attack on the notion came in **Mary Wollstonecraft**'s 1792 work *A Vindication of the Rights of Woman*, in which she argued that the behaviors and traits of her female contemporaries were the product of their environment and **education**. A central argument used by Wollstonecraft to support her claim is that military men of that time, due to their particular environment, behaved in many of the same ways as women. These men, for example, focused much of their attention on their appearance and on their romantic conquests.

Biological determinism has ceased to be a significant issue, as it rests on simplistic notions of human biology and sex distinctions that have been challenged by feminist philosophers since the 1980s. One central challenge of this type has been the claim that what is called biological nature is itself socially constructed. *See also* BODY; CULTURAL FEMINISM; ESSENTIALISM; GENDER; HUMAN NATURE.

BLACK FEMINIST ETHICS. Whether there is a history of black feminist ethics is a complicated question. **Black feminist philosophers**, writers, and activists certainly discussed the values and virtues of black women. Indeed, the nineteenth-century philosopher **Anna Julia Cooper** even held that the moral influence of black women was their contribution to political change. While none of these thinkers could be described as offering anything that could be called an ethical system, it can also be claimed that there is an oral ethical tradition within the African American community, a tradition that is reflected in literature and popular culture. This tradition can be described as one of ethical knowledge that offers shared values and an understanding of the black community.

Most of the work in **feminist ethics** has been done by white Western women. However, in the 1980s, work that is an identifiably black feminist ethics started to be produced, mainly in the United States. Its creators may not always accept the designation of "feminist" due to the history of racism within the feminist movement and feminist theory. In the cases where black feminist philosophers do categorize their work as an explicitly black feminist ethics, this functions as a political statement that not only asserts a black female identity but also provides a critique of the ways that dominant ethical thinking ignores the realities of black existence. These philosophers may claim, for example, that the ideal in the dominant tradition of the **moral agent** as **autonomous** requires a level of personal freedom, one that does not reflect the lived **experiences** of black women.

Alternatively, other philosophers have produced a systematized ethical thought as a component of an overall philosophical theory. Two main reasons can be identified for this. First, it is not always helpful to categorize work in ethics separately from black feminist philosophy more generally, as this may serve to fragment the foundational goal of social **justice**. Second, analyses of injustice, and calls for justice, cannot be made separately from a properly formulated ethics of accountability.

While there is no one way of thinking that is black feminist ethics, there are shared themes within work that falls under this rubric. First, the experiences of black women offer a central **epistemic** and ethical resource. For some philosophers, these shared experiences can offer a moral knowledge for black women to survive, and live well, within a racist society. This knowledge, for example, can help individual black women to learn to develop the specific virtues, such as self-respect, needed for this moral and political task. This picture of situated, concrete individuals, and their particular virtues, also entails a critique of the dominant moral picture of the **universality** of virtues and the **individualism** of moral agents. Some black feminist philosophers also argue that the experiences of black women can provide a resource for the black community as a whole, as they can lead to an understanding of the way that this community functions and could develop. An ethics of **care** is another common theme in black feminist ethical thought. This can be framed either as foundational to the desire for social justice or more explicitly politicized as a direct way to effect social change. Another shared theme is the rejection of derogatory stereotypes both of the **sexual** morality of black women and of black women as morally one-dimensional, fitting them only for servility.

Despite the fact that black feminist ethics is often seen as a particular subfield of the more general field of feminist ethics, it should not be assumed that it only comes out of feminist ethical thinking. Black feminist ethical thinking also comes from the traditions of black theological ethics, and African American communities, as well as from **African** ways of thinking about individuals and communities. *See also* FEMININE ETHICS; RACE AND RACISM.

BLACK FEMINIST PHILOSOPHY. Work in black feminist philosophy has, thus far, been confined to the United States. The line between black feminist philosophy and black feminist social critics is blurred; the categorization of a theorist as either a social critic or a philosopher often depends on the context in which this theorist's work is being considered. Whether they are categorized as philosophers or not, Patricia Hill Collins, Angela Davis, bell hooks, and Audre Lorde are among the foremost U.S. black **feminist theorists** who have had a significant impact on feminist philosophy.

The term black feminist philosophy is hard to apply with any specificity. The contributions of black feminist philosophers to political and social philosophy have gained the most attention, especially for their work on analyses of **oppression**, racism and **race**. This has meant, however, that black feminists' contributions to the other tradi-

tional areas of philosophy—**epistemology** and ethics, in particular—
have been seen in a piecemeal fashion, rather than as being based
on some common philosophical standpoint. In addition, within the
academic discipline of philosophy, black feminist philosophers as
well as philosophers from other minority racial groups have remained
on the margins not only of mainstream philosophy, but even of feminist philosophy. These factors have made it difficult to assess
whether or not there is an identifiable field of specifically black feminist philosophy.

There are few records of any history of black feminist intellectual
thought. Black women's economic and social oppressions greatly
limited opportunities for the type of education they needed to write
what would pass, under mainstream criteria, as intellectual work.
One of the few black feminist intellectuals from the nineteenth century was **Anna Julia Cooper**, who can be seen as offering one of the
earliest articulations of a black feminist philosophy. Cooper's work
contains the hallmarks of black feminism: she critiques the **sexism** in
the black advancement movement as well as the racism in the wom-
en's movement. Cooper discussed these issues within an analytic
framework on race, and a philosophy of **education**. Many of the elements identified by Cooper as central for the liberation of both men
and women of color remain shared elements of modern black feminist thought: the examination of sexism in the black community; the
examination of racism in the feminist community; and the analysis
of race and racism.

Central to black feminist thought is the goal of identification of the
way that the systems of oppression of race, class, and **gender** interlock. These systems affect women in different ways; thus the **experience** of sexism of women of color and of white women is not the
same: there is no "women's" experience of oppression. Moreover,
there is no position from which women of color are able to examine
their situation as "women"; women are women of color, working-
class women, and so on. Indeed, a central critique that black feminists make of feminist theorizing in general (white-dominated feminism) is that the social subject "women" only means white women.
This then serves to marginalize women of color, and their specific
concerns and experiences are rendered invisible. In a fundamental

sense, these concerns and experiences are not counted as part of the oppression of women.

Black feminist theorists also criticize (white-dominated) feminist theorizing for its failure to recognize that racism does not just serve to oppress women of color; it also functions to benefit white women. These benefits can be purely practical in that women of color tend to perform the lower-paid service jobs that enable middle-class white women to focus on their careers. They can also be political; white women are in a better position to attain the social and economic privilege of white men if they are able to show that they are closer to white men than other women. Overall the black feminist critique has had a significant impact on feminist thought, including feminist philosophy; most feminist theorists now attend to differences among women.

Black feminist theorizing in general, and black feminist philosophy more specifically, are not simply critique. The development of **black feminist ethics** and black feminist epistemology are not simply projects that demonstrate the omission of the perspectives and experiences of women of color from these subject areas (feminist and non-feminist alike). Instead, black feminist ethics and epistemology provide alternative ways of talking about and conceptualizing both knowledge and **moral agency**. Patricia Hill Collins has been in the forefront of the development of these projects. For Collins, the experience of black women allows them an epistemically privileged standpoint from which to identify not only truths about black women, but also the creation of new ways to think about criteria for the truth of knowledge claims. Historically, black women have been the objects of knowledge for other knowers; to become subjects or producers of their own knowledge is empowering.

For black women, truth is measured against shared experiences, and the function of knowledge is fundamentally practical: knowledge of survival in a racist society. This shared knowledge provides a basis for both political identity and political action. For Collins, assessment of these knowledge claims for their validity occurs through dialogue within a community; this is something she claims has its roots in **African** oral tradition. This is in stark contrast to traditional epistemology, which holds that knowledge must be **objective** and **universal**, not based on individual experience or agreed upon truth.

Moreover, in the traditional view, knowledge is also knowledge for its own sake, not just for its practical use.

Another central difference between Collins's epistemology and that of mainstream philosophy is that the former is not **value neutral**. For Collins, knowledge claims are also assessed in relation to the integrity of the person making the claims, for this person is morally accountable for the claims. In this way, epistemology blends into ethics; the separation between the two fields of traditional philosophy is neither productive nor relevant for black women. Collins identifies three main elements of the ethics necessary for a black feminist epistemology: the development of a sense of self as a unique individual, one with a capacity for empathy, and the acceptance of the epistemic validity of the **emotions**.

Despite its political and epistemological strength, this type of approach to black feminist thought has been criticized. It appears to rest on the **essentialist** (and thus problematic) assumption that black women have a shared group identity; this then functions to make their differences unimportant. *See also* CARE, ETHICS OF; FEMINIST ETHICS.

BLACKWELL, ANTOINETTE BROWN (1825–1921). American philosopher Antoinette Brown Blackwell was born and raised in New York State. Blackwell studied theology at Oberlin College in Ohio, and in 1853 she was the first woman to be ordained in a major religious denomination in America. After leaving Oberlin, she worked on the lecture circuit and became involved with the women's **rights** movement and other movements for social reform.

Blackwell's 1875 work *The Sexes Throughout Nature* is her main contribution to feminist philosophy. She believed this collection of essays would provide a foundation for a new **scientific** theory of female **nature**. In her work, Blackwell holds to a type of **cultural feminism**, in that she claims the physical and psychological natures of the two **sexes** are different but **equal**. Moreover, she identifies the **oppression** of women with a thwarting of their particular nature. Central to her theory is her feminist critique of the evolutionary theories of Charles Darwin and Herbert Spencer. Blackwell argues that Darwin and Spencer focused only on the evolution of male characteristics and, in so doing, produced a standard by which women are labeled as inferior. Blackwell argues instead that, throughout the different species, females have different but equal characteristics; in humans, for example, female endurance is equivalent to male strength. In analyzing the physical and psychological characteristics of humans, Blackwell does not critique the empirical data she employs. Thus she argues that the male intellect is equally balanced by female insight, and the male instinct for **sexual** love is equally balanced by the female instinct for parenting, without questioning whether these characteristics are natural.

Blackwell's view that the two sexes have fundamentally different natures, however, also leads to an interesting critique of the social roles and treatment of women. She holds that each sex is adapted to its particular function: women bear and raise children; men support and provide for the **family**. She argues that the **division of labor** within a family must follow this design of nature; thus men, as providers, must cook and sew for the family. She holds that for women to take on these roles, as well as their "natural" role as care provider, is a form of oppression. Similarly, preventing women from physical or intellectual activity because they are apparently too weak for such things also goes against their nature, and thus constitutes oppression. *See also* HUMAN NATURE.

BODY. Feminists' concern with the relation between women's subordination and their bodies began as early as the **first wave** of feminism in the eighteenth century. **Mary Wollstonecraft** was the first to recognize that the ideals of **femininity** were played out on women's bodies, through the way that they were cramped and constrained by clothing and rules of deportment. **Second wave feminists** argued that the identification of women with their bodies was a central pillar for, and justification of, the male domination of women. Thus part of the feminist call for self-determination during this time was a call for women to take back control of their bodies, for example, by rejecting cultural ideals of beauty, or by asserting control of their capacity for **reproduction**. During the 1980s there was a trend toward an examination of the way that women were **alienated** from their bodies through, for example, the way that women internalized and acted upon norms of beauty in order to gain the attention and approval of men.

Dominant strands of thought among contemporary feminist philosophers are the examination of an apparent fear of the body within the Western tradition and a theorizing about the body that is primarily influenced by **Luce Irigaray**, **Michel Foucault**, and **Judith Butler**. These types of thought also function to critique earlier theorists for the way they oversimplified the body and ignored differences among women.

The philosophical fear of and disgust with the body in the Western philosophical tradition either comes out of, or provides the ground for, a **dualist** view that the **mind** is superior to the body but also requires transcendence of a hindering body for the acquisition of knowledge. One result of this view is the exclusion of women from the philosophical project because they are culturally associated with the body.

Within **French feminist** philosophy, the complex symbolism of their writing with the body—"feminine writing"—functions as a criticism of the Western philosophical tradition; it is an alternative site for the making of meaning, and developing of knowledge, that is outside **patriarchal** discourse. For these thinkers, **sex** identity is not produced through biology; it is the construct of patriarchal forms of representation of women. Writing outside of this construct disrupts the male order of **language** and knowledge and thus can challenge the dualistic thinking that is the dominant structure of the Western tradition.

The dominant trend in theorizing about the body comes out of **postmodern feminist** thought. Not only does postmodernist thought expose the way that women's bodies are normalized—"disciplined" —to subordinate them to the patriarchal system of power, but it also points to the ambiguities inherent in any claim that the norms of the feminine body **oppress** women. Coming out of the work of Judith Butler is the claim that sex, not just **gender**, is the construct of discourse. To claim that the body is some natural, fixed structure is dangerous, as this underpins the assumptions about the natural, fixed structure of sex difference that justify and form the domination of women. Moreover, the subsequent naturalness of the existence of two oppositional unitary sexes, and thus the assumption of a **sexual** attraction between complementary opposites, supports the **heterosexist** social system.

There is no agreement as to what would count as resistance to the norms of the body. Some feminist philosophers claim that resistance need not take the form of rejection but can come from working within these norms by expanding and replaying them, either through physical change or through decoration. The most radical example of this kind of resistance is Orlan, the French performance artist, who used her body as a canvas to take on different ideal facial features of female beauty through cosmetic surgery. Other feminist philosophers, however, argue that this kind of approach fails to deal with the fact that ideals of female beauty function to oppress different women, such as women of color, in a different set of ways. Thus resistance within the system of norms may implicitly replay, for example, the **racist** elements of ideals of beauty. *See also* AESTHETICS; HUMAN NATURE; OBJECTIFICATION; SOMATOPHOBIA.

BUTLER, JUDITH (1956–). The work of American sociologist and philosopher Judith Butler has had a significant impact on feminist theorizing about the **body**, **gender**, **sex**, and **sexuality**. Her two central works are *Gender Trouble: Feminism and the Subversion of Identity* (1990) and *Bodies That Matter: On the Discursive Limits of "Sex"* (1993).

Butler's work on gender has been the most significant for feminist philosophizing. She argues that gender (**femininity**/woman) is not "real"; it is, instead, the construct of **patriarchal** discourse, and only within the system of **heterosexuality** does gender identity appear coherent. Within this system, men and women are defined in relation to each other—as opposites—and thus gender identity is framed as a relation of mutual dependence. This need for their other is constructed as a sexual need, with the result that human sexuality becomes identified as heterosexuality.

Butler's work is controversial; some feminist philosophers claim that it undercuts political theorizing and strategizing for women's liberation: if there is no coherent concept of "woman," there can be no subject to liberate. *See also* FOUCAULT, MICHEL; LANGUAGE, PHILOSOPHY OF.

– C –

CANON, CRITIQUE OF. The feminist critique of the canon is part of the more general field of feminist **history of philosophy**. The canon critique is grounded in the recognition that philosophy is, at least in part, constructed by particular historical and cultural contexts; thus, philosophy does not fit its own ideals of **objectivity** and **value neutrality**. This recognition is not exclusive to feminist approaches to the history of philosophy; rather, the distinguishing feature of such approaches is their focus on the **androcentric** nature of these contexts and the way that **gender** plays out in the construction of philosophical theories and positions.

The gender bias of the philosophical enterprise surfaces in a variety of ways. It can appear directly through the exclusion of female and feminist philosophers or through the misogynist views of canonical authors; it appears indirectly through the construction of the enterprise as inherently **masculine**—for example, through the identification of **reason** with "maleness."

The earliest feminist canon critique was undertaken in the United States in the 1970s. Initially, the focus was on uncovering the biases against women, or issues associated with women, within the philosophical canon. By the 1980s, it had become clear that these biases could not be redressed by simply "adding" women—or their **experiences**, interests, and concerns—into philosophical theorizing. Feminist philosophers had recognized, instead, that gender bias was deeply ingrained within philosophical thought: in its concepts, ideals, and **methodology**.

During the 1980s, Anglo-American **analytic feminist** canon critique first began to show the influence of the deconstructive readings of texts by **French feminist** theorists, such as **Luce Irigaray**. Attention began to be paid, for example, to the way that the male-female distinction symbolically played out in texts as well as in conceptualizations of reason and its opposites, such as desire. The 1980s was also a period in which canon revision, through the introduction of previously neglected **women philosophers**, began to take shape. This latter project, which is still ongoing, is necessary in order to show that philosophy has not been the sole preserve of men, and also to offer potential foremothers for feminist philosophy.

During this period, Anglo-American feminist philosophers began to ask the further question of whether the canon can be reconstructed, in particular whether it can be reconstructed in such a way that it can support a feminist philosophical enterprise. Some philosophers argue for the outright rejection of the canon, but on the whole, Anglo-

American analytic feminist philosophy has tended toward the preservation of the philosophical canon. Roughly speaking, the revisionist project uses earlier feminist critiques as a springboard to develop new philosophical theories and perspectives. Central examples of this type of project are some of the work in **epistemology** and in the philosophy of **science**.

CARE, ETHICS OF (CARE ETHICS). The foundation of the contemporary philosophical debate on the ethics of care, or care ethics, can be found in the empirical work of **Carol Gilligan**, in particular in her 1982 work *In a Different Voice: Psychological Theory and Women's Development*. Gilligan identifies two ways of thinking about morality: an ethic of care and an ethic of **justice**. The latter can be identified in many ways with traditional moral philosophy, in that it emphasizes **universalizable** moral choices made by **impartial, autonomous** individuals, and the **rights** of such individuals. In contrast, an ethic of care gives moral priority to contextual and particular decision-making, to relationships, and to the responsibilities entailed by those relationships.

Philosophical developments of the ethics of care have focused on exploring the possibility of providing an alternative to the ethic of justice, one that is grounded in the moral **experience** of women's caring for others. However, the questions of whether the two ethics are compatible, whether an adequate care ethic can be developed in isolation from notions of justice, or whether a care ethic should replace the ethic of justice are contentious ones. Because of the association of care with women's cultural and historical roles, some feminist philosophers have claimed that an ethics based on care maintains the subordination of women, as it valorizes cultural ideals of women's roles. Indeed, there is a concern that an emphasis on the development of an ethics of care—as a specifically female ethic— may ultimately serve to limit the **moral agency** of women: only one type of agency (relational) will be best for them.

The introduction of the notion of care into moral discourse, however, does have something important to offer moral philosophy in general. Care is not simply a matter of feeling or intuition; it has a cognitive side: it is a practice that requires judgment, **reason**, and a focus on particular others. In this way, care ethics can allow **emo-**

tions and empathy to play a role in moral decision-making, a role that a justice ethic explicitly excludes.

The concept of care itself is open to interpretation and analysis. Nel Noddings, for example, holds that care talk is the native **language** of women. She frames care in terms not of individuals, but of pairs—the "one caring" and the "cared for"—in terms of the maternal relation. Other feminist philosophers, however, utilize a broader conception that is a "caring for others," which is not identified with women in any particular way.

While care is often incorporated into a **feminine ethics**, it can also play a part in the development of a **feminist ethics**: a politicized ethics. Patricia Hill Collins, for example, politicizes the notion of care for a **black feminist ethics**, specifically the importance of care for maternal practice within African American communities. One central aspect of such care is teaching children the necessary survival skills to live under **oppression**. This maternal care is not understood solely in terms of the dyad of **mother**-child; responsibility for care can also be shared within the female community. Collins sees this latter element as a challenge to capitalist notions of children as (individual) property, and as an impetus—through shared goals of responsibility—for political activism. *See also* CULTURAL FEMINISM; INDIVIDUALISM, ABSTRACT; MATERNAL ETHICS; RELATIVISM.

CAVENDISH, MARGARET (1623–1673). English philosopher Margaret Cavendish, Duchess of Newcastle, was born Margaret Lucas into a Royalist family from the minor gentry. She had little formal **education**, a fact that she regretted. She held a position at the court of Charles I and went into exile to France with the court. In France she met the English philosopher Thomas Hobbes and the French philosophers **René Descartes** and Pierre Gassendi, but it is not clear whether she had much philosophical interaction with them. Cavendish wrote plays and novels as well as natural philosophy. This philosophy is most clearly set out in three of her works: *Philosophical Letters: or, Modest Reflections upon Some Opinions in Natural Philosophy, Maintained by Several Famous and Learned Authors of This Age* (1644); *Observations upon Experimental Philosophy* (1666); and *Grounds of Natural Philosophy* (1668). The *Observations* probably contains the clearest exposition of her philosophical thought.

Cavendish sets up her position in opposition to Descartes's radical **dualism** between **mind** and **body**, holding instead a type of organic materialism. For Cavendish, **nature** is made of one material that she describes as self-moving and self-knowing, as she held that matter is both sensitive and rational. Thus matter produces it own motion: its motion is not the result of an external cause. This also entails that Cavendish holds there cannot be a first cause, although she did not lay claim to the atheism inherent in this position.

This view of nature also means that she rejected the standard notions of the time that humans should control nature, as she holds that humans were not separable in this way. Moreover, she also rejected the accompanying notion that humans, due to their rationality or intelligence, were superior to nature, arguing instead that their only superiority came from physical differences. Cavendish holds that even plant-life has its own form of rationality or intelligence; however, because this rationality is dissimilar from that of humans who judge only by their own standards, it is dismissed or unrecognized.

Cavendish's view of nature and **science** is of interest to present-day feminist philosophers because of its critique of the traditional notion that humans should control nature and because of its rejection of a dualist and mechanist conceptualization of nature. Her natural philosophy, however, cannot be described as a true forerunner of current approaches to either a **feminine** or feminist physics.

CHILD-BEARING. *See* REPRODUCTION, SEXUAL.

CHILDREN. *See* FAMILY.

CHINA, FEMINIST PHILOSOPHY IN. The earliest identifiable Chinese female philosopher is Pan Chao (Ban Zhao), who lived circa 45–114 and was a scholar at the imperial court. She wrote a treatise on the **education** of women, *Lessons for Women* (*Nü Jie*), somewhere between 89 and 105. Pan Chao could perhaps be described as a proto-feminist, as she offered a formulated moral system for women grounded in Confucian ethics. Her focus was on the social order, specifically the order of the **family**, which was the central moral unit for Confucianism. Pan Chao describes the virtues, such as modesty, required for women to maintain harmony and order within the family unit. The relative conservativeness of this discussion is balanced by Pan Chao's more radical claim that women require education in order to develop and to exercise these virtues. She specifically claims that young girls should be educated in the same way as boys to follow the rules of education, in accordance with the ancient "Rites."

On the whole, current feminist intellectual work in China is oriented toward policy-making. Some feminist theorizing is emerging, however, which can be categorized as philosophical in its orientation. This theorizing occurs against the background of the **Marxist** tradition. This tradition recognizes the **gender-**specific **oppression** of women but does not see their liberation as a separable struggle from the liberation of the proletariat. Some feminist theorists in China are beginning revisionist work within this tradition, aiming to move beyond a gender-blind class analysis to one that recognizes a gendered identity of women. Work is being done by some theorists on establishing what this amounts to, and whether this could constitute a vantage point from which to uncover—and correct—male bias in our understanding of the world. The concept of "gender" was introduced in 1993 at a feminist seminar, and it is termed *shehuixingbie* or "social **sex**."

CHRISTIANITY. Feminist critiques of Christianity in general, and proposals for alternatives to the Christian **religion**, can be found as early as the nineteenth century. One strand of feminist thought in this era was a belief in the existence of a pre-Christian matriarchy, a time of peaceful cooperation; this often led to a call for the development of a goddess-centered religion.

In contemporary Western feminist Christian theory, the critique has become more formalized and can be divided into two main groups of thought. One approach comes from within the Christian tradition and focuses on the status of women in the church: for example, the call for the ordination of women. The second approach is the critique of the tradition itself. One central element of this second approach is a critique of the Christian view of women, in particular how the paradigmatic image of Eve was used to justify the subordination of women, because they were seen as the source of sin. Another central element that is closely related to this is the critique of both the **androcentric** nature of the image of God as male, and the

gendered nature of the **language** that is used to describe the divine being.

Of these two approaches, only the latter truly falls into the scope of Western feminist philosophy of religion. Central to this project is the reconstruction of the concept of a male God, a concept that has functioned to reinforce the subordination of women. Feminist philosophical work on Christianity, to date, has been dominated by the work of **Mary Daly**; indeed, the framework of the discourse originated with her post-Christian work of the 1970s. For Daly, God is not identified with a transcendent male being. Such a God is separate from **nature**, and this relation of separation brings with it the relation of "power over." This latter relation, according to Daly, provides the paradigm for, and justification of, the power of men over women on earth. During this early period of her work, Daly argues for the replacement of a **patriarchal** transcendent God with an immanent God who is part of the world.

However, not all feminist work in Christian theology is purely critical in this way. For feminist Christians outside the West (Asia, **Africa**, and **Latin America**, in particular), the Western emphasis on a critique of the "maleness" of the tradition is seen as politically misdirected. These non-Western feminists argue, instead, that political reform and empowerment need to be grounded in a belief in Jesus as the champion of the poor and **oppressed**. *See also* CULTURAL FEMINISM; ISLAM; JUDAISM.

CIXOUS, HÉLÈNE (1937–). The work of **French feminist** theorist Hélène Cixous has been influential in recent developments in literary theory, but it has not been of particular interest for feminist philosophers. She is, however, recognized for her general contribution to the philosophical approach usually called French feminism; it is this general approach that has had a significant impact on Anglophone feminist philosophy. Cixous aims to create a **feminine** form of expression—*écriture féminine*—that challenges the male symbolic order of the Western intellectual tradition. In the traditional male symbolic order, women are constructed in negative terms (e.g., not active) and thus as inferior to men. Cixous aims to write from a position outside this. She advocates a feminine writing that, through its fluidity and mutability, challenges the rigidity of the dichotomous male language and thought and its exclusion of women. *See also* IRI-GARAY, LUCE; LANGUAGE, PHILOSOPHY OF; POSTMODERN FEMINISM.

COIGNET, CLARISSE (1823–?). French philosopher Clarisse Coignet's primary philosophical interest was the establishment of an independent morality that was not grounded in **science** or **religion** but was, rather, a morality solely produced by humans. Her central publication in this area was *La Morale indépendante dans son principe et son objet* (1869), a work influenced in part by **Immanuel Kant**'s moral philosophy. Coignet was interested in the British women's suffrage movement of the time, and she claimed that her goal of an independent morality was connected with the political goals of this movement. Coignet argued that a morality grounded in human freedom and responsibility could serve to liberate women from their subservient status to men, as women would be recognized as individuals possessing **equal** dignity and worth. This liberation, however, did not extend to social and economic freedom for women, as Coignet maintained that the only work natural to women was their biologically destined role of **motherhood**.

COLLINS, PATRICIA HILL. *See* BLACK FEMINIST PHILOSOPHY; CARE, ETHICS OF.

COMPULSORY HETEROSEXUALITY. *See* HETEROSEXISM.

CONSCIOUSNESS RAISING. Consciousness raising was a central strategy for women's liberation during the **second wave** of feminism, particularly for the more radical movement that grew out of other protest movements of the 1960s, such as the civil **rights** movement. Driven by the insight that "the personal is political," small groups of women would meet to share what they had hitherto seen as merely personal or individual **experiences**. This sharing would then lead the group to see common themes in these experiences: that female **oppression** is structural and institutionalized. The participants would then work toward strategies for social and political change.

　　Consciousness raising has played an important role in opening up the possibilities for a specifically feminist mode of gaining knowledge. It allowed women the possibility of seeing beyond **androcentric** biases in knowledge. Moreover, it gave women the power to be the knowers, creators, and subjects of knowledge, which feminist critics claimed had been previously the privilege of men. This critique of androcentric knowledge, and the possibilities of knowledge generated by the experiences of women, can be seen as connected to the development of feminist **epistemology** in the 1980s.

CONTINENTAL PHILOSOPHY. The term Continental feminist philosophy is sometimes used as a convenient way to describe any feminist philosophy that is not part of the Anglo-American **analytic** tradition. This means that it is used to cover analysis and retrieval of the Continental tradition itself, as well as recent **postmodern** philosophy. In the case of feminist philosophical work, it is useful to separate Continental philosophy into these two categories, however loose they may be, to define and examine this work. Thus the specific subject area of feminist work in Continental philosophy is best understood as an examination of this particular tradition—specifically, the critique of the central figures of its historical tradition—and the consideration of ways in which these figures' philosophies may be appropriated for feminist purposes.

Although Anglophone feminist philosophers have reread texts by the central figures from the Continental tradition, they have usually examined **canonical** philosophers as individuals, not as part of a tradition. Moreover, there is usually no general direction of interests or cohesion among such interpretations. The study of these figures within the general context of this tradition is usually only done by European feminist philosophers.

Feminist interpretive work has been done on some of the central figures of the Continental tradition. Given **Immanuel Kant**'s place in the canon, much of this work has been done on his philosophy. However, due to Kant's place in the evolution of the separation of the two systems of analytic and Continental philosophy, the interpretations of him have depended on the particular tradition within which the interpreter is writing. Besides Kant, the philosophies of G. W. F. Hegel and **Friedrich Nietzsche** have generated the most work, as they are viewed as the most fruitful for the feminist enterprise. The writings of **Jean-Paul Sartre** are not of particular interest for feminist philosophy; however, he is considered of importance because of his philosophical connections with **Simone de Beauvoir**. *See also* HISTORY OF PHILOSOPHY.

CONTINENTAL RATIONALISM. *See* AUSTRALIA, FEMINIST PHILOSOPHY IN; DESCARTES, RENÉ.

CONTRACTARIANISM. Contractarianism is the view that political relations have their origins in a contract or agreement: a social contract. Following the publication of American philosopher John Rawls's 1971 work *A Theory of Justice*, there was a renewal of philosophical interest in contract theory. For some feminist philosophers, contractarianism is a promising theory because it is grounded in the rational consent of free and **equal** individuals, devoid of the differences produced by their actual (historical, **bodily**, etc.) circumstances: the same differences that have helped justify the inequality of women. This notion, however, has also been the target of feminist criticism because the unsituated, disembodied self is a "male" notion more reflective of male **experience**, and because women are culturally identified with their bodies. Indeed, it is precisely because of **sex/**bodily difference, and the psychological differences that are supposed to come from this, that the subordination of women has typically been justified.

The foundational premises of the classical formulations of the social contract have also been criticized by feminist philosophers for the way that they exclude women. Women have typically been excluded from the classical theories of social contract because of the way that sex difference is held to produce inferiority in rationality, while the contract is made between rational individuals. Moreover, because the social contract applies only to the public sphere, the subordination of women in the private sphere is ignored; indeed, this omission may even give an implicit sanction to their subordination. Certainly, the social relations between the sexes often remain unexamined by modern theorists and policy-makers alike in their discussions of civil freedom. *See also* INDIVIDUALISM, ABSTRACT; POLITICAL AND SOCIAL PHILOSOPHY; PUBLIC/PRIVATE DISTINCTION; SUBJECTIVITY.

CONTROLLING IMAGES. The term controlling image is used to describe the way that stereotypes have a specific function: to maintain domination over subordinate groups. Even if the stereotype of a group is a "positive" one, it limits or hampers that group or individuals of that group. It dictates what kinds of behaviors are "normal" and penalizes those who step outside of or resist that image. Furthermore, as these images are set by the dominant groups, individuals of subordinate groups may find that they have to work within these images to fulfill their own economic and social needs within existing power structures.

CONWAY, ANNE FINCH (1631–1679). English philosopher Anne Finch came from a wealthy family and appears to have received a good home **education**; she moved in intellectual circles, counting among her friends members of the Cambridge Platonists. In 1651, she became Viscountess Conway. Her only published philosophical work is *The Principles of the Most Ancient and Modern Philosophy*, published first in 1690 in Latin, and then in English in 1692.

Given that Conway's philosophical legacy is only this one work, her philosophy has not been the subject of any particularly detailed study for its own sake; however, her philosophy has been of general historical interest because of her connections to the seventeenth-century German philosopher Gottfried Leibniz. Leibniz appears to have thought well of her work, and it has been suggested that the Leibnizian term "monad" originated with her. Certainly, they share a philosophical vision of an interconnected, vitalist world.

Conway has been of interest to feminist philosophers both because of the critique that she offered of the major thinkers of her period, in particular **René Descartes** and the English philosopher Thomas Hobbes, and because she has been seen as offering a "**feminine**" physics. Conway rejects the mechanistic view of **nature** (such as that of Descartes and Hobbes), holding instead that the created world is an organic unity, one that is alive and interconnected through the **Christian** framework of the hierarchical chain of being. Part of this vitalist view of the world is a monistic view of matter and spirit: they are not ontologically separate. In this way, Conway provides an alternative to the Cartesian **dualism** of **mind** and **body**, a concept that has been a target of criticism for feminist philosophers.

Ultimately, however, Conway's monism offers not much more than a reduction of bodies to spirit. This then means that her philosophy can only be silent on the subject of the behaviors, phenomena, and interactions of bodies; a subject that is of importance for contemporary thinkers. Moreover, Conway maintained the normative distinction between spirit and body held by her contemporaries, conceiving of spirit as superior to body. Despite these limitations, her emphasis on connectivity and the flow of life has been seen as an early example of feminine philosophical and **scientific** thinking.

COOPER, ANNA JULIA (1858–1964). The work of the African American philosopher and teacher Anna Julia Cooper has not typically been an important subject of analysis for either feminist philosophers or historians of black American thought. This is unexpected, as she was connected to the leading figures of the black intellectual movement of her time; her **educational** philosophy, in particular, has been seen to align her with the vision of W. E. B. Du Bois. More recently, however, there has been a development of interest in her work, and Cooper has been credited with offering the clearest and best-argued articulation of early **black feminist philosophical** thought.

Cooper was born Anna Julia Haywood in Raleigh, North Carolina. Her mother was a slave, and Cooper assumed that her father was her mother's master. After emancipation, Cooper began her education at an elementary school. She continued her education throughout her life, earning a B.A. and an M.A. at Oberlin College, and a Ph.D. from the Sorbonne at age sixty-seven. Cooper married in 1877, but her husband George Cooper died two years later. As married women at that time could not teach, this was a significant event of Cooper's career, as it freed her to be a teacher. Cooper supported herself as a teacher and a school principal, and during this time she wrote and spoke publicly on black advancement.

Cooper published her first and best-known work, *A Voice from the South by a Black Woman of the South*, in 1892. It is a collection of essays that she wrote between 1886 and 1892 on racial advancement, racism, sexism, and education. It is because of this work that Cooper has been described as an early black feminist philosopher, even though *A Voice* is her only work on women. The reason for her writing only work on the subject of women is not clear, but it has been suggested that, because the black intellectual movement of the time was male-dominated, there may not have been an intellectual place for analysis and critique of the status of black women. In *A Voice*, Cooper holds that the status of black women, not black men, is the true measure of black advancement. Indeed, she critiques black men for championing ministry as a way of educational and social advancement, as this was at the expense of women, who could not enter the ministry. Simultaneously, she also critiqued the feminist movement for its deliberate and racist exclusion of women of color. She held that the true political and ethical strength of the women's movement could only come from black women, who were subject to both racism and sexism. In this way, Cooper's thought contains the seeds of current black feminist philosophy.

Yet despite this radical position, Cooper tended to ignore black women from lower social classes. Even more problematically, she framed the liberation of black women in terms of the white bourgeois feminist ideology of "true womanhood," which was dominant at that time. Cooper argued that black women should not be actively involved in politics, but rather they should effect change through exerting a moral influence on men. Cooper's motivations for arguing for true womanhood are not clear; she may have thought it would lead white women feminists to recognize and include black women in the movement. Whatever her motivations, this aspect of Cooper's thought may have contributed to the neglect of her work by feminist thinkers. *See also* RACE AND RACISM.

CRITICAL RACE THEORY. *See* RACE AND RACISM.

CRUZ, SOR JUANA INÉS DE LA (1648–1695). Born in Mexico, Juana Inés de la Cruz de Asbaje y Ramírez entered a convent apparently as a means to her goal of a life of study. Sor Juana, a prolific writer of poems, plays, and prose, was an important literary figure of her time. The central sources we have for her philosophical thought are the prose works *Carta Atenagórica* and *Respuesta a Sor Filotéa de la Cruz*, as well as some poetry that includes the poem "Primero Sueño."

Of these works, only the *Respuesta* has been seen to contain feminist thought; her reputation as the first feminist of the New World stems from this work. It was written in 1690 or 1691 as a reply to her bishop, who had criticized her for her focus on non-scriptural studies. This work is a defense of her life, and her pursuit of knowledge, that also functions as a more general argument for the **education** of women. Sor Juana employed her skill at **logical** argument to question the standard arguments against the education of women, but this questioning is also inherent in the actual form of her argument, in particular through its use of irony.

One of her central arguments in the *Respuesta* is that she cannot write on scriptural subjects. This inability arises, she says, not only because this was not the province of women, but because such writing could be heretical as a result of her lack of theological knowledge. At the same time she defends her pursuit of worldly subjects, in particular through a recitation of the biographies of thirty-one wise women from both biblical and historical sources. She frames her inclination for knowledge as natural: part of her God-given nature. This claim functions as an early call for **equality**, in that these inclinations must be satisfied through the education reserved for men, an education that would have included theology. A latent feminism is also present in Sor Juana's consideration of the question of who is to educate women. She recognized that, if men were the teachers, then the intellectual inequality of women would continue. However she also recognized that, if women were to teach men, then they would be persecuted. Thus she offered the progressive possibility of women teaching women. Her work is far from radical, but it is significant for its upholding of the education of women despite the authoritarian structure of the church and its demand for obedience to its dictates. *See also* CHRISTIANITY.

CULTURAL FEMINISM. The term cultural feminism is used to describe a particular strand of feminist thought that values the differences of, for example, women's **experience**, practice, thinking, or virtue; it uses these differences as a foundation for political and social reform both for women and for society as a whole. This way of thinking is also called **gender** feminism.

Cultural feminism was an important strand in nineteenth-century feminist thought, and its first formulation can be found in Margaret

Fuller's *Woman in the Nineteenth Century* (1845). In this work, Fuller argues that women need freedom so that they can discover, and develop, their specifically female faculties. This is not done just on an individual basis; it also needs the collective support of other women.

Cultural feminists of the nineteenth century posited the existence of **feminine** qualities, such as women's intuition, **emotional** sensitivity, and moral superiority, and they argued that these qualities could produce moral and political reform in society. Freedom was necessary for women to develop these qualities, and in this way women's liberation became connected to a larger social reform. Often a matriarchal society was seen as the ideal: one based on pacifism and mutual cooperation. Some cultural feminists of this period also posited the existence of a pre-**Christian** matriarchy, a time of non-violence and cooperation; this view sometimes led to a call for a goddess-centered **religion**.

Cultural feminism is still an important element for contemporary **feminist theory** and feminist philosophy, and contemporary cultural feminist theorists continue to explore many of the ideas of their nineteenth-century predecessors. Within feminist philosophy, as a specific subject field, the social reformist goal remains in, for example, the development of "maternalist" **political philosophies**. Analyses of the foundations of cultural feminist thought are also a central area of interest; theorists have questioned, in particular, whether cultural feminism is founded on the acceptance of a problematic notion of gender difference as biological: **biological determinism**.

Cultural feminist thinking has played out in important ways in a variety of subject fields in contemporary feminist philosophy. It has had an important role in **feminine ethics**, especially in the development of an ethics of **care** grounded in the specific moral experience of women. It is also a part of **maternal ethics**, which posits the **mothering** person-child relationship as the paradigm for ethical relations. For some **ecofeminists**, women's nurturing qualities mean they are more attuned to **nature**, and thus to a privileged understanding of the ways to produce an ecologically sustainable society. The notion of a specifically "women's way of thinking" has also taken a more minor role in discussions of **epistemology** and philosophy of science. *See also* ESSENTIALISM; FIRST WAVE FEMINISM; PUBLIC/PRIVATE DISTINCTION; WAR AND PEACE.

– D –

DALY, MARY (1928–   ). Mary Daly, the American philosopher and theologian, was in the forefront of the development of a feminist theology in the 1970s. She has been a central figure in **radical feminist** philosophizing since the 1970s, and a foundational influence in the development of lesbian studies as an academic subject area. Despite this influence, the complex and challenging nature of her work has meant that she has not been acknowledged within mainstream philosophy.

Daly originally studied Catholic theology, but she became frustrated by the fact that, despite a doctorate in theology, there was little possibility for academic advancement for women in the United States during the 1950s. Indeed, throughout her academic career, Daly has faced rejection by the academic community, in particular in her struggle for tenure at Boston College in the late 1960s. Daly's 1992 autobiographical work *Outercourse: The Be-Dazzling Voyage* offers an account of her academic success in the face of such opposition.

These personal **experiences** have influenced both the content and the style of her work. Autobiographical narrative is a central aspect of her philosophy, and she has been committed to this approach since 1975. Beginning in the 1970s, Daly began to move away from the **Christian** tradition and to position her philosophical work away from mainstream academia and its institutions.

Daly does not reject the **canon** altogether; rather, she commits what she calls "piracy": pulling apart canonical traditions, and using elements of them to construct an alternative philosophy. The central theologico-philosophical influence on Daly's work is the philosophy of **Thomas Aquinas** and the neoscholastics, whose work she studied at the University of Fribourg in Switzerland from 1959 to 1967. From these studies, Daly brought to her own work the notion of transcendence or "Being." She revised Being to "Be-ing," an evolving—rather than static—notion of a search to participate in Being.

In her early post-Christian feminist work of the 1970s, God was identified as this verb: Be-ing. The new conceptualization of God is as an immanent God who is part of the world; thus it forms a rejection of the transcendent God of the **Islamic**, **Judaic**, and Christian religions. For Daly the conception of a transcendent God is problematic, because God is then distant and separate from **nature** and is in a subject-object relation to nature. The rejection of this "I-it" relation is within the **existentialist** tradition and, in particular, reflects the influence of theologians Paul Tillich and Martin Buber. According to Daly, this relation of separation, and its accompanying relation of "power over," is then played out in the societal division of humans into the subject-object categories, with women as the object under the power of men. Within this **oppressive** system of **patriarchy**, positive **feminine** traits, such as compassion, become debased and corrupted. Daly holds, however, that through engaging in the spiritual revolution of the transformative process of Be-ing, women can become liberated.

In her best-known work, *Gyn/Ecology: The Metaethics of Radical Feminism* (1978), Daly realizes that the object status of women is not simply oppressive but destroys them mentally and physically. She now holds that women must free themselves from femininity, as it is a patriarchal construct that imprisons women. They must become, instead, wild, natural women who are engaged in Be-ing. Furthermore, Daly argues, women are oppressed not just by the social constructs of patriarchy but also by the patriarchal structure of reality itself: its **language** and values. These wild women must redefine, and reclaim, patriarchal language about women as a means to female empowerment. In Daly's terms, women must become "spinsters": they must spin new meanings. In 1987, Daly produced a dictionary of these new meanings, *Websters' First New Intergalactic Wickedary of the English Language*, written with Jane Caputi. This revision of language brings with it a transformation of values. Daly claims, for example, that women who are "evil" under patriarchy—challenging, disruptive, powerful women—are in fact "good" women: wild, free women.

In 1979, Audre Lorde wrote an open letter to Mary Daly in response to *Gyn/Ecology*. This letter is an early example of the type of challenge that was raised in the 1980s by women of color to what they saw as the whiteness of feminist theory, and its neglect of the fact that the experience of oppression is not the same for all women. Daly did not reply to this letter, and in a new introduction to the 1990 edition of *Gyn/Ecology*, she stated that she had deliberately chosen—for unspecified personal reasons—not to respond to it.

Daly's work continues to evolve. Perhaps the most significant change is found in *Outercourse*, with her reconception of Be-ing as not connected to a Christian God. Despite the different shifts in her views, from her early interest in traditional Catholic theology, to her most recent work, Daly does not deny the existence of her earlier thought. She chooses, instead, to see her work as a product of multiple selves who are engaged in a continually evolving search. *See also* BLACK FEMINIST PHILOSOPHY.

DERRIDA, JACQUES (1930–2004). French philosopher Jacques Derrida was born in Algeria but lived most of his life in Paris, where he taught philosophy. He is best known for his influential but controversial critique of the texts of the Western tradition through the use of deconstruction, a term that resists definition. In *Of Grammatology* (1967) and *Writing and Difference* (1967), Derrida elaborates the "performance" of deconstruction or the way that deconstruction "takes place."

The relation between the deconstruction of Derrida and feminist philosophy is contentious. Most feminist philosophers view deconstruction as destructive of, rather than constructive for, the feminist enterprise. Those feminist philosophers who have explored the possibilities of deconstruction for feminism would argue that this critique stems from a misunderstanding of what Derrida calls the "event" of deconstruction, or from an unwillingness to undergo a process of self-examination and revision.

Those feminist philosophers who do wish to explore the relation fall into two categories: those who are interested in using deconstruction specifically as a way of questioning **sex** difference, and those who also have the more radical agenda of critiquing feminism itself. Neither of these approaches need entail that these thinkers claim Derrida's work is in itself feminist.

The typical interest of the former group is not in all the elements of Derrida's philosophy but just in the use of deconstruction to subvert **canonical** texts. The Western philosophical tradition, for Derrida, is constructed upon, and through, a series of hierarchical oppositions, in which the upper or superior concept controls the lower, such as **body** and **emotion**. Derrida holds that this hierarchal system of binary opposition is a **patriarchal** model of **language** and labels it phallogocentric. This system places the male as the standard of normality—thus the **masculine** is the source of power and meaning—while its opposite, woman/the **feminine**, lacks power and is outside this male discourse.

The meaning of the concepts of the Western philosophical tradition is dependent on the existence of some **essence**, or object, as a lower disjunct. This then means that traditional philosophy is constructed on central concepts that do not have an independent significance, and thus that the **objective**, **value-neutral**, transcendent language that is required for philosophical discourse is not possible. Therefore the goal of philosophical understanding is nothing more than the goal of control—one that requires both a reductionism and a unification of its objects of understanding.

The resistance to this hierarchical dialectical framework occurs within the text. For Derrida the text has "blind spots," points where there is a gap between the intentions of the writer and the words of the text. It is within such a gap that deconstruction of the text can occur: the examination of the silences of the text, what it conceals, and its internal tensions. In this way, the text provides the material for its own deconstruction.

It is these specific elements that interest those feminist philosophers who wish to explore the possible uses of deconstruction for feminist philosophy. They are interested, among other things, in a deconstruction of what texts do not say about women, and in resisting the hierarchical concepts which control women and the feminine. They aim to expose the blind spots in Western tradition in order to subvert male-female hierarchy. Thus deconstruction is pressed into political use.

What is problematic, however, for most feminist philosophers is that deconstruction must also occur within the feminist enterprise itself. Derrida's deconstruction is not simply negative or destructive, so it does not threaten the enterprise in this way. Its threat comes, instead, from the way that it rejects an analysis which requires entities to uncover and categorize. This type of analysis, however, is a fundamental requirement of the feminist enterprise in that it needs to produce, for example, **gender**-neutral reality, or knowledge. Yet, for Derrida, the patriarchal structuring of difference (through hierarchical opposition) is the foundation of this type of claim about truth, or essence. Moreover, this also means there is no way to conceptualize an entity, or category, of women outside of this mode of discourse from which to critique it, as this would assign them an essence. On the other hand, there is no place within the discourse for critique, as women are only "present" in the sense that they are marked by their absence, or subordination.

This then has the problematic result that there is no space in which to talk about real people: those who actually correspond to this category of women. This is not just a conceptual problem for feminism; it is a central political problem. In order to liberate themselves, women must have an understanding of some kind of self or **subject** to liberate, to protect, and for which to assert **justice**, but the erasure of this concept is a necessary part of the deconstruction of Western intellectual thought.

This is, therefore, the central question for feminist philosophers who want to see Derrida's work as connected to, or as part of, the feminist enterprise. Those who propose this relationship claim that feminism can be strengthened by a process of its own self-deconstruction, as this process can expose the problems of the construction of feminist theory. They argue that, like the Western philosophical tradition, feminist theory provides the material for its own deconstruction. Feminist philosophers who wish to deconstruct feminism point to, among other things, the way that the fixed boundaries and certainties of feminist politics, and the reductionist identification of the causes of women's subordination, lead to an erasure of difference among women within this project, as well as to a refusal to recognize the possibility of a plurality of feminist strategies to remove this subordination.

DESCARTES, RENÉ (1596–1650). French philosopher René Descartes was born in La Haye, France, on March 31, 1596, and studied at the University of Poitiers. In 1649 Descartes went to Sweden to join the court of Queen Christina, but he died shortly thereafter. Descartes is seen as the first philosopher of the modern period and is thus a pivotal figure in the history of philosophy. His first published work was his *Discourse on the Method* (1637). In the *Discourse* he introduced his approach to philosophy and his philosophical system. This was elaborated in his later works: in particular, metaphysics in his best known work *Meditations on First Philosophy* (1641), physics in *Principles of Philosophy* (1644), and psychology and moral philosophy in *Passions of the Soul* (1649). The thought in this last work was developed in part as a result of the philosophical discussions he had in correspondence with **Elisabeth of Bohemia**.

Of the three figures of modern (or Continental) rationalism, the other two being Benedict de Spinoza and Gottfried Leibniz, René Descartes has provoked the most criticism from feminist philosophers. Given the fact that modern philosophy is grounded in, and framed within, Descartes's **epistemology**, feminist philosophers need to offer a detailed and thorough analysis of Descartes's thought. If its roots are antithetical to feminist philosophy, then the modern philosophical project as a whole must be carefully scrutinized.

Within Anglo-American **analytic feminist philosophy**, the focus has been on Descartes's notion of **reason**, and the **dualist** thinking that underpins this notion. An equally important strand of thought can be found in some **French feminist** work that examines Descartes's philosophy in terms of its ethics and its account of the passions.

Among Anglo-American feminist philosophers, few interpreters have argued for ways that Descartes's thought can be of use for feminist philosophy. The majority of work has focused, instead, on analyzing Descartes's legacy of the **masculinization** of reason. One problem with such an analysis is how Descartes's conceptualization of reason is to be initially interpreted. Descartes's contemporaries were typically more interested in his **metaphysics** than his epistemology. It is only since the eighteenth century that Descartes's contributions to epistemology, specifically his introduction of the individual knowing subject, have been considered of central importance. Thus a central question for present-day feminist philosophers is whether they are criticizing Descartes's philosophy itself or cultural readings and appropriations of his thought: what could be called "Cartesianism."

Descartes's philosophical legacy is a rich and complex one; central to this legacy is Descartes's method of attaining certain knowledge. In order to attain this, we must analyze our beliefs and **experiences** of reality through our reason, so that we can find what we can know clearly and distinctly: what is self-evident. In the *Meditations*, Descartes subjects everything to radical doubt only to find there is one thing that cannot be in doubt: his existence as a thinking thing (the "cogito argument"). From this certain foundation, Descartes rebuilds our knowledge of the world, a rebuilding that can only be done through the use of deductive reason. For Descartes, the information we receive through our senses is both unreliable and subjective.

While Descartes maintained philosophical tradition in holding the **mind**, or soul, to be superior to the **body**, the new element that Descartes introduces is that the body is not simply inferior but actually prevents us from obtaining knowledge. Indeed, he holds that knowledge can be obtained only through transcending the body. Descartes no longer maintains a traditional picture of the soul as containing both reason and **emotion**, with reason as the superior element and emotion as the inferior. The Cartesian mind, or soul, is instead simply a thinking thing. It is thus, as he states explicitly, sexless. Emotion is no longer a part of the soul but comes from the body. It is in this way that rationality becomes identified purely with reason; moreover, the attainment of knowledge is the province of the individual knowing "I": a solitary self.

In this initial account at least, Descartes's philosophy may not appear necessarily in conflict with feminist goals. It has been held that these new elements served to produce a very real effect on the intellectual liberation of women of Descartes's time (or at least certain classes of women). Descartes's method does not require the kind of formal philosophical **education** that was considered unsuitable for his female contemporaries. The Cartesian mind as a sexless thinking thing also means that philosophical thought and discourse need not exclude women. Finally, the separation of mind and body at work in Descartes's philosophy carried with it an implicit rejection of claims that women's biology somehow restricted their abilities to think and reason.

This potential of Descartes's works for feminist philosophical thinking of this era can be seen in the fact that many writers and salonistes were influenced by Descartes; for example, **François Poullain de la Barre** employed the Cartesian method to demonstrate that the inferiority of women had no foundation in **human nature**. The effect of Descartes's influence can be seen, in particular, in the work of two early modern female philosophers: **Mary Astell** and **Damaris Masham**. Indeed, in the case of Astell, her feminist philosophy is founded on Cartesian rationalism.

Both Astell and Masham read Descartes's conceptualization of reason differently from current feminist philosophers; both held that the capacity for reason is a human capacity, and thus is possessed by both men and women. They did not see reason as a capacity that is restricted to a search for knowledge, but rather as a capacity that allows us to direct our lives, in particular our moral lives. Thus they did not construe, as modern feminist philosophers tend to do, Cartesian reason as a separate or specialized function. Both Astell and Masham used this understanding of Descartes's view of reason to argue for changes in the lives of the women of that period. Astell focused her attention on women's education, arguing that it was necessary in order for women to develop their capacity for reason. Masham connected women's traditional roles with the need for women's development of reason, arguing that this was necessary for them to be able to rear children properly.

However, even though Descartes's philosophy had this influence on the real lives of women of the intelligentsia, it can be argued that the Cartesian conception of reason ultimately serves not only to exclude women and the **feminine** from philosophy, but to **gender** the philosophical project and its ideals of rationality and **objectivity**. Descartes's conception of rationality requires a division between mind and body that entails the normative dualisms of mind/body and reason/emotion. Given that women and the feminine have been culturally associated with the inferior, or problematic, disjuncts (body and emotion) of these dualisms, this division has the potential both to reinforce these traditional stereotypes and to ensure the separation of women from the philosophical enterprise.

Modern feminist critics differ as to how these potential difficulties are to be analyzed and understood. Thus far, there have been three different types of analysis of the masculine nature of Descartes's conception of reason.

One type of analysis—which comes from the work of Genevieve Lloyd—is primarily grounded in a critical assessment of Descartes's philosophical method. This type of analysis places Descartes's contribution to philosophy within a broader ranging discussion of the symbolic maleness of reason within the **history of philosophy**. In this account, Cartesian rationality becomes a metaphorical overcoming of a feminized corporeality. Women are then left, by default, with the responsibility for knowledge of the world of the senses. Even though the "man of reason" must rise intellectually above this world to attain true knowledge, he will still need its practical benefits. In this way, women are not just excluded from attaining reason, but philosophy as a whole is left with a Cartesian legacy that supports a sexual **division of mental labor**; one in which women have a different, complementary role to play to "male" reason.

Another approach—which comes from the work of Susan Bordo—is to explore Descartes's philosophy as a source of the masculinization of thought in modern philosophy by using a theory of psychological development: **object relations theory**. Cartesian rationalism is depicted as a "flight from the feminine"—the organic female universe or **nature** as "**mother**"—to the security of the modern **scientific** universe. This flight is matched with an epistemological flight from "feminine" ways of knowledge: knowledge that is non-hierarchical, connected to the body, and fails to attain the "masculine" ideals of objectivity and detachment. This separate, knowing "I" of philosophical and scientific reasoning can be explained in terms of the psychological separation of a male child from his mother, a separation that is part of object relations theory. In order to attain a "masculine" cultural identity, the male child must learn to separate himself from his mother and see himself as a detached and **autonomous** entity.

The third interpretation—which comes from the work of Nancy Tuana—grounds an analysis of the Cartesian masculinization of rationality on the concepts and roles traditionally associated with women. The Cartesian conception of reality, with its transcendence of the body and emotion, does not mesh well with traditional conceptions of "woman": a being dominated by emotions and the needs of the body. This tension is not simply on a conceptual plane. The traditionally accepted social roles of women as household manager and mother would have meant that, except in very rare cases, they would have been unable in real terms to find the time necessary to train for, and practice, Descartes's method. Thus, even though Descartes has not explicitly excluded women from the realm and practice of reason, it is only available to women who can, in some way, shed everything that is culturally identified as female.

In contrast to these readings of Descartes, explicitly deconstructionist readings of Descartes have not focused on an analysis of the maleness or masculinity of reason. **Luce Irigaray**, for example, writes on the passion of wonder, and uses Descartes's own words to show how this passion straddles the official Cartesian divide between the physical and the spiritual, and the material and the metaphysical. *See also* CANON, CRITIQUE OF; SUBJECTIVITY.

DIOTIMA OF MANTINEA (n.d.). In **Plato**'s *Symposium*, Socrates, who is the main protagonist, speaks of the importance of love. In essence, Socrates claims that we love beauty in other people and, from that physical love, we ultimately progress to knowing beauty itself. What has been of interest to feminist philosophers of history is Socrates's claim that his philosophy of love is based on an earlier conversation with Diotima, a Mantinean priestess, who is one of only two **women philosophers** mentioned in Plato's dialogues (the other being Aspasia in the *Menexenus*). Traditionally, Diotima has been considered simply a literary device employed either by Plato or the historical Socrates. However, while the evidence for assuming that Diotima is a literary device is strong, it is not conclusive. Thus some philosophers, feminist and non-feminist alike, have considered the possibility that she was a historical figure. One central consideration for assessing this possibility is the fact that Diotima's notion of beauty is not identical with the Platonic notion of the "Form" of beauty; this suggests that her views are those of a real person. A further consideration is whether the literary device of a female, and thus inferior, philosopher would have worked to enhance Socrates's discussion. The fact that this is unlikely indicates that she actually existed. Certainly, if Diotima was indeed an historical figure, her inclusion in Plato's dialogues would make her a significant figure in the history of women philosophers.

DISABILITY. According to the United Nations definition, disability, with respect to an individual, is "any restriction or lack (resulting from an impairment) of ability to perform an activity in the manner or within the range considered normal for a human being." Feminist philosophical interest in disability came to the fore in the 1990s. Feminist theorists have pointed out that, while there is a biological or psychological reality to disability, it is the social construction put on this foundation that produces disability itself.

Feminist philosophers have claimed that both the feminist movement and feminist philosophy can serve to marginalize women with disabilities. Within the feminist movement, for example, one argument often used to support a woman's **right** to **abortion** is the need for the freedom to abort a disabled fetus. In this way, however, the desires and the rights of "normal" women, and the subsequent **alienation** and devaluing of disabled women, become problematically identified with feminism itself. Within philosophy, more specifically, some feminist philosophers are engaged in the project of revaluing the traditional social roles of women, yet their model for these roles is the "normal" woman. A central example of this is the way that the theory of the ethics of **care** is grounded in the actual moral **experience** of women, in particular their experiences as caregivers and **mothers**. This neglects the possibility that some women with disabilities may have a limited range of such experiences and functions.

Despite these difficulties, it is recognized that there is a need for a feminist theory of disability, especially in light of the number of women who are disabled. Feminist theorizing offers, among other things, an analysis of, and response to, the ways that cultural ideals of the **body** have served to **oppress** women. This analysis, in turn, can illuminate the ways that these ideals serve to marginalize the disabled. Failure to achieve these (impossible) cultural ideals in "normal" women leads to a feeling of alienation from one's own body and a devaluing of those who are less than perfect. For physically disabled women, this failure is so magnified that they are not always perceived as "real" women: women who can have **sexual** relationships, children, and so on. Moreover, an inability to achieve such cultural ideals of the body for "normal" women is tied to assumptions about a lack of self-control and of personal responsibility. The disabled represent the existence of the opposite of "normal," as they are culturally understood to lack independence and to have a body they cannot control. *See also* POLITICAL AND SOCIAL PHILOSOPHY.

DIVISION OF LABOR, SEXUAL. While some theorists speak of a "**gender** division of labor," others prefer the term "sexual" over "gender" because it makes clear that the division is grounded in **bodily** differences. Essentially, the division of labor by **sex** is seen to be grounded in the reality of women's capacity to bear children. This sexual difference leads to a division of labor: women remain in the home and raise children, while men work outside the home to provide for the material needs of the **family**. The division is normative, with the women having the lower status or inferior role. **Feminist theorists** recognize, however, that it is difficult to develop a single account of the division that crosses cultures.

Karl Marx and Friedrich Engels offered the earliest identification and analysis of the division. In a standard interpretation of their thought, the division is viewed as a "**natural**" one that originated in primitive society and stemmed from the basic division of labor for producing children. However, Engels did not see the work of women as inferior in some way, as he considered the work of both **sexes** to be of the same importance. According to Engels, it was the advent of the development of agriculture, and thus the development of the male sphere of production, that led to a change in the value placed on women's traditional labor. Women became subordinate, as men now had social and economic power over women. This change in the situation of women coincided with the origins of class society, as this expansion in production brought about the economic benefits of the use of slaves.

There is no one feminist account of the problem with the sexual division of labor. **Marxist feminists** tend to hold that the sexual division of labor serves capital, for example, through the way that women maintain the workers by providing important services, such as caring for the sick. Thus Marxist feminists tend to focus on eradicating gender divisions within the marketplace, as they frame the division of labor as a class issue. **Socialist feminists** offer a more complex account that also analyzes how the benefits that the division gives to men can play a part in the **oppression** of women as a group. A central example of this is the way that "women's work" leads to lower pay for women, due to the fact that they spend time taking care of male workers. The latter then have more working hours, as well as time to learn the relevant skills, so that they can rise up the corporate ladder, and thus have the better paying jobs. Although **radical feminists** agree that **biology** alone is the problem, they do not have a cohesive account of the division. For some, the development of **reproductive** technologies will provide a solution, while others ask whether the division could lead to the development of a specifically female, and thus political, identity. **Liberal feminists** critique the division, in particular, for the way it provides a barrier to **equal** opportunities for women in the public sphere, especially in the workplace. *See also* PUBLIC/PRIVATE DISTINCTION.

DUALISM. The term dualism is typically used by feminist philosophers for the binary oppositional thinking present throughout the Western philosophical tradition. Some of the standard dualisms that have been used to categorize, and thus understand, reality are abstract/concrete, **reason/emotion**, **universal**/particular, subjective/**objective**, knowledge/**experience**, **mind/body**, white/black, and man/woman. What characterizes dualist thinking is not that the disjuncts of each pair are merely different, but that they are mutually exclusive in that one disjunct is defined against the other. Moreover, there is no middle ground: everything falls into one category or the other.

Some feminist philosophers, most notably **Simone de Beauvoir** in *The Second Sex*, have claimed that dualist thinking is a fundamental category of human thought. Certainly there are indications of a version of dualist thinking even in the earliest works of philosophy, those of **ancient Greek philosophy**. Dualist thinking was formalized by **Plato** in the sense that the mind/body distinction was an actual part of his philosophical framework: in order to gain true knowledge, the mind must transcend the body. For Plato, not only is the body a different kind of object from the mind, but it can be a hindrance to knowledge.

A variety of sophisticated approaches are used to analyze and explain the way dualist thinking is structured and how it serves to justify the **oppression** of women. In essence, dualist thinking is considered problematic for feminist philosophy both for its structure and for its connection to power relations. For the discipline of philosophy itself, its very definition relies on its being framed in opposition to the material and the practical, elements that are important components to the definition of feminist philosophy. Moreover, the construction of reality through separation and exclusion is a problematic way of thinking for feminist philosophy, as feminist philosophy aims not only for the inclusion of historically marginalized groups, but for the dismantling of the oppressive thinking that constructs these groups.

Dualist thinking, furthermore, is typically not **value neutral** but normative. In defining one disjunct against the other, the defined comes to be seen as having a positive or superior value, while the defined-against comes to be seen as having a negative or inferior value, precisely because it lacks the qualities of the first disjunct. The value placed on one disjunct over the other is not the result of what the disjunct actually is; instead, the value is grounded in convention or historical association. Furthermore, some feminist philosophers maintain that the construction and affirmation of the identity and value of the "superior" disjunct requires this negative value of its matching opposite. Placed within a system of power relations, such as those of **gender** or **race**, normative dualist thinking then provides a useful justification for the oppression of women or people of color. Some feminist philosophers have also been interested in the ways in which the set of inferior disjuncts and/or the set of superior disjuncts reinforce the others that share the same value. Thus, for example, the desire to control a potentially unruly **nature** is reinforced by fears of the capriciousness of women, which in its turn comes from their lack of rationality. This phenomenon is not necessarily a target of criticism; some thinkers have aimed to show, for example, that the association of women with emotion, or with nature, can be a source of political strength.

The final major element of dualist thinking that has been the subject of feminist criticism is interconnected to the gendering of the disjunctive pairs. Although the initial formulation by Plato of the mind-body relation had a stronger cultural association with the master-slave relation, this relation became over time replaced by a male-female association. This gender association, and the values placed on the disjuncts of male and female, further affirmed the value placed on the other binary oppositions—such as reason and body—which were used to order and understand the world. It is hard to locate a precise moment in the **history of philosophy** in which dualist categories became associated with gender; however, some feminist philosophers point to the radical dualist thinking of **René Descartes** as a defining moment in the **masculinization** of knowledge and truth.

Analytic Anglo-American as well as **French feminist** philosophers have engaged in a variety of strategies to deal with the problems of dualist thinking. Some aim simply to revalue the inferior disjunct, while others aim to erase or disrupt dualist thinking. One example of the latter approach—which comes from French feminist thought—is to take up a position outside the framework of philosophical thought, and then, from this location, to critique cultural representations of female as the negative in philosophical texts. This position then represents a way of thinking and writing outside of dualist constructions. *See also* VALUE HIERARCHICAL THINKING.

DUAL SYSTEMS THEORY. Radical feminists claim that a single system—**patriarchy**—is the root cause of the **oppression** of women. **Marxist feminists**, on the other hand, claim that the root cause of women's oppression is the system of capitalism. Given that **socialist feminism** developed out of both versions of feminism, its proponents recognize the existence of both systems of oppression. However, there are differences in the analyses they offer of the relationship between the two systems: dual systems theory or single system theory.

Dual systems theorists typically argue that patriarchy and capitalism are two separate systems of oppression; thus, before there can be an analysis of the ways in which the two interlock, each must be analyzed in isolation from the other. Critics of the dual systems theory claim, for example, that a separate examination of **gender** oppression serves to restrict this oppression to the domestic sphere, thus obscuring the ways in which women face oppression as women within the workforce. The competing view, a "unified systems" or "single system" theory, aims to analyze capitalism and patriarchy in conjunction with each other, holding that, despite their historically different forms, gender relations have never been separate from class relations. Some feminist theorists have replaced both dual systems and unified systems by theorizing with a multi-systems approach that can include an analysis of other systems of dominance, such as racism. *See also* DIVISION OF LABOR, SEXUAL.

– E –

EASTERN EUROPE, FEMINIST PHILOSOPHY IN. The philosophical tradition in Eastern Europe reflects the diversity of the nations that constitute it; however, the philosophy of **Marxism** forms a common theme within the philosophy of Eastern Europe. Given their different intellectual, political, and social histories, feminist thinkers of Eastern Europe do not always share the same concerns as their counterparts in Western Europe. Often the work of East European feminist philosophers focuses on the limits of the Marxist analysis of the **oppression** of women, and the ways socialism failed to liberate women. In addition, the presence of **war** in some parts of Eastern Europe has led to work on war, nationalism, and violence against women. Some of the most recent feminist philosophy shows the influences of contemporary **French feminist** philosophers, such as **Luce Irigaray**.

ECOFEMINISM. The term ecofeminism was first used by Françoise d'Eaubonne in her 1974 work *Le Féminisme ou la Mort*. Ecofeminism can be characterized as a feminist ecology and an ecological feminism: solutions to environmental problems require a feminist perspective, and **feminist theory** and practice require an environmental perspective. Ecofeminism differs from environmentalism in that it identifies **androcentrism**—as well as anthropomorphism—as the root of both the domination of humans and the domination of **nature**. The ideals and values of maleness—for example, power, **reason**, and civilization—are the hallmark of both these forms of domination. The interconnected dominations of women and nature are justified within the traditional Western framework of **dualist** thinking: civilization/nature, reason/**body**, active/passive, and so on. This way of thinking is **value hierarchical**: one disjunct is superior to the other. In this framework, women and nature are associated with the inferior disjuncts—passivity, non-rationality, etc.—and are thus the subjects of a justified domination. These connections have played out in traditional Western philosophy in a variety of ways; for example, nature and women have been seen as capricious and unruly, and thus needing to be tamed through force: technology in the case of nature, or physical violence in the case of women.

The starting point, therefore, of all versions of ecofeminist theory and practice is the understanding that the liberation of nature requires the liberation of women, and vice versa. However, as with all feminist theories, the definition and boundaries of ecofeminism are contested. Where the disagreement starts is how the connection between women and nature should be understood: as a potential source of power or as the cause of **oppression**. Thus ecofeminists disagree over whether the woman/nature connection should be severed, valued, or reconceived. *See also* ANIMAL ETHICS; BACON, FRANCIS; DUALISM; INDIA, PHILOSOPHY IN; VEGETARIANISM.

ÉCRITURE FÉMININE (FEMININE WRITING). *See* BODY; FRENCH FEMINISM; SEXUALITY.

EDUCATION. Despite the role of education as a central component of the good society, contemporary philosophers of education tend not to pay much attention to issues of women or **gender**. Historically speaking, however, the philosophy of education has been central to discussions of female **equality** within feminist philosophy. As early as the seventeenth century, feminist (or proto-feminist) philosophers began to produce arguments for the education of women. The central figures were **Mary Astell**, **Bathsua Pell Makin**, **Anna Maria van Schurman**, **Sophia**, **Catharine Macaulay**, and **Mary Wollstonecraft** in Europe; and Catharine Beecher and **Judith Sargent Murray** in the United States. In retrospect, it is clear that progress in the education and intellectual development of women was a necessary first step to be taken prior to more broad-ranging arguments for their civil and political equality, although early proponents of female education did not typically conceive of it in this way.

Early proponents of female education offered three main types of argument. Some challenged claims about women's intellectual and moral inferiority through an analysis of the damaging effects of the education, or lack thereof, on the intellect and character of their contemporaries. Others argued that education would enable women to fulfill properly their roles as **mother** and housekeeper. A third group saw education as leading to a kind of empowerment for women. They claimed that a trained **mind** could help women understand, and thus deal with, their subordinate social roles and status, or it could help to prevent young women from making the wrong choices in **marriage**. Within these general arguments for female education, two early feminist philosophers can be identified as producing a systematic or fully worked out philosophy of women's education: Catharine Beecher and Mary Wollstonecraft (in *A Vindication of the Rights of Woman*).

Despite this historical importance, philosophy of education is a minor field in current feminist philosophy. Within this general field, some main subfields can be identified. One is the analysis of a hidden gender "curriculum," broadly speaking an analysis of the interconnections between the theory and practice of education and the maintenance and construction of gender. One obvious example of this is the way that the traditional framing of education as part of the public sphere, which is culturally associated as male, plays out in the way that the profession of teaching is gendered. Female teachers predominate in schools for younger children, while males predominate in institutions of higher education.

Another subfield is also part of the more general field of feminist **history of philosophy**. Central components of this subfield include the reinterpretation of **canonical** works on the philosophy of education, such as those of **Plato** and **Jean-Jacques Rousseau**, as well as the rediscovery of neglected feminist philosophers who developed a philosophy of education.

A third subfield is the development of philosophies of education that are based on an ethics of **care**. Nel Noddings offers an educational theory that is a **feminine ethics** grounded in the ideal of our moral relation with each other: a practical ethic of "caring." In order both to develop and protect this ideal, Noddings argues that we need a proper moral education (broadly conceived). While Noddings does not offer a fully developed philosophy of education, she does recommend ways that schools can be organized; the primary goal of the teacher is to create a specific relation of caring to the student that will produce the ethical development of the latter. This relation is one of involvement with the student, which is aimed at producing intellectual involvement, rather than rote learning or eliciting the correct answer. In practice, schools would then need to be organized to offer such things as more student-teacher contact time (e.g., through having teachers teach more than one subject), open discussions of values and beliefs, and the use of care-oriented service learning.

ELISABETH OF BOHEMIA, PRINCESS PALATINE (1618–1680). Elisabeth of Bohemia, Princess Palatine, was the daughter of Frederick, the Elector Palatine, and Elizabeth Stuart, the daughter of James I of England. After her father lost the throne of Bohemia, Elisabeth first went to the court in the Hague and then to a convent. She appears to have had a strong background in philosophy, and evidence of this shows in her correspondence with French philosopher **René Descartes**, for which she is best known. While some of these letters are simply of a social nature, Elisabeth frequently questions and critiques Descartes on particular points of his philosophical system. Indeed, Descartes's *Passions of the Soul* (1649), was developed in part as a result of her encouragement.

EMOTION. Given the rationalist bias in much of Western philosophy, **reason** has usually been identified as the faculty through which knowledge is acquired and moral judgments are made. Emotion has typically been cast as inferior, or even as a potential hindrance to this faculty. Prior to the thought of **René Descartes**, the emotions and reason were usually conceived as related in some way, or as part of the same entity: the **mind** or soul. Within Descartes's radical **dualist** framework, however, the mind or soul is a purely thinking thing in opposition to the **body**, which he saw as the seat of the emotions. In this way, it is not just that reason is the capacity for knowledge, but rather reason needs to transcend the body in order to obtain knowledge. This conception of knowledge and its ideals underpins much of the modern Western philosophical enterprise, for example, in the ideal of the detached **objective** observer of **scientific** inquiry.

The reactions of feminist philosophers to this dismissal of emotion within the Western tradition have been varied. For early feminist philosophers, such as **Mary Astell**, the connection of the emotions with the body—and the subsequent separation of the mind as a sexless thinking thing—were seen as potentially liberating for women, as this meant that female biology need no longer be seen as a hindrance to their rationality.

In contrast, those current philosophers who engaged in critiquing and rereading the **canon** often point to the way that the cultural association of women with emotions and the body has resulted in the exclusion of women and the things associated with women (such as child care) from the traditional philosophical enterprise. Other feminist philosophers have begun exploring the emotions themselves, through looking at the way emotions are socially constructed, through bringing out their cognitive elements, or through providing a fine-grained analysis of a specific emotion.

An examination of the **epistemic** value of emotion is often a component of many of the subfields in feminist philosophy. Within **feminist ethics**, for example, a dominant theme has been the reevaluation of the role of emotion for moral decision-making and moral knowledge. The ethics of **care** and **maternal ethics**, in particular, have come to be associated with this reevaluation, because of their developments of ethical alternatives that are grounded in women's **experience** of caring for others. Given the centrality of the situated knower for feminist epistemology—and thus the situated emotional responses of the knower—some philosophers are also engaged in exploring the variety of ways in which the role of emotion informs the conception, acquisition, and attribution of knowledge. It has been asked, for example, whether women's emotional responses to their **oppression**, combined with political reflection, can place them in a position of epistemic privilege.

ENGELS, FRIEDRICH. *See* MARXIST FEMINISM.

ENVIRONMENT. *See* ECOFEMINISM.

EPISTEMOLOGY. Epistemology, or the theory of knowledge, has traditionally been concerned with the justification of knowledge claims in general, including the question of skepticism: whether knowledge is possible at all. An examination of the **canon** shows that epistemological issues and concerns are central to the Western philosophical enterprise, or at least at the heart of current interest in the canon.

Within the canon, men have been framed as "knowers." Women have been explicitly or implicitly excluded from access to knowledge, or they have been labeled as incapable or not fully capable of knowledge. This exclusion occurred in a myriad of different ways. On the most basic level, this exclusion was the result of women's lack of **educational** and economic resources, as well as the male-only orientation of academic disciplines. More subtly, the symbolic and cultural association of "maleness" with **reason**, traditionally the source of knowledge, served to undermine women's epistemic authority. Moreover, the epistemological project itself contained, and was grounded in, male bias. Knowledge claims were presumed to be **value neutral**, yet they were grounded in the **experience** of middle- and upper-class Western men, and ignored any differences in the experience of women. Indeed, feminist epistemologists claim that even the ideals of the epistemological project are biased, in that they are grounded in male experience and privilege.

Early feminist philosophers were well aware of the **oppression** that was the corollary of this exclusion. **Mary Wollstonecraft**, among others, criticized the debilitating effects of the combination of a lack of educational resources and the **socialization** of women that produced women's development of sensibility over rationality. Both Wollstonecraft and **Sophia** criticized so-called knowledge about women—knowledge that kept women in subordinate roles—claiming that it was, in fact, the product of male prejudice and self-interest.

The focus of these early feminist philosophers was ultimately on demanding women's inclusion in the epistemological project. Assertions of women's capacity for reason were typically tied up with claims for the **equality** of women. It was not until the 1970s that feminist philosophers started to question the traditional epistemological project itself, and in the 1980s the subject area of feminist epistemology took shape. At this point feminist philosophers began to question, in a variety of different ways, whether it was enough to include women in the epistemological project or whether the project could allow for the inclusion of women at all.

Some feminist philosophers point to the way that the mainstream epistemological project excludes the possibilities of "women's ways of knowing," which are rooted in women's different experiences of "reality." This notion of women's knowledge, or ways of knowing, is often associated with **radical feminist** thinking; for some radical feminists, women have an intuitive faculty that can be a source of knowledge. This notion, however, is not particular to radical feminism. For some **ecofeminists**, women's connection to **nature** means that they have a knowledge of the way the world is interconnected, a knowledge that is not available to men. Because of the underlying assumption of this type of thinking—that there is a unitary set of "women's" experiences—it has been criticized as problematically **essentialist**.

The predominant way of critiquing the epistemological project, however, is to question the concepts of knowledge and reality that are currently prominent in mainstream epistemology. While these concepts have a long history, their explicit formulation can be traced back to **René Descartes**. The Cartesian knower is a solitary individual whose task is to gain understanding or knowledge of a reality that is independent of human knowers. This knowledge or understanding is gained through reason, which, for Descartes, functions alone. The **emotions**, the **body**, or any other of the historical particulars of an individual are seen as hindrances to the successful acquisition of an **objective** knowledge of reality. Moreover, once free of these hindrances, this individual can generate a **universal** account of knowledge. The notion of a solitary knower is not exclusive to the rationalist tradition: even though the knower of the empiricist tradition gains knowledge through reason in conjunction with the senses, this knower is often conceived of as independently attaining knowledge.

This conception of reality with its radical **mind**/body **dualism** is not, as it was originally intended, **gender** neutral. Essentially, the cultural associations of women with the body and the emotions means that "femaleness" is framed in opposition to reason. Moreover, the ideals of the Cartesian project are only apparently gender neutral. Feminist philosophers have argued instead, in a variety of different ways, that the ideals of **objectivity**, the objective knower, and the universality of knowledge do not reflect general human ideals and experiences, but rather those of middle-class Western males.

Much of the impetus for feminist epistemology as a subject field originally came from this questioning of the **masculinist** nature of the ideals of reason, objectivity, and knowledge of the traditional epistemological project. However, feminist epistemology is not simply a critique; it is also a reconstructive project. There is no such thing as *a* feminist epistemology, but rather different epistemologies. There is no tendency, moreover, to demarcate epistemology from other subject fields in philosophy; in particular, it is closely connected to feminist philosophy of **science**. However, an overall sense of the project can be encapsulated with Lorraine Code's germinal question: "Is the **sex** of the knower epistemologically significant?"

Central to the feminist reconstructive epistemological project, and in contrast to the dominant tradition, is the concept of the situated knower. This concept means that the historical particulars of knowers, such as their embodiment, emotions, relationships with others, and social status, affect both their access to knowledge and the way their knowledge claims are expressed, justified, and accepted as authoritative. The effects of these historical particulars need not be understood as negative or limiting; one possibility, for example, is whether the emotional response to repression can offer the possibility of epistemic privilege. In giving epistemic significance to situated knowers, feminist epistemologists are challenging the ideals and objectives of the traditional epistemological project: the possibility of a universal account of knowledge produced by detached, abstract knowers.

There is no one way in which this notion of situated knowledge is approached. Feminist epistemological theories are often divided into three types of approach using Sandra Harding's 1986 taxonomy (from the most radical to the least): **postmodernist**; feminist standpoint theory; and feminist empiricism. The latter two are part of the **analytic feminist** project.

Feminist empiricism, broadly speaking, questions the rigid dichotomy that is traditionally drawn between the ideal of a pure objective knowledge and the political values and social location of the knower. Feminist empiricists argue instead that these latter elements can, and should, inform empirical inquiry. The claim is that this approach not only furthers the goals of feminism but also improves empirical inquiry itself, because it requires inquiry to be answerable to an actual community of knowers, rather than to unrealizable ideals of objectivity.

Feminist standpoint theory, in essence, approaches the situated-ness of knowledge by claiming that some socially situated perspectives can be epistemically privileged. Drawing on **Marxist** standpoint theory that claims epistemic privilege for the proletariat, these feminist epistemologists claim that the standpoint of women offers epistemic privilege for understanding, for example, gender relations under **patriarchy**. Standpoint theory does not automatically grant such privilege to women as women, but rather to politicized (i.e., feminist) women. Moreover, there is no one standpoint of women. The recognition of the multiple oppressions experienced by women of color has led some philosophers to identify a specifically black female standpoint as part of a **black feminist philosophy**.

A postmodernist approach holds that our "epistemic world" is composed of the multiplicity and fragmentation of perspectives that arise from the differences of situations among women due to class, **race**, **sexual** orientation, and so forth. In this way, the postmodern approach also criticizes the essentialist thinking that underpins the notion of "woman," both as an object of knowledge and as a knowing subject: the notion of a women's standpoint.

In the most recent work in feminist epistemology, theories and perspectives from each of these three categories have been used to inform and improve the others; thus current theorists tend to resist an easy allocation into these three categories. There has also been some critical reflection on the feminist epistemological project itself. It has been questioned whether this project, because it is grounded in a Eurocentric philosophical tradition, is open to charges of ethnocentrism. The central aspects of this project are also open to a similar challenge. For non-Western women, there is a concern that an emphasis on the epistemic privilege of the oppressed may romanticize, and thus neglect, the material situation of that oppression; it may also serve to gloss over the ambiguities non-Western women may encounter in the application of such a notion to their lives.

One response to these types of concern comes from Jane Duran's work on global feminist epistemologies. Duran argues that one strand—although not the dominant strand—in Western feminist epistemology is the appropriation by feminist theorists and activists of cultural knowledge as well as the traditional methods for gaining that knowledge. Duran argues that this is also taking place within non-

Western communities and cultures: it is not simply a project of Western feminism. A central strength of Duran's understanding of feminist epistemology, and her use of it as a lens to examine global epistemologies, is that it allows for a culturally sensitive analysis of global feminist epistemologies, an analysis that offers informative cross-cultural comparisons between feminist knowledges and knowledge acquisition. *See also* EPISTEMOLOGY, MORAL; HUME, DAVID.

EPISTEMOLOGY, MORAL. Prior to the 1980s, there was no work that could properly be called feminist moral **epistemology**. Since the 1980s, however, developments in epistemology and **feminist ethics** have given rise to questions about moral knowledge. One element of particular importance that comes from feminist epistemology is the concept of the situated knower: the recognition that the concrete and historical particulars of the knower affect both access to knowledge and the authority of claims to knowledge.

Feminist critics of the dominant paradigm of ethics in Western philosophy have pointed to the ways in which ethics is framed on a "**scientific**" model—a search for moral knowledge—specifically, knowledge of abstract rules and formulas that can be applied **universally**. In conjunction with these criticisms, some philosophers have offered alternative ways of constructing moral knowledge, often emphasizing understanding over certainty and guarantees of correctness. In these alternative epistemologies, there is a greater emphasis on knowledge of particulars, especially the knowledge of particular individuals in their concrete and historical contexts. This is in contrast to the goal of reliability and correctness in moral judgment central to the dominant paradigm and the corresponding need in this paradigm for an **impartial** agent who judges cases in the abstract, free of the particular features of a situation that may hinder rational thought and decision-making. *See also* EXPERIENCE; RELATIVISM.

EQUALITY. The question of whether men and women are equal, and in virtue of which characteristics are they equal, has been an important issue in the history of Western philosophy. The earliest systematized account of **sex** equality can be found in **Plato**'s *Republic*, where he argues that equal work and **education** for women are part of the requirements of the ideal state.

Feminist philosophers from the eighteenth and nineteenth centuries were part of the burgeoning feminist movement for women's civil **rights**: the right to vote and to own property. Given that the traditional justification for the denial of rights to women was that they were not capable of **reason**—a criterion for holders of rights—these early philosophers typically aimed to show women's equal capacity for reason. This claim also entailed the need for additional arguments that showed that any apparent differences in rationality were the effects of differences in education and **socialization**.

Equal rights, equality of opportunity, and **gender**-neutral laws formed the goal of the **second wave** of feminism in the 1960s and 1970s. There were differences of opinion as to how this goal could be achieved. Theorists with a more conservative vision held that equality could be accomplished within the existing system. Those with a more radical vision held that this would only lead to a superficial equality, and that true equality could be achieved only through a rejection of the system itself.

Since the 1980s a questioning of the concept of equality itself, from a variety of different viewpoints, has led to its becoming an area of debate. In particular, it has been asked whether true equality can be achieved only through a recognition of sex difference, and the subsequent development of policies that reflect this difference. There has been a recognition that gender-neutral laws, for example, may ultimately produce discriminatory results, in particular in the private sphere of **marriage** and **family**. Moreover, this "formal" equality assumes that the goal is sameness to men, as well as affirming—rather than questioning—the value of the roles that have typically been the province of men. In addition, feminist theorists have recognized that equal opportunity could not be produced solely through legal equality in education and employment, as this would ignore the structural inequalities generated by differences in socio-economic background. In response to these difficulties, feminist theorists have argued, for example, for changes in laws regarding maternity leave and in support of more nuanced **affirmative action** policies. On the whole, this has meant that the debate about actual equality has become the province of feminist legal theorists.

The central area of concern in the contemporary equality debate for feminist philosophers has been in the conceptual arena of difference, identity politics, and gender. Anglophone feminist philosophy has been greatly influenced by the analyses of difference that have come from Europe, in particular from Italian, **French**, and Spanish feminist philosophers. These analyses, implicitly or explicitly, reject both the notion of equality, as this assumes sameness, and the notion of difference, as this assumes that difference is connected to biology. Furthermore, these theorists claim that the equality/difference debate only has meaning within a system of **language** that has been constructed by **patriarchy**.

Another reason standard feminist thinking about equality has come under attack (especially from theorists of color) is that it ignores or minimizes the social realities of women of color, or specific differences among women. Finally, non-Western philosophers have started to question whether the **universalizing** Western conception of equality has a potentially colonizing nature for non-Western women. *See also* JUSTICE; POLITICAL AND SOCIAL PHILOSOPHY.

ESSENTIALISM. The term essentialism is sometimes used by **feminist theorists** interchangeably with **universalism**. For many feminist theorists, however, a clear distinction can be made between the two concepts. Universalism is a claim that women's characteristics (or those of other groups) are the same across culture, history, class, **race**, and so forth. Essentialism also includes a claim that these characteristics are innate, fixed, and unchangeable: there is an essential "woman's" (or "man's") nature. While universalist claims still offer problematic generalizations about women, they do not necessarily entail claims that these are specifically "womanly" characteristics.

The claim of a specifically female nature has, historically, been grounded in biology; in current debate, it has often come to mean simply a shared characteristic, without necessarily being grounded in some theory about female biology. The particular characteristics of "woman's" nature tend to vary depending on whether the notion is being used by a feminist or a non-feminist. In the case of the former, positive characteristics—such as peacefulness—are attributed to women. Conversely, the essentializing of non-feminists tends toward negative characterizations, such as the claim that women are overly **emotional**.

The use of essentialisms was an important component of the arguments of **first wave feminists** for women's **equality**. The notion of an essentialized woman was used, in particular by **cultural feminists**, to argue that women's different characteristics were something to be affirmed, not devalued. First wave **liberal feminists** invoked an essentialized **human nature**—usually characterized by **reason**—that both **sexes** shared. The problem of essentialism surfaced with critiques in the period after **second wave feminism**. Some theorists claimed that, in demanding equality for "women," feminists of the second wave ignored differences among women, for example, of race and class. Thus "women" signified only women of a certain group: white, middle-class, and privileged.

The question of which feminist theory is essentialist is not a simple one. The charge is most often leveled at cultural feminism, but not all cultural feminists are essentialist. **Radical feminism** is also usually considered essentialist, because of its use of a timeless and cross-cultural notion of "woman" who is the subject of male domination. It may also be present in some forms of **ecofeminism**: in those cases when ecofeminism is grounded in generalizations about the relation of women to **nature**. The charge of essentialism has been leveled at the work of **French feminists** such as **Luce Irigaray**; however, her supporters maintain that Irigaray is writing about the symbolism of "woman" within Western thought, not the actual nature of women.

Despite the fact that "women" is a problematic notion, some theorists do not wish to abandon it completely, for political purposes. Some theorists have considered whether there can be a strategic use of "woman" as a political identity.

Since the 1980s, discussions of essentialism have grown increasingly complex. Feminist theorists have shown that **gender** identity is not separable from other elements of our identities, such as race or class. Essentialist notions of "women" not only produce this separation but serve to frame other elements of identity as surplus or added extras. Moreover, some theorists claim that the notion of "woman" serves to normalize and delineate certain social, cultural, and sexual behaviors. **Judith Butler**, for example, has claimed that the notion of "woman" is framed in opposition to "man," which then reinforces the assumption that human sexuality is identified as **heterosexuality**.

Essentialist thinking may also be present within the feminist philosophical enterprise itself. Claims within subfields such as **epistemology** or **aesthetics** about the existence of a "**feminine**" or "female" way of thinking, experiencing, or framing the world rely on essentialist thinking. Some work in the feminist **history of philosophy** also runs the risk of essentialist thought through the critiquing of historical texts for their neglect of "women," the **experiences** of women, or women's issues. Thus this type of analysis of historical texts may problematically smooth out, or neglect, differences among women. *See also* BIOLOGICAL DETERMINISM.

ETHICS. *See* ANIMAL ETHICS; BIOETHICS; BLACK FEMINIST ETHICS; CARE, ETHICS OF; ECOFEMINISM; EPISTEMOLOGY, MORAL; FEMININE ETHICS; FEMINIST ETHICS; LESBIAN ETHICS; MATERNAL ETHICS.

ETHICS OF CARE. *See* CARE, ETHICS OF.

ETHICS OF JUSTICE. *See* CARE, ETHICS OF; JUSTICE.

EXISTENTIAL (EXISTENTIALIST) FEMINISM. Existential **feminist theory** draws on ideas found in the work of G. W. F. Hegel, Edmund Husserl, Martin Heidegger, and **Jean-Paul Sartre**. It is usually identified with the pioneering thought of **Simone de Beauvoir** in her 1949 work *The Second Sex*. However, other feminist philosophers have drawn from the existentialist tradition, most notably **Mary Daly**.

Essentially, existentialist feminism locates the **oppression** of women in their **universal** status as "Other" or object. Existentialist feminists ground this notion on the general existential notion of the relation between self and Other, where the subject self defines itself in relation to a subjugated Other. It is through this relation that the subject self is able to achieve transcendence. The crucial difference for existential feminists is that this relation is not individual, but one of groups: women are permanently Other to men, who are defined as positive or the norm against a negative (female) Other. For existentialist feminists, liberation for women will come about through individual transcendence: becoming a self-realizing, authentic self. Indeed, it is the ethical responsibility of the individual to realize her potential as a free, self-creating subject. *See also* CONTINENTAL PHILOSOPHY; SUBJECTIVITY.

EXPERIENCE. Within the feminist movement, the individual and collective experiences of women are of central political significance. The sharing of personal experience within **consciousness-raising** groups has been a crucial strategy for identifying, and thus being in a position to resist, institutionalized sexism.

This political use of the experiences of women also contributed to philosophical theorizing about the possibility of a specifically feminist mode of gaining knowledge, or the possibility of "women's knowledge." A foundational part of the task of feminist philosophy is to explain the experiences of women and to offer theories that can have, among other things, the practical effect of addressing and altering the experiences of women. At minimum, feminist philosophers are wary of theories that reject personal experience; indeed, for many feminist philosophers, the varied experiences of women can provide an important political and **epistemic** resource. The use of women's experience in this way need not entail commitment to a view that there is some **universal** set of women's experiences, nor that these experiences are related to some kind of **essential** female nature.

The use of women's experiences as a resource has been of particular interest for work in **feminist ethics**, **feminine ethics**, and epistemology. Such theorizing typically rests on identifiably shared experiences, but it can also use individual experience as a basis. Specific justifications for the **methodological** use of women's experiences are, for example, that it can bring out different aspects of a philosophical or **scientific** problem or that it can identify the ways in which there are moral and political dimensions to knowledge. This use of women's experiences, and the theorizing about this use, also functions as a critique of mainstream theories of knowledge and morality; these theories frame knowledge as universal, obtained by an impersonal, **objective**, individual knower.

Given that differences in personal experience are traditionally not supposed to account for differences in philosophical theories or viewpoints, work that uses personal experience as an epistemic resource may often be rejected by mainstream philosophy. A central reason for this rejection is that philosophical work is expected to produce universal results as the end products of an objective process. In response, feminist philosophers often point out that, historically, the philosophical project itself has reflected and been grounded in the experiences of men; thus this type of criticism may be groundless.

– F –

FACT/VALUE DISTINCTION. *See* VALUE NEUTRALITY.

FALSE CONSCIOUSNESS. The term false consciousness comes from the **Marxist** tradition. Within this tradition, the term is employed to describe the thinking that prevents the development of a true class consciousness: a recognition by members of the working class of a unity among their desires and needs that will ultimately lead to revolution. Essentially, false consciousness is a distorted perception of reality in which, for example, others are perceived as potential competitors for scarce goods, and work is viewed as a necessary evil for the acquisition of those goods. Blinkered by this false reality, the working class is unable to see how these ways of thinking ultimately maintain the dominance of the **capitalist** class.

Feminists have adopted this term, in particular to explain how it is that many women do not have a feminist consciousness; indeed, many women may even explicitly reject feminism. Essentially, the realities of women's lives produce and confirm a false consciousness; this functions both to prevent women from recognizing their own **oppression** and to maintain male dominance. Some women, for example, have learned to identify their value solely in terms of their status as **sexual** objects; this identification is further reinforced by a distorted "feminist" consciousness that defines this way of thinking as a form of **postfeminist** liberation. *See also* CONSCIOUSNESS RAISING.

FAMILY. The institution of the family plays an important, if ambiguous, role in **political and social philosophy**. Traditionally, the family

is not only the site of **reproduction** but also, as a **heterosexual** institution, the site of private relations between individual men and
women.

For some feminist philosophers of the **first wave** of feminism, the
family was seen as the location of women's power. Women were prevented from entering the public sphere but could affect it indirectly
through their moral influence on husbands and children. For other
feminist philosophers of this era, however, the family was the barrier
to true **equality**, as women's traditional duties prevented them from
having the time to enter the workplace or political life.

The institution of the family often plays a complex role in traditional political philosophy. While their theorizing about **justice** and
rights did not include the private sphere, and thus women, **canonical**
male philosophers often spent a surprising amount of time discussing
family relations and paradigms of the good family. Women's role
was typically seen as one of producing good citizens. Unlike early
feminist accounts of the power of this role, however, this type of account ultimately made women invisible within the state, as this role
was performed within the private sphere.

Many of these original issues remain in contemporary feminist
philosophical work on the family. The family is still identified as the
site of the moral development and training of future citizens, but this
is now regarded as entailing state recognition and support of domestic labor, rather than being the responsibility of only women. Even
though feminists often resist traditional family structures, they recognize that outside the West, these structures will be harder to break
down. Thus it is generally agreed that there needs to be continued
focus on analyzing how the family is an economic trap, particularly
for non-Western women, and on offering solutions within traditional
family structures.

Feminist philosophers have often supplemented these critiques by
placing them within an analysis of the family as a political construction: the family is not a natural production. What goes on within fam-
ilies, for example, the lack of legal protection against domestic
violence, cannot be understood apart from the legal system; what
constitutes a family, for example, the paradigm of the nuclear family,
is the product of laws and political systems. Inclusion of the family
as a legitimate area of concern for political philosophy—as a political

entity—challenges the traditional notion that the family should be out of the reach of state interference, as well as the standard political theorizing that focuses on, for example, the relation of the non-situated individual to the state.

There is no general agreement over how much the family contributes to **gender** injustice and the power relations between men and women: whether it is the primary cause or not. There is some disagreement, moreover, about whether the traditional family structure is, by definition, **oppressive**. Some philosophers have argued that maintaining the traditional family is important for women. Such philosophers claim that women are more inclined to nurture, whether due to their psychology or biology; thus the solution for women's inequality is to value and support the role of carer.

Feminist philosophical work on the family is not restricted to abstract theorizing; it also entails the development of practical solutions for social justice. These solutions for equality can be reformist in nature, for example, state day care. They can also be more radical, premised on the assumption that only true freedom of choice can produce equality: for example, through multiple parenting as a new way of forming and legalizing non-subordinating relationships among adults and children. *See also* DIVISION OF LABOR, SEXUAL; PUBLIC/PRIVATE DISTINCTION.

FASHION. *See* BODY.

FEMININE ETHICS. There has been a long tradition of debate within traditional moral philosophy over the notion of the existence of a "women's morality," one aligned with the traits of **femininity**. In **ancient Greek philosophy**, for example, some of the female Pythagorean philosophers argued that women and men had different virtues and moral responsibilities. Within the philosophical **canon**, the view that morality is **gendered** has typically led to the devaluation of traditionally feminine virtues and characteristics, such as **emotionality**. This view is often connected to arguments for the reinforcement of women's traditional social roles—for example, in the philosophies of **Immanuel Kant** and **Jean-Jacques Rousseau**.

Contemporary feminine ethics continues with this notion of morality as gendered but develops it in a different vein, with the intention of revaluing those aspects of human life that have been traditionally identified as feminine, such as **caring** or compassion. This revaluation may then lead to the development of a separate female ethic or to the addition of these aspects into mainstream **masculinist** ethics to produce a more balanced and inclusive picture of morality.

As both feminine ethics and **feminist ethics** are women centered and founded in some way on the moral **experience** of women, there are clear connections between the two. They differ, however, in their goals. The goal of feminine ethics is to develop a way of thinking that can be seen to be a women's way of thinking or that somehow comes out of the moral experiences of women (for example, experiences of **motherhood**). This has meant that the charge of **essentialism** has sometimes been leveled at feminine ethics: that it argues for a fixed "woman's" nature. Ethicists who self-define as feminist, on the other hand, see the development of ethical theories and perspectives as part of the feminist political commitment to end the **oppression** of women (and other oppressed groups), rather than as a revaluing or understanding of women's different moral experiences that need not entail political and social change.

Despite these definitions, it can be hard in practice to categorize works in these two areas. **Carol Gilligan**, for example, argues for the existence of different moral "voices" of men and women, yet she sees her work as feminist because she maintains that these two voices are different but **equal**. **Maternal ethics**, an ethics grounded in the experience of mothering, can potentially be a feminine ethics or a feminist ethics, or both. *See also* BLACK FEMINIST ETHICS; CULTURAL FEMINISM.

FEMININE WRITING (ÉCRITURE FÉMININE). *See* BODY; FEMININITY; FRENCH FEMINISM; IRIGARAY, LUCE; LANGUAGE, PHILOSOPHY OF; SEXUALITY.

FEMININITY. Feminist philosophers define femininity as the ideology that dictates appropriate **gender** behavior for women through a system of rules (such as those that govern personal appearance), roles (such as the role of wife), and socially valued traits (such as nurturance and empathy). The ultimate purpose of the ideal of femininity is to make women pleasing to men.

Simone de Beauvoir was the first feminist philosopher to recognize what is now an accepted tenet of feminism, that these roles, rules, and traits constitute a cage for women, a cage constructed by **patriarchal** society. She argues that not only are women forced to play these roles, but they acquiesce in their own **oppression** through an internalization of these roles, and thus an internalization of their own inferiority. Both Francophone and Anglophone feminist theorists have followed Beauvoir in holding that femininity is constructed as the negative, inferior "Other" to **masculinity**; the latter construct is identified as the positive norm within patriarchal society. Indeed, masculinity needs the Other both for its definition and its higher status or value relative to femininity. Thus, despite the fact that the ideal of masculinity is also a social construction, it functions differently from the ideal of femininity.

In Anglophone **feminist theory** in general, this notion of femininity as social construction is often used to provide the framework for arguments for political change. If femininity is a social construction, then those roles and characteristics attributed to women—which are seen as justifications for their inferior social status—are not innate or a product of their biology. Thus **equality** would be the result of the abolition of gender. Not all feminists, however, are committed to the abolition of the masculine/feminine binary. Some argue that the path to equality is to revalue the traits associated with the feminine. Moreover, for some Third World feminists, the possibility of a self-construction of femininity for women could be a means to empowerment.

In contemporary Anglophone feminist philosophy, a frequent use of the concepts of femininity and masculinity is to demonstrate the devaluing of women and the feminine in the Western philosophical tradition. This tradition constructs reality within a framework of a set of normative **dualisms** such as rationality/**emotionality** and civilization/**nature**. The "top" disjunct is the superior, and these superior disjuncts are the elements that are culturally associated with men. Thus reality replays the cultural valorization of men and the masculine.

At present, the most influential work on femininity comes from

French feminist thought. In French feminist philosophy, the masculinity of the discourse of traditional philosophical thought is challenged for its erasure of the feminine. Femininity is thus a metaphorical position outside the dominant discourse, a position that can allow a critique of the patriarchal symbolic order through the autonomous construction of "feminine" expression and **language**: an *écriture féminine*. This concept of feminine writing breaks with the more mainstream notion that there is a fixed construction of femininity. Feminine writing is seen as writing "with the **body**": it is a writing that symbolically represents women's bodies and **sexuality** and their shifting nature. *See also* FOUCAULT, MICHEL; SEX.

FEMINIST ETHICS. Many historical feminist philosophers have been interested in issues of morality, but there is little that amounts to any kind of feminist tradition. Typically the work of these early philosophers focuses on **gendered** morality, and thus tends to fit better under the category of **feminine ethics**.

Ethical issues have always been an important component of contemporary feminist philosophy. It was not, however, until the late 1980s that book-length treatments of feminist ethics as a specific topic were published. Thus far, most feminist ethicists have been white Western women. There is some work being done by male philosophers and by philosophers of color; however, the latter may not always accept the designation of "feminist," due to the history of racism within both the feminist movement and **feminist theorizing**.

Offering a precise definition of feminist ethics can be problematic. It can be hard to draw clear boundaries between it and the other women-centered ethics of feminine ethics and **maternal ethics**. Moreover, given the influence of the work of psychologist **Carol Gilligan** on feminist ethical thinking, feminist ethics is held by some philosophers, feminist and non-feminist alike, to be interchangeable with the ethics of **care**.

Feminist ethics can be distinguished from these other ethics due to its prioritizing of the analysis, and elimination, of the subordination of women (and of other **oppressed** groups). Feminist ethicists offer new perspectives on "applied" issues through their awareness and analysis of relations of power: for example, the inequalities in health care delivery among different groups. Feminist ethicists have also established new areas of examination. For example, the standard view of cosmetic surgery is that it is simply a matter of free choice, whereas feminist ethicists point to the ways that women undergo unnecessary surgery because of their internalization of **patriarchal** standards of beauty.

On the theoretical side, feminist ethics functions as a critique of the ideals, concepts, and concerns of traditional ethics. Feminist ethicists challenge the **canonical** tradition for its lack of concern for women's interests, its neglect of issues of particular importance to women (the private realm in particular), its denial of women's **moral agency**, and its devaluation of the moral **experience** of women and the characteristics culturally associated with the "**feminine**." Feminist ethicists have argued that the traditional picture of the moral agent is a construct of male ideals and is antithetical to the lived experience of women. The traditional moral agent is an **autonomous** and **impartial** decision-maker. Because of the nature of this being, "his" rational choices will be made independently of particular historical and cultural contexts. Thus, if he decides well, he makes choices that can be **universally** applied. Feminist ethicists have pointed to the way that this ideal excludes women. For example, women have not always been seen as rational, or their experiences in their traditional roles of wife and **mother** are not those of an independent individual.

For some feminist philosophers, this male bias means that the canon must be rejected altogether. Others respond to this bias by seeing feminist ethics in terms of a reversal—for example, privileging the moral experience of women or offering a direct substitution of "feminine" values for "**masculine**" ones. The potential problem with this latter approach is that it will substitute one bias for another, rather than offering a fully human ethics. Typically, however, the aim of those working in feminist ethics is to counter male bias in ethics through a reconceiving of the norms and a broadening of the scope of philosophical ethics itself. The areas that have generated particular interest are **equality**, impartiality, moral agency, autonomy, and moral **epistemology**.

Alison Jaggar offers a widely accepted set of minimum conditions for theoretical adequacy of any feminist ethics: feminist ethics recognizes that there are differences in the situations of men and women;

works toward an analysis of and resistance to the subordination of women; can encompass the moral issues of the private realm as well as the public; and acknowledges the moral experience of women.

Some **postmodern feminists** have also argued for a feminist ethics, despite claims that the postmodernist deconstruction of the ideals and concepts of traditional Western moral philosophy leads to a nihilistic stance. The postmodernist approach is characterized by a resistance to the reframing of traditional moral philosophical concepts, a resistance to the development of a unitary feminist morality, and an insistence on the multiplicity of moral values and choices. *See also* BIOETHICS; BLACK FEMINIST ETHICS; FEMINIST ETHICS AND SOCIAL THEORY; LESBIAN ETHICS; OBJECTIVITY.

FEMINIST ETHICS AND SOCIAL THEORY (FEAST). FEAST is a professional society in the United States. According to its mission statement, it is "dedicated to promoting feminist ethical perspectives on philosophy, moral and political life, and public policy."

FEMINIST THEORY. Early feminist theorizing focused on the goal of social and political **equality**, although there was no one account of how such equality could be accomplished. This early theorizing about equality fell into two rough categories: it could be achieved within the existing system, or it required an overturning of the existing **patriarchal** system. Starting in the 1980s, with the development of theorizing about **sex** difference and **gender**, the ideal of equality became an area of debate, in particular because it flattens differences among women. The goal of current theorizing is better understood as the uncovering and analysis of the **oppressions** experienced by women: their differences and interconnections, their causes, and the formulation of strategies for their removal. There is no one feminist theory and thus no one analysis or solution. Moreover, the wide variety of feminist theories that exist tend to resist easy categorization. Some of the most central theories are: **anarchist feminism, black feminism, cultural feminism, ecofeminism, existentialist feminism, French feminism, global feminism, liberal feminism, Marxist feminism, multicultural feminism, postmodern feminism, psychoanalytic feminism, radical feminism,** and **socialist**

feminism. *See also* FIRST WAVE FEMINISM; POSTFEMINISM; SECOND WAVE FEMINISM; THIRD WAVE FEMINISM.

FILM, PHILOSOPHY OF. *See* AESTHETICS.

FINCH, ANNE. *See* CONWAY, ANNE FINCH.

FIRST WAVE FEMINISM. The term first wave feminism (or old wave feminism) refers to the period of challenges to the legal and social inequalities of women from the mid-1800s to 1920 in the United States and the United Kingdom. Activists worked for, among other things, female suffrage, the **right** of women to own property, the reform of marital laws, and **education** reform. Much of the feminist philosophy of this era reflects the concerns of these activists. **Harriet Taylor Mill**, for example, holds that allowing married women to work outside the home, and removing all laws related to **marriage**, would give women both personal and economic independence.

Feminist philosophy of this period was not just within the **liberal feminist** tradition; there was also a strong current of **cultural feminist** thought. While the two strands of thought shared a common goal of social reform, they differed in their understanding of this goal. Essentially, liberal feminists aimed toward **equality** of the **sexes** produced through civil and political rights and freedoms. Cultural feminists held that the liberation of women, understood as the opportunity for women to develop their cooperative nature, would benefit women as individuals. They held that it would also benefit society overall through the feminization of culture. *See also* SECOND WAVE FEMINISM; POSTFEMINISM; THIRD WAVE FEMINISM.

FOUCAULT, MICHEL (1926–1984). French philosopher and historian of thought Michel Foucault was born in Poitiers, France. For most of his academic life he was Professor of the History of Systems of Thought at the Collège de France. Three stages can be identified in his work, stages in which he examined different subject matter and employed different methodologies. In the earliest work from the 1960s, he focused on such things as madness and medicine, reflected in his book *Madness and Civilization*. In the second stage from the

1970s, he explored the relations between power and knowledge in punishment and in **sexuality**, which he set out in *Discipline and Punish* and *The History of Sexuality*. The third and final stage was on ethics.

Foucault's *The History of Sexuality* has been an important influence for **postmodern feminist** philosophical work on the **body, sex,** sexuality, and the relations between knowledge and power. On the whole, however, Foucault's philosophy has been of little interest; his work tends more to be the object of appropriation and use. Indeed, for many feminist philosophers, his writings are best known through **Judith Butler**'s analysis and use of his ideas. Typically, Foucault's thought is not transmitted in its pure form; rather, it is usually mixed with other postmodern work. There are three main reasons for the lack of interest in Foucault's philosophy as a whole: he does not say much about constructions of **gender**, he is not a feminist per se, and his account of **subjectivity** may be in tension with the feminist enterprise. This latter element is a problem that many feminist philosophers see as common to all postmodern theorizing.

Foucault rejects the notion that power comes from centralized sources. Power is not something one individual "has" over another; rather, it is a set of material discursive practices that construct individuals. Power, in Foucault's account, is exercised on the body, but the subjection of individuals is not imposed on them, for example, by force. Individuals correct and discipline themselves in accordance with politically created norms. Even sex and sexuality are the product of discourse. Knowledge and power are interconnected, which means that knowledge is not in itself independent; it is tied to systems of social control, and thus it is a tool of **oppression**.

For feminist philosophers, this provides a radical departure from more conventional conceptions of gender and sex. Feminists usually see gender alone as constructed: a mutable social overlay on a fixed sex. Foucauldian reconceptualization of gender has allowed feminist philosophers to offer new analyses of the way that the norms of **femininity** serve to oppress women. In these new types of analysis, femininity is the normalization of the female body through a set of disciplines enacted on the body. To be feminine requires the individual to follow the norms of femininity: women subject themselves to a set of disciplinary practices, such as the adornment of the body to please men. Foucauldian feminist philosophers recognize the ambiguities inherent in this type of analysis; success in these practices subordinates women, but it may also offer power to an individual because of her increased appeal to men.

Feminists influenced by Foucault also explore relations between gender and sexuality. Judith Butler is the best known of feminist theorists on the subject of sexuality, and she draws on *The History of Sexuality* for her analysis of the relations between sexuality and gender. For Butler sexuality, specifically **heterosexuality**, is an **epistemic** category—one that is constructed through discourses of power—while gender is a set of regulatory practices for human behavior that function to support the system of heterosexuality. The identity of men or women is constructed in opposition to the other; this means not only that their identity is one of mutual dependence, but that this dependence is constructed as a sexual need for the other.

Because it seems to be in tension with the feminist project, this type of use of Foucault has been the subject of criticism. Foucault's analysis of power is about the way networks of power constitute individuals; however, without the possibility of one group constructing another, Foucauldians can only talk about the gendering of individuals; they cannot discuss gender relations. The intelligibility of the notion of gender relations is important for feminist philosophers; without this notion they cannot explain how the system of gender is perpetuated, or why it is more oppressive to women.

If, as Foucauldians claim, individuals are constituted by social practices, then the feminist call for **autonomy** for women is undercut. More generally, without the notion of a stable subject, feminist politics becomes dissipated. The struggle against the oppressive system of gender requires that there be some notion of a female sex to be liberated from this system. Thus, on the level of particular phenomena, a Foucauldian analysis of gender is useful as it shows ways that a **patriarchal** system controls women. On the more general level, it fails the feminist project, as it cannot offer an identifiable political subject to liberate.

FRENCH FEMINISM. The term French feminism was originally coined by feminists in the United States and the United Kingdom to define the work that began coming out of France after the student revolt of 1968, in particular the work of **Luce Irigaray**, Julia Kristeva, and **Hélène Cixous**. On the whole, however, these French thinkers tend to hold that there are more differences than similarities in their goals and methods. French feminist thought is grounded in **Marxism**, psychoanalysis, and poststructuralism, and it is influenced by the thought of, among others, **Jacques Derrida** and Jacques Lacan. French feminist thought is far from derivative, however, as it is also a rejection of these male theorists for their failure to provide an adequate account of **sex** difference.

For some feminist philosophers, these French feminists are more properly placed under the general category of **postmodernist**. For others, the use of the term French feminism serves to emphasize a distinct shared perspective among these thinkers in their work on sex difference, **femininity**, and **language**, for it is this shared perspective that has been highly influential outside France. Of the three central figures, only Irigaray has specifically addressed philosophy and the philosophical tradition. Thus, while Kristeva and Cixous have had a great influence on feminist theorizing in general, their work is rarely discussed by philosophers. Even though French feminist work was originally eschewed by Anglophone philosophers because of its complexity and challenging writing style, it is now a central influence on feminist theory throughout the West.

French feminists, like all feminist theorists in one way or another, are engaged with examining sex difference: the foundation of the subordination of women. Anglo-American feminist philosophers tend to engage in discussions of whether liberation can be best achieved through **equality** or through the revaluing of difference. French feminist work is an implicit rejection of this type of analysis, because this analysis assumes both that difference is connected to biology and that equality is about sameness. Moreover, these alternatives are challenges within society, whereas French feminists aim to challenge the existing framework of discourse that gives these terms meaning.

In essence, French feminists, through an examination of sex difference within the intellectual context of French philosophy and psychoanalysis, claim that sex difference is produced through the operation of discourse, not biology. Sex identity is the construct of **patriarchal** forms of representation and knowledge.

In the patriarchal symbolic order, women are represented as the negative "Other"; this notion of otherness is influenced by **Simone de Beauvoir**'s analysis of woman as Other. For contemporary French feminists, however, the Other is understood as the symbolically feminine. It is not so much constructed through relations between self and other (which is Beauvoir's account) as through relations of meaning within the symbolic order. Thus femininity is male defined and has no meaning or existence outside patriarchal discourse.

In response, French feminists aim to create a different structure of thought and speaking, a "feminine" form of expression—*écriture féminine*—that operates outside the male symbolic order. These theorists do not write as the woman that is found in male discourse, but rather outside this discourse. In this way, feminine writing serves to disrupt **masculine** language and to make visible its exclusion of woman and the feminine.

For Irigaray and Cixous, to do feminine writing is to write "with the **body**" or to "write the body": this writing symbolically represents women's bodies and **sexuality**. This speaking position is one of both critique and meaning-making, but like female sexuality, it is no one thing: it is multiple and fluid. There is disagreement among feminist theorists over the interpretation of the "body" in this context: whether it is a complex metaphor or also has some biological significance.

For Cixous, feminine writing has the power to challenge the dichotomous—male—thinking and writing of the Western intellectual tradition within which women can only be conceived of in male terms as a negative: for example, as "not man" and "not active." Furthermore, it is within this framework that dominance and submission have existence and meaning. Feminine writing is fluid and changing like female sexuality. Thus it forms a challenge to the male writing of the Western intellectual tradition which, like male sexuality, is linear and rooted in one location. Feminine writing is not a negative enterprise; for Cixous, writing with the body opens up the possibility of female knowledge, a knowledge that comes from desire, not **reason**.

For Irigaray as well, feminine ways of speaking are not just resistance and subversion but are also needed for the exploration of new ways of knowledge. Irigaray aims to show what has been left out of Western phallocentric representations. Women are not represented in the philosophical tradition, as social language is masculine; female sexuality does not have an existence, as it has no cultural representation. Thus the female has been left out of the knowledge generated by the Western intellectual tradition.

Irigaray resists the definition of woman as the negative or Other of man, for in the patriarchal symbolic order, woman only exists as a reflection of man. She does not, however, offer an alternative conception of female sexuality—of what this sexuality is in reality—as this would replay the maleness of the concept that sexuality is one thing. She holds, instead, that female sexuality is unstructured, fluid, and multiple.

In creating a feminine language, a language of female sexuality, Irigaray aims to subvert and resist Western philosophical thinking. It is by using this female language that Irigaray offers criticism of the "male" language of **science** and **logic** in Western philosophy, which then leads to her critique of the central concepts and ideals of the Western tradition, such as neutrality and **universality**. Her work functions as a critique of Western philosophy, as it resists the dominant structure of meaning: **dualist** thinking. Moreover, her critique itself is a philosophy: it is meaning-making. This is not in the sense that it is a unified or unique system; female language is multiple and even inconsistent. In traditional philosophical thinking, these characteristics are problematic, as language is conceived as a fixed set of semantic elements that are open to dissection and analysis. The function of female language, however, is not the same as that of male language; its goal is not to individuate and identify in order to achieve knowledge, but to produce understanding and relationship. *See also* CANON, CRITIQUE OF; CONTINENTAL PHILOSOPHY; IMAGINARY, PHILOSOPHICAL; SUBJECTIVITY.

FREUD, SIGMUND. See PSYCHOANALYTIC FEMINISM.

– G –

GENDER. Gender is the set of socially constructed behavioral and psychological characteristics associated with **masculinity** and **femi-**

ninity. Feminists began using the term gender in the 1960s for the social construction of what it means to be a woman, or a man, as distinct from the biological **sex** of an individual. The significance of this distinction was that it undercut the problematic notion of **biological determinism**: that women's biological sex determined a specific set of psychological characteristics and social roles. Instead, feminists claimed, only biological sex is fixed, while psychological and intellectual characteristics are the product of **socialization**, specifically the **patriarchal** socialization that controls women's social realities.

In the 1980s, theorists began to challenge the intelligibility of both the sex/gender distinction and the conceptualization of gender in this system. Theorists claimed that the physiology of the sexes, as well as gender, could be affected by social interpretation and construction. In some cultures, for example, the physical attributes of women are partly formed through their level of nutrition, which in turn is dictated by their lower social status. Moreover, even though the sex/gender distinction challenges the problematic notion of biological determinism, it still shares the same assumptions about the fixed nature of human biology.

Theorists call attention to the fact that individuals are not gendered simply as a man or woman; gender is constituted and understood within other hierarchical systems, such as **race** and class. The romanticized **motherhood**, for example, of nineteenth-century American white women was part of their femininity and was constructed against the gender/race appropriate roles of black female slaves, who were seen as breeders with little attachment to their children. Thus masculinity and femininity are not unitary notions; rather the discussion should be of masculinities and femininities as a group of notions that share characteristics in the way that family members resemble each other.

In this way the feminist philosophical debate on gender moved from analysis of the sex/gender system to a questioning of whether "woman" has any **essential** or unitary meaning. The current debate has been dominated by the work of **Judith Butler** on gender identity. For Butler, gender identity is a fluid and unstable notion, and thus one cannot claim that one "is" a woman. Butler argues that it is only within the system of **heterosexuality** that gender identity appears coherent, and in its turn supports this system.

In Butler's account, gender identity is wrapped up with heterosexuality as part of the identity of men and women: they are defined in relation to each other. Thus they are mutually dependent, and this need for the other is also constructed as a **sexual** need for their other: their partner. Gender, for Butler, is a set of regulations for human behavior that functions to support the system of heterosexuality. Femininity/woman is not "real" but artificial—a set of codes performed on the surface of a **body**, male or female. Butler aims to demonstrate this notion that gender is performance through showing how drag is a parody of that performance. Parodying these codes serves to destabilize them, and thus to subvert the discourse within which women are **oppressed**.

Butler does not mean that there is some "subject" beneath the performance who can choose what to perform; rather the performance of gender is what constitutes this apparent subject. Thus the notion of a self is also destabilized, for there is no self on which gender is performed. In these ways, Butler is critiquing the claim that the separation of gender from sex can liberate women, for she holds that the acceptance of a totalizing unified concept of gender serves merely to reaffirm oppression. She argues that only outside the system of binary thinking can we understand how gender binaries function to oppress, and she claims that feminists should consider the possibility of polymorphous identities as a replacement for gender.

For many feminist theorists, Butler's rejection of the coherence of gender identity is problematic. The feminist political goal of the end to women's oppression, and the analyses and strategies that accompany that goal, must be grounded in some kind of unified concept of woman: a subject to liberate. There is no agreement among feminist philosophers on how this issue is to be resolved. Certainly, feminist philosophers now recognize that past generalizations about "women" have been false and overly simplistic. Thus some are considering, for example, ways that claims about "women" can function just as strategies for the feminist political goal, without having any ontological significance. *See also* FOUCAULT, MICHEL; SUBJECTIVITY.

GENDER FEMINISM. *See* CULTURAL FEMINISM.

GILLIGAN, CAROL (1936–   ). Psychologist Carol Gilligan is probably the best-known proponent of the ethics of **care**. Her major work is *In a Different Voice: Psychological Theory and Women's Development* (1982). Gilligan makes three main claims in this work: that there are two ways of speaking about moral problems (the voices of "care" and "**justice**"); that care must be included in some way in the moral domain; and that a focus on care is characteristically female. While all three of these claims have been the focus of feminist criticism, the third claim has drawn the most criticism. Gilligan has qualified these three initial claims in more recent years, but her studies still find a connection between women and care.

In *In a Different Voice*, Gilligan's main target is the work of educational psychologist Lawrence Kohlberg. Kohlberg developed a six-stage scale of moral development; the highest stage is a **Kantian** approach in which the person adopts a **universal**, **impartial**, **autonomous** point of view. While not all males are certain to reach this top level, females are far less likely to reach it, and typically remain at stage three on Kohlberg's scale. This third stage is where a person conforms to conventional moral norms in order to gain the approval of others.

Gilligan argues that instead of this indicating women's moral inferiority, these differences point to a different—but **equal**—way of thinking about morality: a different moral "voice." In Kohlberg's view of moral development, morality is framed as an ethic of justice in terms of **rights**, fairness, and an impartial application of universally applicable principles. Contrary to this, the "different voice" of women identified by Gilligan, the ethic of care, frames morality in terms of responsibility, relationships, and a contextualized answering of moral problems.

Gilligan does not hold that this different voice is innate. Instead, she grounds her explanation of its existence on social **object relations theory**, claiming that the different voices of men and women are the product of different processes of separation in childhood from the primary caretaker, usually the **mother**. In essence, social object relations theorists hold that the female child does not completely separate from the mother; thus her sense of self as a woman becomes identified with relationality and caring. In the case of the male child, the development of a **gendered** identity is achieved through a distancing and separation from the mother. In this way, therefore, the moral voices of men and women reflect their differing **experiences** of attachment with others. Men are able to assume a position of **objectivity** in making moral decisions, whereas women make these decisions within a framework of connectedness with others.

The relationship that Gilligan sees between the two ethics is not completely clear. Originally in *In a Different Voice*, Gilligan claimed that the justice and care orientations could converge. In later work, she claims that justice and care are two different perspectives through which to see a moral situation that can be alternated by most individuals. Here Gilligan uses an analogy of the visually ambiguous figure of the duck-rabbit (an image that viewers can interpret it as a duck or a rabbit) to clarify the relationship between the two moral perspectives: the two perspectives are related, but cannot be easily integrated.

The strength of Gilligan's claim about the relationship between gender and moral voice has often been misinterpreted. Gilligan is clear that she is not making universal claims about all men or all women, but about tendencies in their thinking. Even this more limited claim, however, may still leave her work open to charges of **essentialism**: the claim that there is a fixed "woman's" nature. Gilligan responds to these charges in more recent works, where she states that the different voices are learned, rather than **biologically determined**. Even with these charges answered, some feminist critics maintain that an unpoliticized analysis of the connections between gender and care—the type offered by Gilligan—will not serve to further the liberation of women, and may instead reinforce gender **oppression**. *See also* FEMININE ETHICS; FEMINIST ETHICS; SUBJECTIVITY.

GILMAN, CHARLOTTE PERKINS (1860–1935). Charlotte Perkins Gilman, the American philosopher and feminist, was born in Hartford, Connecticut. She is probably best known for her works of feminist fiction, such as "The Yellow Wallpaper" (1892) and *Herland* (1915). Gilman developed a social philosophy grounded in Reform Darwinism, the theory that humans are active participants in their own evolution. Her central argument is that women's **oppres-**

sion is the main impediment to social progress, and that human progress requires the active participation of women in the social world.

In her 1898 work *Women and Economics: A Study of the Economic Relation Between Men and Women as a Factor in Social Evolution*, Gilman aims to demonstrate the relation between women's oppression and the thwarting of human progress. She argues that the economic and social dependence of women on men is unnatural and that this dependency relation affects both **sexes**. Gilman holds that women are parasitic on men and that this has stunted women's development. As their survival depends on male support, women have been forced to develop only those characteristics that will help them get this support, specifically those characteristics that are pleasing to men. In their turn, men's progress is hindered by the burden of this relationship.

Gilman argues that only sweeping social change can dismantle this relationship and thus make human progress possible. In her 1911 work *The Man-Made World; or, Our Androcentric Culture*, Gilman calls for a matriarchal world to replace the **androcentric** world; she holds that this world would be one that reflects women's characteristics of cooperation and peacefulness, as opposed to the destructive characteristics of men. She depicts the progressive nature of the female world in her 1915 novel *Herland*, a utopian vision of a matriarchal society.

Gilman's criticism of androcentric society is wide ranging. She saw that male bias extended throughout culture; it was not just present in institutions such as **marriage**. In *His Religion and Hers: A Study of the Faith of Our Fathers and the Work of Our Mothers* (ca. 1923), she critiqued the male bias both in the **history of philosophy** and in the philosophy of her contemporaries. She argues for a philosophy that also incorporates women's philosophy, claiming that this is the only way to produce a truly human philosophy: one of human progress. *See also* CULTURAL FEMINISM.

GLOBAL FEMINISM. As with all **feminist theories**, the definition and boundaries of global feminism are contested. Global feminist theory does not just focus on women's **oppression**, but on the multiple oppressions **experienced** by women of all cultures and nations. A central focus on **gender** oppression is seen as something of more concern for privileged women in the First World, whereas the central concern of global feminists is the way that political, economic, and social policies and practices oppress peoples of the Third World. Global feminists, therefore, often focus on making visible the control of people and resources that support international capital. The analyses of gender oppression offered by global feminists are often made within the context of how "globalization" affects women. Global communication systems, for example, may help liberate women through access to information; however, these systems also allow industries to operate in areas where the (female) workforce is cheapest.

The conceptual divide between First and Third Worlds is a double-edged sword for global feminists, as it produces tendencies in Western feminist theorizing to view Third World women not only as constituting a **universal**, but as "Other" (outside or in opposition to the Western "norm").

This division of worlds also brings with it the assumption for Western feminists that Third World women are unable to provide the proper tools of analysis of their own oppression. The reasons for this assumption are the impression that these women cannot see beyond their culture, and that they do not have the social advantages, such as **education**, of white Western women. Furthermore, global feminists point to the way that this conceptual divide hides the fact that the two are connected in reality: for example, the oppression of Third World women can provide economic benefits to women of the First World through the production of cheap consumer goods. These analyses can then mean that global feminists hold that, before women can achieve their own specific liberation, the alleviation of oppressive political, economic, and social policies and practices is necessary. Some global feminists have adopted the word "womanist" (originally coined by Alice Walker) to bring out this primary commitment to all Third World peoples. *See also* EPISTEMOLOGY; INDIA, FEMINISM IN.

GOLDMAN, EMMA (1869–1940). The **anarchist** and feminist philosopher Emma Goldman was born of Jewish parentage in czarist Russia. Much of the information about Goldman's life can be found in her 1931 autobiography, *Living My Life*. Goldman was given little formal **education**, but the period she spent in St. Petersburg exposed her to revolutionary ideas and writings. In 1886, she emigrated to New York, where she worked in a factory making overcoats. Goldman credits the trial and martyrdom of the Chicago anarchists—the Haymarket martyrs—as the catalyst for her move from mere sympathy with revolutionary ideals to revolutionary activism. She is buried with the Haymarket martyrs.

Goldman's anarchist philosophy leads to and underpins her feminist philosophy. The cornerstone of her **political philosophy** was her belief in individual freedom and development; her anarchism does not imply some kind of state of chaos but rather requires the absence of government. She criticizes the way that the state controls people, not just through its laws and physical forces, but through such state-sanctioned institutions as schools, the church, and **marriage**. Goldman argues that once people are free of such government, they will quite naturally cooperate and aid each other. Her notion of the freedom of the individual is thus sharply contrasted with the individualism of capitalist America. She holds that once there is a new social order, **human nature** has a measure of flexibility that would allow it to change in this way; however, she also maintains that this nature has some core elements that are immutable, specifically the love of freedom.

In Goldman's feminist philosophy, this belief in freedom took the form of a belief in **sexual** freedom for women. In 1911, she published some of her lectures, including four feminist essays, as a collection, *Anarchism and Other Essays*. In "Marriage and Love," she argues that the ideal relationship between the **sexes** is one of complete independence and **equality** in a partnership of free love, whereas the institution of marriage is one of economic dependency and subsequent **oppression** for the woman. Goldman sees the institution of marriage as an economic arrangement that restricts the freedoms of both sexes, albeit to a different degree. The man is not free in that he must pay; far worse, the woman becomes a useless dependent. Goldman draws parallels with the infantilization of the worker produced by capitalism and the infantilization of women produced by marriage: both stunt the growth and independence of humans, and then offer humiliating charity to support them. She rebuts claims that the institution of marriage serves to protect children and claims instead that only in a state of freedom can women truly love their children and partners.

In "The Traffic in Women," Goldman argues that capitalist exploitation of labor and social hypocrisy create **prostitution**. She demonstrates how the low wages of working women force them into prostitution and how, once women have become prostitutes, the sexual double standard will keep them on the margins of society. The other two essays, "Woman Suffrage" and "The Tragedy of Women's Emancipation," form a critique of the women's liberation movement. In keeping with her anarchist views, Goldman argues against the women's liberation movement, claiming that its supporters do not recognize that real liberation for women is connected to personal and sexual freedom.

GOUGES, OLYMPE DE (MARIE DE GOUZES) (1748–1793). Marie de Gouzes, born in Montauban, France, was the self-educated daughter of a butcher; she lived in Paris during the period in which she was writing. Olympe de Gouges is the name under which she wrote plays as well as political pamphlets. Her philosophical writings have a theoretical basis; typically, her arguments are grounded in natural law, and she critiques the arguments of other philosophers. Her writings also have an activist component, in that she often includes a call to action for the social and political change she is discussing. In keeping with this activism, Gouges sometimes explicitly called for greater solidarity among women to work for these changes.

Her work is provocative for its time, for her calls for the **rights** of women were calls for the rights of *all* women and men. She was the first feminist to see what is now called the interconnections between sexism and racism. Her 1788 *Réflexions sur les Hommes Nègres (Reflections on Black Men)*, which argues for the **equality** of black people and against the existence of natural racial differences, is one of the earliest critiques of the treatment of people of color.

Gouges's best-known work is also her most philosophical. She claimed that the French *Declaration of the Rights of Man and Citizen* did not cover women, and thus it was necessary for her to write her 1791 treatise *Déclaration des Droits de la Femme et de la Citoyenne (Declaration of the Rights of Woman and the Female Citizen)*. Based on natural law, she argues for the equality of women: specifically, for political equality; equal opportunity in **education** and employment; equal protection under the law; and the right to property after **mar-**

riage. Gouges ends her call for the equality of women with a critique of the treatment of black people and a renewed call for the equality of all people.

Gouges's last work, *Les Trois urnes, ou le Salut de la patrie*, was an argument that government in France should be chosen by a general vote. It was her attempt to publish and distribute this work that led to her arrest on suspicion of being a royalist; she was found guilty and sentenced to death. It would appear that her views on the equality of women were also a factor in her death sentence. *See also* RACE AND RACISM.

GOURNAY, MARIE DE (MARIE LE JARS DE GOURNAY) (1566–1645). French philosopher Marie de Gournay was born in Paris, where she lived most of her life. Little is known about her childhood, but it would appear that she was mainly self-educated. She admired and was a friend of Michel de Montaigne, who gave her the title of "fille d'alliance" (adopted daughter). Gournay wrote the preface for the 1595 edition of Montaigne's *Essays*, which also functioned as a philosophical defense of them. Gournay was well known among the intellectual circles of her time. The Dutch philosopher **Anna Maria van Schurman** refers to the influence of Gournay on her own work. While many of Gournay's works contain feminist themes, her two explicitly feminist works are *Egalité des hommes et des femmes* (*The Equality of Men and Women*), published in 1622, and *Grief des Dames* (*Complaints of Women*), published in 1626.

Egalité is original in that Gournay argues against her male opponents by explicitly drawing on arguments for the **equality** of women from works written by men. Among the philosophers cited are Seneca, Montaigne, Plutarch, and **Plato**. Her work is also notable for being an early defense of the view that, beyond basic biological differences, **sex** differences are a product of the environment. Moreover, she appears to hold that all humans are fundamentally equal: for example, she claims that the only difference between the ruler and the ruled is that the former has been given the power to look after the latter. *Grief* is an argument for the inclusion of women in intellectual debate, and a criticism of those who wish to exclude women. She critiques the sexism of those who automatically find the writing of women to be bad, but who admire men even when they have nothing but their sex to recommend their conversation or writing.

– H –

HEALTH CARE ETHICS. *See* BIOETHICS.

HEGEL, GEORG WILHELM FRIEDRICH. *See* ALIENATION; CONTINENTAL PHILOSOPHY; EXISTENTIAL FEMINISM; *SECOND SEX, THE.*

HETEROSEXISM/HETEROSEXUALITY. Heterosexuality (a **sexual** relationship between people of the opposite **sex**) has been an important issue for feminism since the 1970s. Feminist philosophers have focused on the clarification of concepts of heterosexuality, and on analyses of the ways that heterosexuality is valued and privileged. The fundamental question is whether the social behaviors that make up the institution of heterosexuality are natural or socially constructed. The term compulsory heterosexuality—first used by Adrienne Rich—refers to the assumption that heterosexuality is innate, and therefore justifies the resulting social reinforcement of heterosexuality.

For some feminist philosophers, heterosexuality is a political and ideological system that functions to maintain the subordination of women. They claim, for example, that the system of heterosexuality reinforces the sexual **division of labor**, as well as socially dictated norms of **gender** behavior, such as passivity and vanity in women. However, not all groups of women are subordinated in the same way by heterosexuality. It has been claimed that "normal" female heterosexuality is identified with the sexuality of white women. The boundaries of female heterosexual behavior are formed by being set up in normative opposition to social constructions of women of color, who are stereotyped as problematically oversexed and assertive. Thus not only do women of color function as the inferior group, against which appropriate behavior is framed, but they can be excluded from the social acceptance that accompanies this behavior.

Feminist philosophers have also analyzed how heterosexism, the assumption that heterosexuality is the norm, makes women reluctant or unlikely to challenge this system. The system is invisible: heterosexuality is so much the norm that sexuality itself has become identified with it. The assumption that heterosexuality is the norm also functions to assert its superiority over homosexuality; this plays out in the ways that homosexuals are subordinated by being labeled as deviant or being made invisible. *See also* LESBIAN PHILOSOPHY.

HILDEGARD OF BINGEN (1098–1179). Hildegard of Bingen was born in Bermesheim near Alzey, Germany. She entered the double monastery on Mount Disibod when she was about fifteen and later became its abbess. Hildegard was not exclusively a philosopher-theologian; her extensive writing covered a range of topics, including drama and **science**. Her best-known philosophical-theological work is *Scivias* (*Know the Way*).

Strictly speaking, Hildegard of Bingen cannot be considered a feminist, or even a protofeminist. However, her contribution to the discussion of the relations between the **sexes** has been acknowledged; she was the first thinker to set out a systematized account of **sex complementarity**. Hildegard held that the sexes were different in their knowledge, relation to God, and virtue, but she argued that these differences were **equal**.

For Hildegard, the creation of men and women in the image of God was a reflection of the bisexuality of the divine. Hildegard held, furthermore, that this meant both **masculine** and **feminine** elements were present in the human soul, and that each sex should aim to develop its "opposite" side or elements. This is reflected in Hildegard's personification of the virtues as female knights, characterizing the virtues as containing both male (e.g., strength) and female (e.g., grace) elements. The goal of wisdom for both sexes, which Hildegard identified with self-knowledge, was understanding their nature as men or women; even though the content of their knowledge would differ, the goal was shared.

HISTORY OF PHILOSOPHY. The feminist examination of the history of philosophy can be seen as providing one of the central catalysts for the feminist philosophical project. There are three main strands in this field. **Canon critique** started in the 1970s, and was one of the earliest forms of feminist history of philosophy. On its most basic level, it is the project of examining texts for their exclusion or marginalization of women, and their neglect of women's interests, such as child-rearing, that come out of women's lived **experience**. At a more complex level, it can be the examination of texts for **gendered** concepts: for example, the way that **reason** is represented as **masculine**. The second central strand of feminist history of philosophy is the consideration of possible ways in which the canon can be appropriated for feminist use, although some feminist philosophers maintain that the sexism of the canon is too engrained for the canon to form a politically legitimate foundation. The third central strand is the recovery of neglected or forgotten **women philosophers** from the past.

Coming out of these strands is one of the central projects of feminist history of philosophy: the examination of the enterprise and ideals of philosophy to find whether, at its very core, it is a gender-neutral enterprise. A particularly common claim of this type of approach is that traditional ideals reflect cultural ideals of masculinity as well as the experiences of men that are the result of their political and social status. Thus philosophy itself is not a natural kind, but a gendered construction. In addition, some philosophers ask whether the intersectionality of gender with **race** and class also played a part in the construction of philosophy itself.

These projects have prompted recent work in Anglo-American feminist philosophy on the meta-questions of the history of philosophy. Feminist philosophers challenge mainstream accounts of the project of the history of philosophy, in particular for the abstraction of philosophy from its context, and for the framing of the history of philosophy as a series of attempts to answer a set of timeless questions. They offer feminist history of philosophy as an alternative approach, one that simultaneously examines texts within their particular historical and cultural contexts and assesses the way that these texts can speak to present-day feminist thought. These historians of philosophy are also engaging in self-reflection on their own project: for example, through the assessment of whether gender alone is the most fruitful lens for the examination of historical texts.

HOBBES, THOMAS. *See* CONTRACTARIANISM; CONWAY, ANNE FINCH.

HUMAN NATURE. For feminist philosophers, the question of whether there is a fixed, identifiable human nature has been a pivotal but controversial issue. With any philosophical discussion of human nature, feminist and non-feminist alike, the problematic question of **sex**-differentiated natures is inevitably raised. The notion of a human nature has been accompanied by a history of denial of some of its constitutive characteristics to women, with the result that women have been denied full humanity and its attendant privileges and **rights**. Indeed, the differences in the natures of the two sexes were seen as both the cause of and justification for their differences in social status.

The traditional notion of a single, although divided, human nature has its roots in **ancient Greek philosophy**. Human nature was sometimes framed in terms of a simplistic **dualism** between soul or **reason** and **body**. A more complex notion of a divided soul with the distinct, but interactive, elements of reason and the non-rational was developed in the philosophy of **Plato**. In both conceptions, reason is the superior element. Feminist philosophers have argued that reason is only superficially **gender** neutral, for historically it has been metaphorically and culturally associated with men or "maleness." Thus early philosophical notions of human nature are suspect.

Prior to the eighteenth century, the notion of sex-differentiated natures was framed in terms of women's relative lack of the capacities that were identified as the particular characteristics of human nature. During the eighteenth century, the notion of a gender-hierarchical continuum along a shared nature began to be replaced by theories that maintained that psychological and intellectual differences were grounded in biological difference. The question of the relationship between women's biologically different capacity for **reproduction** and their **oppression** has remained central for feminist philosophy.

More recently, feminist philosophers have focused on the question of what it means to say that women and men have different natures, and indeed, whether this question itself is legitimate. The more general issue of human nature became subsumed in the 1980s into the sex/gender debate and the **essentialism**/anti-essentialism debate. Some feminist philosophers, however, have continued to maintain the notion of a specifically human nature for its political power. One of the two main approaches to this is the use of the notion of a shared human nature for the claim that women's rights are specifically human rights. This claim requires an understanding both of a human nature with its attendant rights and of the specific way that women's oppression is linked to sex difference. The other main approach is to frame human nature in terms of human functioning and thus argue for social policies and rights that will produce **equal** opportunities for the human flourishing of both men and women. This latter approach has been seen as fruitful for the creation of policies to aid Third World development. *See also* BIOLOGICAL DETERMINISM; LIBERAL FEMINISM; RADICAL FEMINISM; SOMATOPHOBIA.

HUME, DAVID (1711–1776). Scottish philosopher David Hume is often seen as the foremost Anglophone philosopher. Hume's most important philosophical works are *A Treatise of Human Nature* (1739–1740), *Enquiries Concerning Human Understanding* (1748), and *Dialogues Concerning Natural Religion* (1779). He is also known as an essayist and historian. Hume was born in Edinburgh and studied at the university there. After completing his university studies, he lived for a time in France, then went to England in 1737 in order to publish the *Treatise*. He was never accepted for an academic position, but he was librarian for the Edinburgh faculty of advocates.

Hume's major work, *A Treatise of Human Nature*, has thus far been the most fertile for feminist discussion. Hume's account of the virtue of chastity in the *Treatise* (III.2.12) has generated the most attention. Hume argues for the double standard of male/female chastity, claiming that it is based on social utility: men need the assurance of paternity in order to shoulder the costs and responsibilities of rearing children, and this benefits society as a whole. On the one hand, Hume can be condemned for the fundamental sexism of his different standard for the virtue of women. On the other, Hume can be praised for recognizing that the greater propensity for chastity in women is merely the product of a necessary **socialization**. Thus, for Hume, the subordination of women is not justified by any natural inferiority. This is in contrast to prevalent views of the time: for example, that chastity was an innate characteristic, or punishment for the natural immorality of women.

Throughout many of his works, however, Hume explicitly states that women are intellectually inferior to men. This view may not be of much concern, as it reflects a common cultural view of the time. The question has been whether it plays out in Hume's philosophy more generally. One consideration is his view that women's intellectual weaknesses stem in part from their greater tendencies toward what he calls the "violent" passions. For Hume, it is the calm passions that are requisite for the truly moral individual. Even though he does not state this, this view entails that women are less likely to achieve full moral development.

For Hume, the potential of the calm passions for control over the violent passions has led people to misidentify them as purely an operation of our intellect: **reason**. Thus he does not adopt the dominant view of traditional philosophy of the **dualism** between reason and passion, a view that feminist philosophers claim identifies the former as **masculine** and the latter as **feminine**. Some interpreters have questioned whether it is the case that other concepts instead become masculinized or feminized for Hume; for example, the "male" philosopher must struggle with a "female," and potentially unruly, imagination. On the whole, however, Hume's anti-rationalist project has been seen as open to feminist reconstruction. The fact that the passions and relationality, concepts that have been traditionally aligned with the feminine, play a central role in his account of knowledge and morality has had a particular appeal for work in both **feminist ethics** and **feminine ethics**, as well as work in feminist **epistemology**. In the case of Hume's epistemology, feminist readings have also contributed to the recent development in Hume scholarship—which originated with Norman Kemp Smith—of no longer reading Hume as a purely negative skeptic. Instead, Hume is also seen as offering a positive account of knowledge, a "naturalized" epistemology.

Although the work of Annette Baier should not be categorized as solely informed by feminist interests and issues, it has been in the forefront of feminist reading of Hume's work for its previously neglected positive project; Baier sees this as a pertinent project for contemporary philosophy. Of specific interest for feminist epistemologists is a social epistemology that Baier identifies in Hume's philosophy. Instead of allowing epistemic authority to the proofs generated by a distant abstract reason, Hume allows that custom of thought, and some social behaviors, can provide validation. Custom alone is not enough; it must survive reflective scrutiny. This scrutiny is a moral one in the Humean sense of morality: what is useful for human well-being, broadly conceived. In this way, (informed) passions as the source of morality become connected to reflection. This, however, is not the reflection of the lone individual; rather, collective and cooperative reflection establishes what is to count as knowledge. Given the epistemic significance of both **emotion** and the situated knower for feminist epistemology, it could be claimed that Hume is a "woman's epistemologist."

As part of her work on Hume's moral philosophy, Baier considers the ways Hume's moral theory connects with **Carol Gilligan**'s work on the moral perspectives of women. In essence, for Hume, the task of morality is directed toward the problem of human cooperation. Like the moral life of women identified by Gilligan, Humean moral life is characterized by connectivity, the concrete, and a reliance on custom or convention. Central elements that can be identified in Hume's thinking as "female" on a Gilligan-type account are: Hume's claims that morality is ultimately based on feeling; that **justice** is a virtue that has its origins in cooperative **family** life; and that some virtues are relational. *See also* CANON, CRITIQUE OF.

HYPATIA: A JOURNAL OF FEMINIST PHILOSOPHY. The journal *Hypatia* is devoted to the publication of feminist philosophy. It has been published in the United States since 1986. The journal is named after Hypatia of Alexandria, one of the most famous teachers of philosophy in late fourth- and early fifth-century Alexandria, the epicenter of learning at that time.

– I –

IMAGINARY, PHILOSOPHICAL. The philosophical imaginary is a way of philosophical enquiry, developed by the **French feminist** Michèle Le Doeuff, that has influenced feminist rethinking of textual interpretation. Unlike Jacques Lacan, who uses the term in a psychological context, Le Doeuff uses the term in the context of the imagery in written texts. She argues that, while philosophy is often claimed to be a rational, abstract, and **logical** enterprise—rather than a story or a picture—philosophical texts contain many different pictures, symbols, and metaphors.

This philosophical imagery, however, is traditionally held to be of no importance for textual interpretation. Le Doeuff argues, instead, that these images should be seen as part of the philosopher's enterprise, and examined accordingly. She states that such images cannot simply be dismissed as tools for the philosopher who wants to communicate with a non-philosophical audience. She shows that there is no one way these images function. They can point to difficulties in the text, and they can also work for the text if they support an element, or elements, needed by the system that the system itself does not contain.

Le Doeuff does not justify her approach as a "woman's" approach. She does, however, recognize that criticism of her approach will be rooted in stereotypes of the way women are supposed to read philosophical texts, with a focus on the stories, and with an inability to see a complete system for the details. *See also* CANON, CRITIQUE OF.

IMPARTIALITY. The concept of moral impartialism is present in different forms in both the two major traditions, **Kantianism** and Utilitarianism, of modern Western moral philosophy. Moral impartialism, in its essence, is the requirement of **equal** consideration of all involved parties without favoritism or bias. Thus impartialism requires the **moral agent** to remain detached from the situation, and to employ rational, rather than **emotional**, moral thinking.

With the development of feminist synoptic interpretations of the philosophical **canon** in the 1980s, the ideal of impartiality started to be criticized for its **masculinist** nature. It has been argued that, historically, impartiality has been an inaccessible ideal for women as moral agents, due to the cultural association of women with the emotions, and the way that the traditional female roles (of wife and **mother**) have meant that women's lives are bound up in a network of relationships and attachments.

More recent criticism has focused on whether, given the inherently social nature of the self, this ideal can be achieved, as it requires us to **reason** detached from our history, embodiment, and social location.

Moreover, feminist philosophers have questioned whether impartial reasoning is applicable to personal relationships, especially given the fact that impartialism may require that we put these relationships to one side for the welfare of strangers.

In part as a response to these difficulties, work is being done on demonstrating the moral value of partiality. Marilyn Friedman, for example, argues that partiality is valuable because it is essential to the promotion of close personal relationships, which are themselves necessary for human fulfillment and well-being. This does not entail, however, that all personal relationships are inherently valuable or unproblematic,

In **political philosophy**, impartiality has also come under feminist criticism, in particular for its role in theories of **justice**. It has been argued that impartiality can serve, in practice, to disguise or even promote social hierarchies. The impartial application of **gender**-neutral workplace leave policies, for example, ignores the greater need women have for personal leave, as women typically bear the responsibility of the caretaking of ill family members. While this may not indicate that feminist philosophers should abandon the notion of impartiality for political philosophy altogether, it does show that it should be treated with caution. *See also* FEMINIST ETHICS; OBJECTIVITY; UNIVERSALISM.

INDIA, FEMINIST PHILOSOPHY IN. A number of feminist theorists and cultural critics living in the West originally came from India: for example, Chandra Mohanty, Uma Narayan, and Gayatri Spivak. Their position as both outside and inside the Western world has been the driving force for their analyses of the problematic nature of Western **feminist theorizing** about Third World women. They have shown, for instance, that it has been hard for Western theorists to avoid creating **universalizing** theories about Third World women: theories that marginalize the differences between these women. Despite their contributions to **global feminist** thought, Mohanty, Narayan, and Spivak cannot be labeled Indian feminist theorists.

Any feminist philosophizing that comes from within India about the liberation of women in India, or theorizing about a specifically Indian feminism, will need to draw on Indian intellectual and cultural traditions. There are potential problems with the development of an

Indian feminist philosophy. The subject field itself is distinctively Western in that it assumes a certain amount of unity in philosophical tradition and in feminist goals; however, the intellectual and cultural traditions available to Indian feminist thinkers are diverse and complex. Moreover, it is unclear how useful many of these traditions could be for the empowerment of women. Within the Hindu tradition, for example, is the figure of the powerful goddess, but she is a force for both good and evil. The physicist and **ecofeminist** activist **Vandana Shiva** can be credited with the first successful development of a specifically Indian feminist philosophy; it is based on the traditional **feminine** principle of *prakriti* (the energy that pervades matter), and respect for this principle.

INDIVIDUALISM, ABSTRACT. Abstract individualism is the term for the notion that the characteristics, desires, needs, and interests of human individuals are inherently pre-social, rather than connected to and constituted by social context. This notion of the ultra-individualist self is a fundamental component of traditional moral philosophy, classical liberal political theory, and some theories of the philosophy of **mind**.

Within traditional moral philosophy, this notion of the self entails that the task of the moral philosopher is to find ways to produce cooperation among such separate individuals. Within the philosophy of mind, this notion plays out in the way that psychological states are assumed to be identifiably individualist states.

Arguably, the most important manifestation of this notion of the individualist self is within classical liberal political theory. This theory, in its most basic form, is grounded in the assumption that human beings are separate individuals with potentially competing desires, interests, and needs. The aim of the state is to allow for the maximum fulfillment and **equal** treatment of the interests, desires, and needs of each individual, in so far as this does not infringe on the fulfillment of these goods for other individuals.

Feminist philosophers have criticized this notion of the self in a variety of ways. One criticism is that the notion of the self as individualist in this way is conceptually flawed; rather, it is precisely because humans are situated in a social context that they have desires, interests, and so forth. Another criticism of this notion of the self, one that comes from **object relations theory**, is that it is a "male" self. Philosophers who make this claim argue that, within **patriarchal** society, the **masculine** identity of the male child is achieved both through recognizing himself as different from his **mother**, and also through a necessary separation from her. Thus masculine identity is framed in terms of, and produced through, separation and individuation. *See also* CONTRACTARIANISM; LIBERAL FEMINISM; POLITICAL AND SOCIAL PHILOSOPHY; POLITICAL SOLIPSISM; SUBJECTIVITY.

INTERNATIONAL ASSOCIATION OF WOMEN PHILOSOPHERS (INTERNATIONALE ASSOZIATION VON PHILOSOPHINNEN). The International Association of Women Philosophers (IAPh) was founded in 1974 and is located in Berlin, Germany. According to its mission statement, its goals are "to promote communication and co-operation among women engaged in philosophical activities; to stimulate philosophy in the light of feminist criticism; to improve working conditions for women philosophers; to raise public awareness of their discrimination in history and present times and to promote the study of their work." The association is open to all schools of philosophical thought.

IRIGARAY, LUCE (1932–). Little biographical information is available about Luce Irigaray, as she prefers to keep her life private. Of the major **French feminist** thinkers, only Luce Irigaray is considered a philosopher. Irigaray claims that **sex** difference may be the central philosophical issue of our time. She argues that the questioning and exploration of sex difference will bring the whole Western philosophical and psychoanalytic tradition into disarray. This is because to explore the question of the relations of sex difference is to explore the relations between subject and world, and subject and others, for the subject of all intellectual discourse previously has always been man. Irigaray's focus in her critical readings of philosophical texts is to disrupt this **masculine** discourse, to show how it excludes women and the **feminine**, and to introduce new possibilities of a feminine speaking and knowledge.

For Irigaray, women are represented in the **patriarchal** symbolic order as the negative "Other." Thus woman and femininity, because they are male defined, have no meaning outside male discourse; rather, woman is merely a reflection of man. Irigaray claims, however, that this reflection need not be rejected out of hand, as women can use it as a way of subverting their male definition. Irigaray's strategy is for women to reflect back their own reflections—only magnified—in order to mimic them, and thus show that woman and the feminine are nothing more than male constructions. Irigaray holds that the approach to resisting and subverting this order should not be to produce an alternative concept of woman or the feminine. To aim to create such a concept, she claims, would not be to escape male discourse, for its creation would replay the "sameness" of women that is part of male discourse.

By taking up this position outside male discourse, Irigaray offers a critique that aims to make visible the effects of this symbolism on texts and, because it is mistaken as real, on the lives of actual women. The central effect of this symbolism is to place women outside the philosophical tradition and thus to generate a male-defined and created knowledge that is not neutral or **objective**, but **gendered**. By taking up this position, she produces readings of texts that have multiple meanings and that are deliberately open to multiple interpretations. In this way both the content of her work and her writing itself function as a philosophical critique of male philosophical discourse: they are not structured, linear, and grounded in a reductionist set of concepts.

In the case of female **sexuality**, Irigaray points to the way that it does not have a cultural representation within male discourse, and thus does not have an existence within this discourse. Irigaray does not resist this non-existence by offering an alternative conception of female sexuality—of what this sexuality is in reality—as this would be to replay the maleness of the concept that sexuality is one—male—thing.

Irigaray aims, instead, to create a different structure of thought and speaking: a "feminine" form of expression (*écriture féminine*) that operates outside the male symbolic order. This is a **language** that is not the language of philosophers, but one which women will speak "between ourselves." This writing symbolically represents women's **bodies** and sexuality; its speaking position is one of critique, but like female sexuality, it is no one thing: it is multiple and fluid. Thus, as this new language—"written with the body"—comes from a specific position that is consciously not neutral or objective, it has no one meaning or truth. This disrupts the "male" discourse of the Western philosophical tradition, which is premised on the existence of an objective truth discoverable by **reason** alone. It also serves, simultaneously, to make visible the tradition's exclusion of woman and the feminine.

Irigaray's work functions as a critique of Western philosophy, and this critique itself is a philosophy, although not in the sense that it is a unified system or only one system. Instead, it is one of fluidity, even inconsistency. The creation of this language is not simply a resistance and subversion of the intellectual tradition; it is meaning-making. It leads to the exploration of new ways of knowledge: female knowledge comes from the (metaphorical) female **body**.

For Irigaray, the **dualism** of Western philosophical thought is grounded in symbolically male **logical** relations, such as disjunction and conjunction. Within this discourse these logical relations are **epistemologically** necessary, as they identify and individuate the objects of knowledge. In the traditional picture, rationality is one of these stable forms, identifiable through its oppositional relation to body and desire. This means, for Irigaray, that it will not be enough to claim that women are rational, as women are symbolically outside reason. The multiplicity and fluidity of female language forms a different set of relations, one of relationship and the expression of the fluidity in symbolically male and female relations, such as those between rationality and the body. The function of female language is not to identify, individuate, and separate in order to achieve knowledge, but to produce understanding and relationship. *See also* CANON CRITIQUE; CONTINENTAL PHILOSOPHY; SCIENCE, PHILOSOPHY OF; SUBJECTIVITY.

ISLAM. Currently there is feminist work from a variety of disciplines on reading Islamic texts for their views of women and women's social status, in particular for what such texts may state or imply about **equality** of the **sexes**. This work is both of historical interest, and of use to present-day discussions of social reform. In addition, there is work that demonstrates how interpretations of Islamic texts have been distorted by being read through the lens of **patriarchal** ideology. However, despite the role of medieval Islamic philosophers in transmitting **Aristotle** to the Latin West, and in developing the debate of the relation between **reason** and faith, feminist philosophers have shown little or no interest in Islamic philosophy itself. *See also* CHRISTIANITY; JUDAISM; RELIGION, PHILOSOPHY OF.

– J –

JUANA INÉS, SOR. *See* CRUZ, SOR JUANA INÉS DE LA.

JUDAISM. Jewish feminism, as a specific intellectual and political movement, originated in the 1960s and 1970s. Within Jewish **feminist theorizing**, there has been a two-pronged struggle against **sex** inequalities in Judaism, and against anti-Semitism both within and outside the feminist movement.

Women were traditionally excluded from full participation in the Jewish **religious** community as well as from access to a religious **education**. The role of women was seen as a supportive role for the faith of men. Since the inception of Jewish feminism, significant advancements have been made in raising the status of women within Judaism; for example, since the 1970s, women have been able to become rabbis within the Reform, Reconstructionist, and Conservative movements.

For Jewish feminists working within a theologico-philosophical context, the question of the exclusion of women from religious knowledge is not simply a question of access, but a question of the male bias within the structuring of this knowledge. There is little doubt that the sacred texts are sexist and exclusionary, and that their interpretation has traditionally been the province of men. The question has been how this male bias should be addressed. Some Jewish feminist thinkers have asked whether this exclusion is simply a product of culture and history, which would mean that it is open to challenge and change. Other thinkers have aimed to reinterpret traditional texts to include women and to revise the tradition through the recovery of texts written by women. A third approach has been to critique the way the male imagery and **language** used to describe God in the sacred texts serve to reinforce existing male-female power structures, and to ask whether this can be resolved through the introduction of **gender**-neutral or female imagery. *See also* CHRISTIANITY; ISLAM.

JUSTICE. The changes and developments over time in the feminist philosophical debate on justice reflect those of **feminist theorizing** in general. For **liberal feminism**, the dominant theory of the early stages of the **second wave** of feminism, justice (along with **equality** and liberty) is a central value. The liberal feminist view of justice is grounded in traditional liberal political theory, which understands justice as the fair and equitable distribution of resources among separate, equal individuals. For liberal feminists, injustice is the various ways that **sex** discrimination plays out in society. Thus justice requires equal opportunity and **rights** for women as the means to ending this discrimination. Accordingly, feminist philosophizing about justice in the 1970s and 1980s focused on analyzing the concept of equality and the legitimacy of means (such as **affirmative action**) to achieve this goal.

The current debate on justice, both domestic and international, reflects different strands of thought that began in the feminist philosophizing of the 1980s. One major strand is the critique of the philosophical tradition and thus of traditional theories of **political philosophy**. These theories are criticized for their foundation in a problematic picture of **human nature** as potentially conflicting **autonomous** and separate individuals operating within the public sphere. Thus women are dropped from the framework of justice, as this picture contrasts with the way that women's traditional roles of wife and **mother** confine them to the domestic (private) sphere and bind them to a network of relationships and attachments within this sphere.

The other major strand is the development of different analyses of women's subordination that go beyond the liberal feminist account. Underpinning these analyses is the claim that justice will not be achieved simply through legal and political measures aimed at ending discrimination. There is no agreement about what a just society will be, or the theoretical approach that will lead to this end; there is a basic agreement, however, that a just society requires the dismantling of **oppressive** social hierarchies.

Some feminist philosophers aim to revise traditional theorizing in order to develop a specifically feminist theory of justice. Part of this project includes the analysis of central aspects of justice, such as **universality** and **impartiality**, because these ideals have historically been inaccessible to women. Other feminist philosophers have drawn on the distinction between the female-oriented ethic of **care**, and the male-oriented ethic of justice, to question the value of justice for feminism. They claim that the "maleness" of justice means that it is inadequate to include and value women's thought and **experience**. For some philosophers, this then means that a feminist theory of justice is not possible. A slightly less radical version of this view questions whether justice—though an important value—is the only value for feminism, and thus whether it should be combined in some way with the perspective of care.

Other feminist thinkers wish to retain the goal of justice, even if they do not necessarily aim to produce an actual theory of justice. They aim, instead, to revise the traditional notion of justice as distributive. This position grows out of the recognition that, in the traditional paradigm of the just society, only legal and economic **gender** injustice can be changed; oppressive gender ideology will still remain. In this type of revisionist view, injustice can be understood as institutionalized oppression, and justice as empowerment. With this revision comes a different notion of who is recognized as a recipient of justice. Oppression is not just experienced by individuals, but by individuals because of their membership in a particular group. In this way, social justice will also be directed toward the achievement of the liberation goals of oppressed groups. *See also* INDIVIDUALISM, ABSTRACT; PUBLIC/PRIVATE DISTINCTION.

– K –

KANT, IMMANUEL (1724–1804). German philosopher Immanuel Kant was born on April 22, 1724, in what was then Königsberg, East Prussia. Kant started university in Königsberg in 1740 but did not complete his degree; during the following years he worked as a teacher of children. Kant's first publication was *Thoughts on the True Estimation of Living Forces* (1747). In 1754, he resumed his university studies, and this period also marked the commencement of his philosophical career.

Kant's contribution to the discipline of philosophy has afforded him recognition as one of its pivotal figures; however, he has been frequently criticized by feminist philosophers, both for the explicit sexism in his works and for the **masculinist** nature of his philosophy. While there is no doubt that Kant's views on women are inherently sexist, the fundamental question asked by feminist philosophical readers of Kant is what this entails for our understanding of his philosophical theories. Current feminist critique of Kant's philosophy does not explore the whole spectrum of his philosophy; rather, it has tended to focus on Kantian ethics and the Kantian conception of rationality. Of these two, the analysis of Kantian ethics has dominated discussion among feminist philosophers.

The crucial texts for feminist criticism of Kantian philosophy have been *Observations on the Feeling of the Beautiful and Sublime* (1764) and the works on ethics, in particular *The Groundwork of the Metaphysics of Morals* (1785). It is in the former, earlier work that Kant sets the stage for his views on ethics and rationality that have been the central target of critique. In this work, Kant espouses a **sex complementarian** view of the different moral natures of the **sexes**. He holds that men are more naturally inclined to reflection and **reason**, while women are more naturally inclined to the **emotional** and the "beautiful." It is this **aesthetic** sense, or their "beautiful understanding," that prompts women to recoil from ugly actions: actions that are morally wrong. Despite his emphasis on the emotional nature of women, Kant is not claiming that women are completely bereft of the capacity to reason; rather, he holds that the development of their rationality would not serve what he sees as their moral and social function. For Kant, it is the institution of **marriage** that defines women's function. He views marriage as a joining of the two complementary natures of the sexes: feeling (female) and rationality (male). Within this relationship, the two sexes then have complementary roles, with women's role being to help refine their husbands and inspire them to lead a moral life. Kant held that this moral influence of women in the home would, ultimately, aid the civilization of humanity itself.

While Kant's discussion of the nature and role of women seems irretrievably sexist, the philosophically troubling question is whether his account of the different natures of the sexes plays out in his moral philosophy itself. Feminist philosophers have argued that, on the most immediate level, the essential structure of Kant's philosophy, combined with his "philosophy of women," leads to an identification of the Kantian **moral agent** as male and to the explicit exclusion of women's capacity for moral agency. Feminist philosophers claim that this identification of morality as male holds, even if it is true (as some Kantian scholars argue) that interpreters have placed too much emphasis on rationality over the Kantian "good will" in understanding Kant's moral philosophy.

In Kant's account, women, as humans, have the capacity for reason that is necessary for morality, but women must be **educated** and encouraged to act based on their finer feelings. There are three main tensions between Kant's moral theory and his views of women. First, women to all intents and purposes, are not truly moral agents. Second, women are essentially being treated purely as a means to an end: the civilization of society (specifically men). Finally, women cannot develop or perfect their rational nature.

For Kant, morality is a matter of duty. Actions that are motivated by desires or inclinations such as self-interest or sympathy may conform to our duty, but they are not moral acts; instead, we must do our duty for the sake of doing our duty. It is through our reason that we can know which actions have moral worth, specifically through the application of the **universal** law of morality: the "categorical imperative." Kant's dictum requires that we should only act in such a way that we can also will that our maxim or principle of action should become a universal law. At stake in this universalizability of our actions is the recognition that our actions in a particular situation should be those that would be done by, or accepted by, any rational being. This concept of moral agency does not necessarily exclude women, for as human beings, they are rational beings. However, in Kant's account of women's specific nature, moral agency would not be particularly relevant or useful for women's nature or their function.

Inherent in the moral law is the notion of the rational individual as an **autonomous** "maker" of the law; this moral decision-making is independent of custom or subjective inclinations and desires. In tandem with this, the respect that we show for the rationality in others requires that we do not restrict the autonomy of others. Feminist philosophers argue that the ideals of independence and autonomy, required for a Kantian moral agent, exclude women, in the sense that women's role in marriage is, by definition, one of support and responsibility for another. For Kant, the human capacity for rationality does not just mean that we are the makers of the moral law that directs our actions; it also means that we should act in such a way that we treat humanity (in ourselves or in others) as an end in itself: we can never use rational beings purely as a means to our ends. Assuming that Kant truly does think that women are rational beings, their role in marriage contradicts Kant's claim of the universality of the categorical imperative of treating humans as ends in themselves. Moreover, Kantian duties are not just to others; as the makers of the moral law, and out of respect for our humanity, we also have duties to ourselves. We must develop any mental and physical capacities, which will include autonomy, that produce and enhance our rational decision-making. Indeed, moral maturity is premised on the development of our rational nature. Given the realities of women's social and moral role for Kant, it is unlikely that women would have the opportunity for this self-development.

Feminist philosophical analysis of Kantian ethics, however, stretches far beyond this kind of textual and historical criticism. It has been argued that the problem with Kant's moral philosophy is not simply the way it explicitly excludes women, but the fact that many of the Kantian moral ideals and characteristics are antithetical to the moral **experience** of women. This is a dominant strand of criticism within the subject field of **feminist ethics**, and one that has been heavily influenced by **Carol Gilligan**'s identification of a female-oriented ethic of **care**.

Gilligan's psychological studies reach the conclusion that there is an identifiable tendency in women to see emotions, personal relationships, and context as the relevant factors for moral decision-making. However, there is no room within Kantian moral philosophy to value, or even recognize, this "female" way of thinking. Kantian moral philosophy values characteristics traditionally identified as male (such as detachment and rationality), while devaluing those (such as sympathy and emotionality) traditionally identified as female. The autonomy necessary for the Kantian moral agent is achieved by freedom from the emotions, and thus relations with others. Moreover, in order to apply the categorical imperative, the agent must do so abstractly, thereby losing sight of the particular histories and contexts involved in the decision-making.

That is not to say that all Kantian moral ideals are potentially in tension with feminist ethical and **political** thought; for example, the individual and political need for women's autonomy has been a central issue both for feminist theorizing and for the feminist movement itself. Given the strength and complexity of the ideal of Kantian autonomy, some philosophers have considered the possibility of reconceiving this ideal for feminist use.

Feminist work on Kantian rationalism, like that on his moral philosophy, can also be divided into the critical and the reconstructive. Kantian rationalism is problematic in that the role of reason is both to judge from a vantage point outside the particular perspectives of those involved and to formalize those perspectives into a unified whole; this feat is quite simply not possible for human capabilities. Moreover, Kant posits an **individualistic**, unconnected self, failing to recognize that, in fact, the self is historical, embodied, and framed by social relations. An example of reconstructive feminist work on Kantian rationalism is Adrian Piper's claim that the rational Kantian self would welcome the cognitive challenges provided by experiences of human difference, and as such, could provide a resource for dismantling xenophobia.

Work on Kant is in the process of development. For example, there is a burgeoning interest in areas that are currently a subsidiary focus of the feminist study of his work, such as political philosophy and aesthetics. *See also* CANON, CRITIQUE OF; COIGNET, CLARISSE; IMPARTIALITY; SUBJECTIVITY.

KNOWLEDGE. *See* EPISTEMOLOGY; FOUCAULT, MICHEL.

– L –

LANGUAGE, PHILOSOPHY OF. During the 1970s, feminist philosophers turned their attention to the study of language. Compared with other fields of feminist philosophy, however, feminist philosophy of language remains a minor area of study.

In the traditional philosophical view, language is **value neutral**. As language is considered mainly expressive or descriptive, philosophers aim to study language abstracted from its social settings. In contrast, feminist philosophers have demonstrated the variety of ways in which language is not neutral but can reinforce the dominant **patriarchal** ideology. Moreover, they have emphasized the way that language is socially located, and thus cannot be studied in isolation or abstraction. Some feminist philosophers of language question whether the philosophical topics of study themselves, such as meaning and reference, are indeed as value neutral as traditional philosophy takes them to be. A final central difference between the two approaches is that traditional philosophy of language tends to see the field as one with reasonably clear-cut boundaries, whereas feminist philosophy of language tends to intersect with other areas of study, such as literary theory. The main strands of feminist work in the philosophy of language have come from both Anglo-American **analytic** philosophy and **French feminist** philosophy.

Within French feminist philosophy, the most influential work on meaning and expression has been that of **Luce Irigaray** and **Hélène Cixous**. Irigaray's woman's language *"parler-entre-elles"* (speak between ourselves), and Cixous's *"écriture féminine"* (**feminine writing**)—in which she "speaks the **body**"—are feminist strategies as well as philosophies of language. Both Irigaray and Cixous see the meaning of a word as produced by its relation with other, oppositional words: for example, the meaning of the word "female" means "not male." For Cixous these are hierarchical oppositions that reflect actual social power relations and that are kept in place by force, whether through intellectual or physical force. Cixous sees that these **masculine** forms of thought and discourse are not the only way to discover and express truths, and she offers an alternative mode of expression, one that can express the sensations and feelings of the woman writer. Irigaray also sees that there must be a language different from that of the philosophers and linguists that women will speak "between ourselves." This language is not grounded in a fixed set of semantic elements that our task is to analyze, but is rather fluid and associative, functioning to produce understanding and relationship.

Early Anglo-American feminist philosophical work in language in the 1970s showed the influence of the analytic philosophical approach: philosophical understanding is achieved through language analysis. Feminist philosophy of language of this period can be characterized by its focus on the analysis of sexist language: for example, an analysis of the use of "man" as a supposedly neutral term for "human." Some philosophers argued that, because these two words cannot be used interchangeably in all social settings, women are implicitly excluded from some social settings. Others drew the more radical conclusion that terms such as "man" and "he" cannot be used neutrally at all.

The discussions of the 1970s brought out the dual role language can play in the **oppression** of women. First, women are "marked" as women through the use of **sex**-specific words, pronouns, and naming. This highlights their differences from the "male norm" and, by implication, their apparent inferiority. Second, women are silenced. They are either excluded as speaking subjects, or their voices are not recognized as having authority or credibility.

This early work raised one of the central questions within feminist philosophy of language: is the goal of feminist philosophy simply to eradicate sexist language and adopt a "neutral" voice, or should women search for their own feminist "voice" to express their **experiences** and call for liberation? One provocative variant of the latter approach is that of **Mary Daly**, who aims to uncover the "lost" meanings of words in order to transvalue them. Daly produced *Websters' First New Intergalactic Wickedary of the English Language* (1987), written with Jane Caputi. For Daly, this reclaiming of words is a means to female empowerment. Thus "spinster" becomes a woman who "spins," disentangling the knots of patriarchal **false consciousness**, and weaving a connected feminist consciousness.

With the growing development of work on sex and **gender** in the 1980s, feminist philosophers of language have started to examine the ways that sex and gender are not pre-linguistic "givens"; rather they are created by our discursive practices. To say that "X is a woman" may appear to be a value-neutral description and nothing more. However, in order for this statement to function as a description for us as listeners, it requires that we have already accepted a background set of meanings and norms for sex and gender. The notion that there is some kind of unitary or fixed meaning of "woman" has been challenged by (among others) **Judith Butler**, who argues that there is nothing that is "woman": it is the creation of patriarchal discourse.

Some of the most recent work in Anglo-American feminist philosophy of language expands the issues and areas covered by the analysis of language. Catherine MacKinnon, for example, argues that **pornography** is more than just "words": it constructs what women are and what can be done to them, as well as silencing them. Within the study of philosophy itself, feminist philosophers have asked whether women should aim to speak in the neutral language of philosophy, or whether they should adopt different approaches to philosophical **methodology**, such as personal narratives. While it may appear that adopting the neutral philosophical voice will give women's voices authority, it can also be questioned whether this may come at too high a price: the denial of their particular gender identity. *See also* LOGIC; SUBJECTIVITY.

LATIN AMERICA, FEMINIST PHILOSOPHY IN. The history of Latin American thinkers writing about women and women's **rights** includes the French/Peruvian feminist and socialist Flora Tristan (1803–1844) and **Sor Juana Inés de la Cruz** (1648–1695) of Mexico. In terms of work that can be categorized as an explicitly feminist philosophy, the Uruguayan philosopher Carlos Vaz Ferreira wrote a pro-feminist treatise, *Sobre Feminismo* (*On Feminism*), in 1918; opinions differ as to how important this work was for the suffragist movement of the time.

The development of feminist philosophy as an academic discipline in Latin America is still in its early stages. The first formal gathering of feminist philosophers—the International Conference in Feminism and Philosophy in Latin America—was held in Mexico in 1988. Latin American feminist philosophers share similar interests with feminist philosophers from North America and Europe: for example, in offering analyses of the concept of **gender**, in exploring the connections between gender and rationality, and in critiquing the **canon**. Typically, Latin American feminist philosophers have a stronger interest in political practice than their American and European counterparts.

LE DOEUFF, MICHÈLE. *See* IMAGINARY, PHILOSOPHICAL; METHODOLOGY.

LEIBNIZ, GOTTFRIED WILHELM. *See* CONWAY, ANNE FINCH; DESCARTES, RENÉ; MASHAM, DAMARIS CUD-WORTH; NATURE.

LESBIAN ETHICS. Even though some earlier work could be categorized as lesbian ethics, it was not until the 1980s that lesbian ethics became an identifiable field of philosophical study. While lesbian ethics could not have developed without the analyses and critiques of traditional ethics provided by **feminist ethics**, it is an independent field of study. One central reason for this is that lesbian ethics finds much of its roots and support in the lesbian community rather than in academic discourse and institutions. Indeed, the way that this community is conceived, whether as a small community of intimates or as interconnected with the larger community of those fighting for **justice**, dictates how a particular thinker will conceive and practice lesbian ethics.

Lesbian ethics offers a double challenge to traditional moral philosophy. It goes beyond a critique based on **gender** to a radical particularist view based on the moral concerns and **experiences** of lesbians. The other central way that lesbian ethics challenges traditional moral thought is through a **Nietzschean** transvaluation of values.

Sarah Lucia Hoagland, the best-known exponent of a lesbian ethics, rejects the traditional framework of evaluating morality in reference either to "rightness" of character or action. Instead, she reframes ethical discussion within the context of what will bring about the development of someone's integrity and **agency**. While freedom of choice is given the moral weight, rather than what is actually chosen, Hoagland can avoid charges of moral arbitrariness. She holds that lesbian ethics is not a practice of isolated individuals; rather, moral choice is made within, and for, the lesbian community.

Not all work in lesbian ethics is confined to theory. There is also work done on "applied" or "practical" ethical issues, such as the legal issues surrounding lesbian parenting. Journals specifically devoted to lesbian ethics include *Gossip: Journal of Lesbian Feminist*

Ethics (1986–ca. 1988) and *Lesbian Ethics* (1984–), both published in the United States. *See also* LESBIAN PHILOSOPHY.

LESBIAN PHILOSOPHY. Lesbian philosophy became an identifiable philosophical field during the 1980s. On the whole, those philosophers who self-identify as lesbian philosophers, or as writers of lesbian philosophy, resist any explicit definitions of the concepts of "lesbian" or "lesbian philosophy." A central reason for this is that lesbian philosophy can be seen as part of lesbian culture, which is no one thing. The knowledge generated by lesbian culture may simply be about that culture—for example, the examination of the meaning of the concept of lesbian, or of contested behaviors such as sadomasochism. At other times, it may be knowledge that is relevant for feminist philosophizing more generally, such as the functioning of lesbian **sexuality** within the wider discussion of male—that is to say **oppressive**—constructions of female sexuality.

Some of the projects of lesbian philosophy parallel those of the wider feminist philosophical project in the questions they pose to traditional philosophical thought. Lesbianism itself presses on the framework of traditional **dualist** categories of men-women and male-female sexuality; and the construction of a history of lesbian thought offers a critique of male-biased histories of the philosophical tradition. Thus far the central and most fully formulated project of lesbian philosophy has been the development of a **lesbian ethics**, one that is fruitful for the lesbian community and also functions as a challenge to the dominant tradition of moral philosophy. Among the journals and newsletters published in the United States on lesbian philosophy is the *Society for Lesbian and Gay Philosophy Newsletter* (1988–).

LIBERAL FEMINISM. Liberal feminism was the earliest form of **feminist theory** and it has often, mistakenly, been identified with feminist theory itself. As with all contemporary feminist theories, a variety of positions can be called liberal feminism; however, they share a common foundation in the fundamental tenets and ideals of classical liberal theory: **autonomy**, **equality**, and self-fulfillment. Central to liberal theory is a normative **dualist** picture of **human nature** in which the mental, understood as the distinctive human capacity for rationality, is valued over the physical. This capacity is viewed as the means either to individual self-fulfillment, or to individual autonomy. Moreover, the equal capacity for rationality of all human beings entails their fundamental equality.

Given that, historically, women were not considered fully rational, or to share the same type of capacity as men, the strategy for eighteenth- and nineteenth-century feminist philosophers was to demonstrate women's equal capacity for rationality. Thus a central task for these philosophers was to explain away any apparent evidence to the contrary. The liberal feminist claim that the capacity for rationality of both **sexes** is equal need not commit its proponents to the claim that this capacity is the same; until women are no longer subject to external **socialization**, it remains unproved.

The dualist picture of human nature has political significance for feminists because it underpins the claim that physical differences, and thus the sex of an individual, are socially unimportant. Liberal feminists argue that physical differences should not affect **rights** or opportunity, and they identify sex discrimination—discrimination based on physical differences—as the barrier to female equality.

In order to achieve equality, liberal feminists hold that all humans need the maximum possible amount of liberty. Liberal feminists argue that, without this, there cannot be a just distribution of social goods based on merit; instead, there will be an unjust distribution that will privilege men: the already socially advantaged group. Typically, liberal feminists have aimed to secure equality through reforms in the public sphere, especially in the workplace. Feminist philosophical work in this area has focused on the examination of the pivotal ideals of **justice** and equality as well as on analyses of particular political strategies to attain these ideals, such as **affirmative action**.

While the liberal feminist movement is responsible for many important legal and social reforms in the West, it has been criticized as a movement just for white, middle-class, Western women that ignores the concerns and needs of minorities and non-Western women. In addition, the goal of liberal feminism is reform—not revision—of the system in order to achieve the inclusion of women and their opportunity for self-fulfillment within that system. Its critics claim that this means liberal feminist analysis can only focus on the more superficial causes of the **oppression** of women at the expense of an analysis of deeper and less visible causes, such as economic institutions. Without this deeper level of analysis, the different barriers to equality faced by women of color will remain hidden.

Feminist philosophical criticisms of liberal feminism have focused on the problematic concepts of the liberal tradition that are still present in the liberal feminist analysis, as well as on the way that these concepts affect its adequacy as a **political philosophy**. A central feminist philosophical criticism of the dualist liberal picture of human nature—our rational nature—is of its underlying male bias. Not only have women been traditionally associated with the **body**, and thus devalued, but the conceptual distinction between body and **mind** reflects the **experiences** of men who, for example, were not responsible for taking care of the physical needs of children. This separation of the mental from the physical is interconnected with the liberal view that our needs and desires are not the products of a social and material context. In this view, we are independent of others. Moreover, the needs and desires of others may conflict with our own. This notion of a solitary, **individualistic** self—a fundamentally egoistic self—has been criticized by feminist philosophers for being inconsistent with the experience and biology of women. Thus this concept of an individualistic self is not politically useful for the feminist enterprise. For some feminist philosophers, this is a crucial problem that liberal feminism must overcome in order to become an adequate political philosophy. *See also* POLITICAL SOLIPSISM; REASON; SUBJECTIVITY.

LOCKE, JOHN. *See* ASTELL, MARY; MASHAM, DAMARIS CUDWORTH.

LOGIC. Compared with other fields of feminist philosophy, there has been little feminist work on logic, but logic has been seen as a useful tool for feminist philosophy. Logic can be used to expose the errors of sexist arguments and to cut through these arguments to uncover the unspoken propositions that underlie them. However, some feminist philosophers hold that even logic must be held up to scrutiny for its sexist bias, similar to the way that **language** has been examined for bias in feminist philosophy of language. Given logic's central status within philosophy, this is a controversial project. In the standard account, logic is the tool that can show the structure of language and the structure of truths, free of the difficulties and ambiguities of natural language; it is an abstraction, absent of bias and value free.

Some feminist philosophers have criticized logic for the way it frames **reason** as **masculine**. **Luce Irigaray**, for example, sees the fundamental logical principles of the principle of non-contradiction and the principle of identity as symbolically male. Both principles assume the possibility that things are stable forms and thus can be distinguished one from another. For Irigaray, stable forms, individuation, and identity are symbolically phallic.

Other feminist philosophers have argued that different logics are used for different purposes: for example, for creating social consensus or for enforcing the consistency of ideas. Support for this latter view comes from the history of logic, most notably in the work of Andrea Nye, who traces the history of different logical theories from **Ancient Greece** to Gottlob Frege. She holds that there is no one logic, but different logics with different motivations and uses.

One of the examples Nye gives to illustrate her thesis is the political use made of the logic of medieval philosopher Peter Abelard, a use that was not inconsistent with the way Abelard viewed his logic: as the weapon of an intellectual battleground, with logical arguments forcefully and rightfully establishing one's authority. This was a period in which the Catholic Church wished both to consolidate its political power and to enforce and reinforce belief among its followers. One of the ways it did this was by rationalizing the conflicting elements of canon law through the use of Abelard's logical principles, producing a unified body of law applicable across nations. In this way, logic became pressed into the service of the church's suppression of dissent and heresy. The masculine nature of this enterprise (and also the other enterprises within the history of logic), and its accompanying exclusion or dismissal of women, is covert and complex. Women are excluded from Abelard's logic because it is the logic of the communications of the medieval male world. Training in Abelard's competitive logic functioned as a preparation for men ambitious to rise in the growing bureaucracy and expanding hierarchy of the church; this career was closed to women.

If Nye is correct, then it must be recognized that, despite the tradition that logic is an independent abstraction, it is a form of human communication. As such, logic is rooted in a socio-cultural context;

it is not timeless, nor is it free of the motivations and biases of its speakers. *See also* ANALYTIC FEMINIST PHILOSOPHY; VALUE NEUTRALITY.

LUGONES, MARIA. *See* MIND, PHILOSOPHY OF.

– M –

MACAULAY, CATHARINE (CATHARINE SAWBRIDGE MACAULAY-GRAHAM) (1731–1791). During her lifetime, the English writer and philosopher Catharine Macaulay was celebrated as a public intellectual and political radical. The extent of her public recognition can be seen in the fact that her ideas and work were an acknowledged influence on some of the leaders of the American Revolution. Although she wrote prolifically on history and politics, including an eight-volume republican history of the seventeenth century, she wrote only one work of feminist philosophy: *Letters on Education with Observations on Religious and Metaphysical Subjects* (1790). In this work, Macaulay argues that the human **mind** is sexless, and thus that women should receive the same **education** as men. She further argues that the social **equality** of women is not just essential for their personal development but is a necessary component for a morally excellent society.

MAKIN, BATHSUA PELL (fl. 1673). The erudition of English philosopher Bathsua Pell Makin is clear from the fact that she was a tutor to Princess Elizabeth at the court of Charles I, a position that usually would have been reserved for a male tutor. It is the argumentative strategy for the **education** of women employed by Makin in her 1673 work *An Essay to Revive the Antient Education of Gentlewomen, In Religion, Manners, Arts & Tongues* that makes her philosophy of historical interest. Makin does not simply argue for women's education; she also critically examines her own proposal for women's education and provides replies to potential objections. While the central thrust of Makin's *Essay* is an argument for the better education of women and the benefits this will bring them, it is important to note that Makin's argument is framed within the general social utility of women's education. She states that educated women will be in a better position to help their husbands and educate their children, while a general improvement in the education of women will benefit the country as a whole. *See also* SCHURMAN, ANNA MARIA VAN.

MALESTREAM. The term malestream, which combines "male" and "mainstream," has been widely adopted by some feminist philosophers to describe traditional or mainstream philosophy. The first use of the term is attributed to Mary O' Brien in her 1981 work *The Politics of Reproduction.*

MAN. *See* ESSENTIALISM; GENDER; SEX.

MARRIAGE. Historically, marriage has been a central issue in discussions of women's **equality**, and it remains an important component of contemporary feminist calls for liberation. Feminist philosophers have critiqued the institution of marriage because it reinforces the domination of women by men, either through the domination of one individual by another, or through the way that a **patriarchal** society has set the social and economic conditions of marriage in ways that benefit men.

Analysis of the marriage contract, and its differences from other contracts, is a central focus for feminist philosophers. They argue that, unlike other contracts, there is no formal setting out of the terms of the arrangement, nor can the terms be changed according to the wishes of the contractors; rather, the terms are defined by the state. Another type of critique of marriage as a contractual relation— influenced by **object relations theory**—points to the concept of the contract itself, made between two equal consenting individuals, as one that comes out of a historically **masculine** way of thinking about human relations: it reflects men's social experiences and privileges.

Feminist philosophical work on marriage has produced a variety of analyses of the **oppression** of marriage for women; these analyses typically depend on the particular kind of feminist theory held by the author. **Liberal feminists** tend to focus on strategies that will give women the opportunity to have marriage and **motherhood** as well as a career. **Marxist feminists** usually hold that marriage has similarities to **prostitution**: women sell their person for economic survival. **Radical feminists** typically focus on the actual relation between the **sexes** within the institution of marriage; for example, they point to the way that women are pushed into marriage through the patriarchal ideology of marriage as the fulfillment of the needs of women.

Discussions of marriage are of interest to feminist philosophers, not just because of the centrality of these discussions in feminist arguments for women's liberation, but also because of their presence in philosophical work in the **canon**. For many canonical philosophers, most notably **Immanuel Kant** and **Jean-Jacques Rousseau**, the traditional institution of marriage—with women in the subordinate role—was a component of the development of men as moral agents and political citizens. *See also* FAMILY; GOLDMAN, EMMA; POLITICAL AND SOCIAL PHILOSOPHY.

MARXIST FEMINISM. The identification of the Marxist feminist position is complicated by the existence of competing interpretations of classical Marxist theory and by changes in Marxist thought over the decades. Moreover, for many **feminist theorists**, including self-defined Marxist and **socialist feminists**, there is no precise boundary between Marxist and socialist feminism. The main distinction between the two is that Marxist feminists see class under capitalism as the primary lens for analysis of the situation of women, while socialist feminists analyze the situation of women under the interconnected systems of both capitalism and **patriarchy**. For Marxist feminists, the subordination of women to men is not a primary system of **oppression**; it is the historical product of a particular form of capitalism. Thus Marxist feminists do not see any fundamental opposition in the relations between men and women; rather, they hold that the dismantling of capitalism will bring about the end of patriarchy. On the whole, Marxist feminism has had the most support in the United Kingdom and Italy.

The intellectual foundations of the Marxist feminist analysis of women's subordination lie in Friedrich Engels's 1884 work *The Origin of the Family, Private Property, and the State*, in which he outlines what is often seen as the classic Marxist position on what he called "the woman question." Engels argues that the historical source of the subordination of women is the sexual **division of labor**, which he sees as a constant in every society. The division between women's work of the domestic sphere and men's work of production does not, however, automatically lead to the subordination of women; rather, this will depend on the particular mode of production within a given society. According to Engels, the advent of the development of agriculture—and thus the development of the male sphere of production—led to a change in the value placed on women's traditional domestic labor and the rise of men's economic power over women. This change in the situation of women coincided with the origins of class society, as this expansion in production led to the economically beneficial use of slaves. Engels identifies an accompanying change in the relations between men and women. Rather than staying as a natural pairing between **equals**, **marriage** became an economic institution with the sole purposes of ensuring a man's control over property and procuring his future heirs. Thus marriage is the primary institution of women's subordination, as it makes women economically dependent on men.

While Engels's picture of the origins of women's situation has a great deal of explanatory power, it has been the subject of critique by contemporary feminist theorists. A central criticism is that it is not evident, beyond Engels's possibly inaccurate account of its historical origins, why women are the lower-paid workers as well as the service workers for the labor force. Moreover, contemporary feminist philosophers have questioned why the sexual division of labor remains. Most Western women are in the workforce but still tend to have the primary responsibility for labor in the home. One of the tasks for contemporary Marxist feminists, therefore, has been to offer an analysis of this continuation of the sexual division of labor, an analysis of how this division of labor ultimately benefits capital.

For Marxist feminists, the full liberation of women will occur only with the dismantling of capitalism, but temporary solutions have been offered for the particular harms caused by the form of the labor division under modern capitalism. Solutions typical of the 1960s and 1970s are the socialization of housework and wages for housework. More recently, Marxist feminists have turned their attention to the way that the labor division plays out in the workplace; for example, women earn less than men and tend to be directed toward work that is "women's work": caring and service work. One popular solution for this is a call for the introduction of a system of comparable worth among jobs.

For non-Marxist feminist theorists, Marxist feminism fails because it offers a **gender**-neutral analysis of women's oppression: it sees capitalism as the ultimate source of the oppression of women. Thus, for example, it cannot explain why particular forms of oppression, such as domestic violence, are typically only the **experience** of women; nor, ultimately, can it allow for the recognition that women's oppression serves in a variety of ways, not just economically, to benefit men.

In response to these criticisms, some Marxist feminists have aimed to produce what Heidi Hartmann has termed a "marriage" between feminism and Marxism: an analysis that does not give priority to either form of oppression but examines the ways in which these separate systems of oppression reinforce each other. Other theorists have argued that the two systems are not analytically independent in this way. These theorists claim that patriarchal ideology is not the exclusive site for the production of women's oppression, and thus that women's oppression cannot be analyzed independently of the economic relations of capitalism. The development of these sorts of revisionist approaches to Marxist feminist theorizing has meant that it is not always possible to make any clear distinction between Marxist feminism and socialist feminism. *See also* DUAL SYSTEMS THEORY.

MASCULINITY. Masculinity is understood as the ideal of the appropriate **gender** behaviors, traits, and roles for men. Thus men are expected, for example, to act in an assertive manner, to be rational, and to be the primary wage earner. Philosophical work on masculinity is usually done by men and typically focuses on the ways that men, like women, are trapped by gender expectations. However, for feminist philosophers, similarities between the restrictions caused by the constructs of **femininity** and masculinity stop here. Within **patriarchal** society, masculinity is seen as the norm and is constructed against a negative, inferior "Other": femininity. Thus both masculinity and femininity serve to **oppress** women, whereas men are only subject to the ideology of masculinity. *See also* BEAUVOIR, SIMONE DE.

MASHAM, DAMARIS CUDWORTH (1659–1708). Damaris Cudworth was the daughter of a well-known Cambridge Platonist; she married Sir Francis Masham in 1685. While her philosophy shows her father's influence, she was also a follower of the seventeenth-century English philosopher John Locke. Her two philosophical works are *A Discourse Concerning the Love of God* (1696) and *Occasional Thoughts in Reference to a Virtuous or Christian Life* (1705). Her correspondence on philosophical issues with both John Locke and German philosopher Gottfried Leibniz has also been preserved.

Within Masham's philosophical works, several early feminist arguments can be found on the status of women. Like many other feminist philosophers of this period, Masham decries the lack of formal **education** for women. In Masham's case, this critique is filtered through her **Christian** beliefs. She holds that women have the same rationality as men, but she argues that without a development of their **reason**, women will lack the knowledge necessary both for proper faith and to answer criticisms of Christianity. Masham explicitly blames men for women's underdevelopment of their reason, claiming that this is due to the fact that men view women as little more than the bearers of a dowry. Masham also offers an early critique of the double standard for the **sexual** behavior of men and women; she argues that making chastity the sole measure of women's virtue restricts their moral life, as she holds that chastity is just one of the many virtues of a Christian life.

MATERNAL (MATERNALIST) ETHICS (MATERNAL THINKING). Maternal ethics can be either a **feminine ethics**, a **feminist ethics**, or have aspects of both types of ethics. Essentially it employs a **mother** and child relationship in some way as a basis for the development of a new ethical approach. For many theorists, "mother" means a "mothering person," someone who can be either male or female.

Virginia Held argues that traditional moral theories were developed for the public realm: to provide guidelines for contractual relations between **equal** strangers. This, however, is only part of the picture of the relations and activities of our moral world. Held argues that there is also the need for moral theory that begins from the private world, with the mothering person-child relationship as a paradigm for ethical relations.

Another major proponent of maternal ethics, Sara Ruddick, argues for a notion of maternal practice grounded in the mothering **experience** of women (although she holds that both **sexes** can mother). Maternal thinking is not simply **emotional** response; rather, the goals of maternal practice are the preservation, growth, and social acceptability of children. The specific traits needed to achieve these goals are then the virtues of that practice. Ruddick's notion of maternal practice reframes the notion of good in terms of knowledge and perception, while traditional moral philosophy narrowly frames good in terms of choice and action. Ruddick draws connections between maternal thinking and opposition to militarism. This is not to say that all women oppose **war**, or that women are "naturally" pacifists, but that the maternal task is fundamentally in conflict with the activity of war.

While maternal ethics is, strictly speaking, a development of contemporary feminist philosophy, it is possible to find elements of this type of ethical thinking in much earlier thought: for example, in the work of **Christine de Pizan**. Pizan's maternalist ethic surfaces within her **political philosophy**, specifically in her account of the relationship of subjects to their sovereign. For Pizan, the mother-child ethical relation provides the paradigm for the political obligations of subjects and rulers. Like the child, the political subject has a duty to obey; like the mother, the sovereign is responsible for the moral and material well-being of the subject. Moreover, just as the child learns from the mother, subjects learn by example from the sovereign. Thus, in order for their subjects to develop a good character, sovereigns must themselves be of good character. *See also* BLACK FEMINIST ETHICS; CULTURAL FEMINISM; CARE, ETHICS OF.

MEN. *See* ESSENTIALISM; GENDER; SEX.

METAPHYSICS. There has been little discussion of metaphysics by feminist philosophers. Those who have done work on metaphysics have tended to remain critical of the subject; indeed, some feminist philosophers have claimed that metaphysics, due to the untenability of its very subject matter, should be rejected completely. As the philosophical study of reality, metaphysics is both an analysis of the nature of reality and a search for what is real; it raises ontological questions of the nature of being or existence. The foundational requirement of this metaphysical project is the assumption that both reality and being are fixed. In contrast, feminist philosophy is fundamentally a **political philosophy** for social change. Its fundamental requirement is the call for the change of the **oppressive** reality of women's existence and the rejection of spurious theories about the nature of women's being.

Feminist critique of metaphysics began in the 1980s and is primarily a historical critique. Both the questions of the traditional metaphysical project and the theories used to explain the nature of reality and being are seen to be irretrievably male biased, as they are based on **experiences** and ways of thinking that have been associated with men. A central problem is the requirement of traditional metaphysics for us to take a **value-neutral, objective** position from which to understand reality, a position outside the particular perspective of our situated self. This ideal of intellectual detachment does not reflect the material and social reality of women, who have historically been tied to the concrete demands of the domestic sphere.

The ideal is also grounded in the rejection of the **feminine**. The transcendence of the situated self and the material world is simultaneously transcendence of those things that have been metaphorically associated with the feminine. This **dualist** nature of reality, a reality constructed through separation and exclusion, has been a particular target for feminist philosophy for the way it provides conceptual legitimacy for the marginalization, and subsequent subordination, of particular groups.

The ontological question of the nature of human being has also been the subject of criticism for its male bias. This search is not **gender** neutral; it is a search for the nature of male being. One type of approach to this problem, offered by feminist philosophers, has been a reformist approach that aims to revise the concept of human being to include what can be identified as women's ways of being and perception. A more radical approach is to argue that even what it is to be male and female are constructs of a male reality. This makes the question of human being, and thus metaphysics more generally, an empty inquiry.

For some feminist philosophers this history of male bias need not entail the complete rejection of metaphysical study; rather, the perspectives and experiences of women can be used to press upon and revise traditional notions of reality and being. However, beyond a potential revision of dualist thinking, it has not been clear how gender plays out in having a perspective on reality. For example, is there only one perspective or multiple perspectives for each gender? Even if this notion of a gendered perspective were clear, there remains the need to establish whether this has an effect on our concepts of reality.

It has also been argued that the task of a feminist metaphysics is not to identify a gendered perspective but to examine the ways in which our views about reality inform or maintain oppression: there is a sense in which reality is political. Thus a specifically feminist metaphysics is a possibility, as an examination of the nature of reality and being is part of the feminist political project. *See also* SUBJECTIVITY.

METHODOLOGY. Feminist critics have analyzed the ways in which philosophical methodology reflects, or may even reinforce, the dominant ideology. Janice Moulton, for example, has argued that aggression, a trait that has a different social meaning and value for men and women, has been incorporated into the standard paradigm of philosophical technique: the adversary method. In essence this method frames different philosophical viewpoints and arguments as being in opposition or competition. The aim is to defeat opponents' arguments through, among other things, challenging their foundational assumptions, exposing their inconsistencies, searching for argumentative fallacies, and showing how their premises lead to unintended conclusions that are untenable.

This linking of aggression with philosophical ability serves to exclude women from philosophy, as it requires behavior that is not culturally constructed as **feminine**. Moreover, an approach that focuses solely on defeat of an opponent also serves to limit philosophy itself; for example, knowledge cannot be produced through dialogue, while subject matter that does not lend itself easily to an adversarial approach is ignored. Furthermore, the **history of philosophy** becomes both distorted and a limited resource, as it is read merely as a series of triumphs or failures among competing views. Some feminist philosophers have considered the possibility of developing new methods, such as narrative techniques; new ways of approaching the history of philosophy are also being developed, such as Michèle Le Doeuff's philosophical **imaginary**.

Some feminist philosophers have asked whether feminist philosophy, given its connections to the feminist movement, requires philosophical methods of its own that have a political or ethical dimension. They point to the tension between standard philosophical methods, which have as their goals **universal** and **objective** truths, and the fact that the feminist movement relies on **consciousness raising**—a collective examination of personal **experience**—as a method of gaining knowledge for political action. *See also* ANALYTIC FEMINIST PHILOSOPHY.

MILL, HARRIET TAYLOR. *See* TAYLOR MILL, HARRIET.

MILL, JOHN STUART (1806–1873). English philosopher John Stuart Mill was the son of philosopher and social reformer James Mill (1773–1836). John Stuart Mill's childhood education and achievements are famous; he was taught Greek when he was three and logic when he was twelve. In 1823, he started work for the East India Company and after his retirement was a member of Parliament for Westminster (1865–1868). During his period in politics, he worked actively to gain the vote for women. In 1851, he married **Harriet Taylor**, with whom he had had an intellectual and emotional relationship since they first met in 1830. Mill's major published works are *On Liberty* (1859), *Utilitarianism* (1861), and *The Subjection of Women* (1869). His *Autobiography* was published posthumously in 1873.

The Subjection of Women is viewed as a significant work of early feminist philosophy, in particular because it provided a theoretical grounding for the feminist activism of that period, and many of the issues raised by Mill continue to be part of feminist debate. Furthermore, *The Subjection* is unique in that it is the only major feminist work written by a male philosopher from the Western **canon**. Despite Mill's arguments in this work about the relation of overall happiness to the liberation of women, feminist philosophers have not considered Mill's feminism to be explicitly grounded in his Utilitarian thought.

The early roots of Mill's feminist philosophical thought can be found in his essay on divorce written for Harriet Taylor in 1831 or 1832. Although Mill focuses on the question of divorce in this early essay, he also says that the question of **marriage** cannot be considered without understanding how it affects women. Mill argues that what marriage ought to be, and which laws should cover marriage (and thus divorce), could only be clarified when it has been established whether it is a relationship between two **equals** or not. Mill makes his views plain on this matter: there is no **natural** inequality between the **sexes**. Mill develops his analysis of the connection between equality and marriage in *The Subjection of Women* and it is a core theme throughout the work.

In the first chapter of *The Subjection*, Mill argues that the legal inequality of women has no basis in the overall happiness of society; rather it is a vestige of historical relations between the sexes that were based solely on men's physical power over women. Mill then replies to potential objections to the equality of women. He focuses, in particular, on the claim that it is a fact of nature that women are not equal to men. He holds instead that we cannot know the true nature of the sexes; what appears to be the nature of women is the result of repressive **socialization**. This issue of the nature of women, and the role of **gender** socialization, is one that has been central for modern feminist philosophy, especially in the 1970s and 1980s.

In chapter two of *The Subjection*, Mill discusses the repressive state of marriage for women generated by the laws of England. However, he does not wish to dissolve the institution and he posits his own ideal of marriage: a voluntary companionate relationship between two equals. Even though Mill argues for the legal equality of women—for example, in property ownership—he does not promote the desirability of employment for married women. Instead he sees the customary sexual **division of labor**, with married women in a domestic role, as the best for both women and society.

In chapter three, Mill tackles objections to women being given the vote or holding political office that are based on sex stereotyping. Mill repeats his claim from the first chapter that, because women have been artificially socialized, it is impossible to know their true nature. The remainder of this chapter has troubled modern feminist philosophers, as Mill appears to accept certain sex stereotypes in his discussion of whether women should take part in public life; he makes generalizations about women's tendencies toward the practical and their capacity for intuitive thinking.

In the final chapter, Mill argues that the civic and legal equality of women will bring benefits to society in general, not just to women: first, because individuals of both sexes can only develop morally if they are raised in a society grounded in **justice** and equality; second, because more people will then be available to contribute to society. Here Mill is thinking of the potential moral contributions of women to society through their role as the **educator** of the character of their children.

There is some ambivalence on the part of feminist scholars toward the actual philosophical content of *The Subjection*. Mill's discussion of equality and respect in marriage has sometimes been seen as a potential model for intimate relationships. However, Mill is often criticized for not challenging the traditional sexual division of labor. Mill specifically states in chapter two of *The Subjection* that, when women marry, they choose a domestic life in the same way a man chooses a profession. Feminist philosophers argue that, without the possibility of economic equality (the ability to earn an income), women cannot achieve true equality. If women have the primary responsibility for the **family**, moreover, then they have little opportunity for individual growth and fulfillment.

In light of these difficulties, some feminist philosophers have aimed to uncover the causes, philosophical or psychological, of Mill's apparent inability to move beyond the status quo. Mill's empiricism, for example, may have meant that he did not advocate radical change in the situation of women, as he could only base his arguments on the empirical facts of the lives of Victorian women. *See also* FIRST WAVE FEMINISM; HUMAN NATURE; LIBERAL FEMINISM.

MIND, PHILOSOPHY OF. Feminist philosophical examination of the traditional questions in the philosophy of mind started in the 1980s. As with much of feminist work in the traditional areas of **ana-**

lytic philosophy, this examination has taken the form of both critique of this area and attempts at its revision for the feminist philosophical project.

In the case of critique, feminist philosophers have challenged both the conceptual framework of the philosophy of mind as well as some of the specific issues within the philosophy of mind. The central problem for feminist philosophers is that the subject area of the philosophy of mind is grounded in the usually normative **dualism** of mind/**body**. The superior disjunct of mind has historically been associated with men; the inferior disjunct has been associated with women, because of their cultural and biological ties to their bodies. Even if mind and body are not explicitly associated with the two **sexes** in traditional philosophical texts, the two entities are metaphorically **gendered**: for example, the mind needs to control an unruly body.

Because of this central problem, feminist critique of the philosophy of mind usually focuses on questioning the coherence of the conceptual separation of mind/body and on challenging the normativity of this split by revaluing elements, such as **emotion**, that are associated with the **feminine**. This type of critique has meant that even the contemporary work in mainstream philosophy to dismantle or solve what is known as the mind/body problem, or to analyze specific "mental" states, can be seen as suspect; this is because this mainstream work assumes some version of the conceptual divide between mind and body as a basis for its investigations. For these reasons, feminist philosophers have even criticized the name of the field itself, preferring the alternative name for the field: philosophy of psychology.

Of the specific questions within the traditional field of the philosophy of mind, the most important for feminist philosophers has been the problem of personal identity. If, for example, the personality and memories of a person were to be transferred to the body of another, the puzzle is then whether they are the same individual. In the standard account, the defining feature of the self and its survival is its continuous psychological identity over time. Thus, in this particular case, it is plausible to claim that they are the same person. This notion of the self is then, by definition, a purely psychological entity that is independent of both the body and social relations—a notion that ultimately makes these elements of human life irrelevant to the identity of the individual.

Feminist philosophers have argued that this notion of the self is not coherent; rather, the self must be understood as embodied and embedded. Any proposed notion of the self cannot be understood separately from its original formation within a network of social relations, such as parent-child relations. Moreover, these social relations construct gender identity, yet the standard account of the self requires a gender-neutral individual.

Feminist philosophical revision of the field of the philosophy of mind has also focused mainly on the question of personal identity; this revision is explicitly political in nature and has served to expand the range of issues in the field. Feminist philosophers have examined psychological states for their political interest: for example, whether **anger** can be a political emotion that produces knowledge and a desire for social change. Others have considered the question of what is the "I" of personal identity, and how—if women are not born but made—does the "I" come into existence.

Maria Lugones has pressed on the notion of the "I" as a fixed or distinguishable identity through her examination of the way that a person of a particular **race** has different identities, each constructed by the particular "worlds" the person inhabits. We can gain knowledge of others, and of the way that we are seen by them, through "traveling" to the worlds of others. This account is politically significant; it suggests a way of coming to understand difference, one that does not simply reflect the standpoint of the dominant group's perception of the difference of marginalized groups. *See also* INDIVIDUALISM, ABSTRACT; PSYCHOANALYTIC FEMINISM; SUBJECTIVITY.

MODERN RATIONALISM. *See* AUSTRALIA, FEMINIST PHILOSOPHY IN; DESCARTES, RENÉ.

MORAL AGENCY. For philosophers, the standard concept of the moral agent is a self who is the maker of choices about the right acts to perform. Within the Western philosophical tradition, the (ideal) moral agent is conceived of as an **individualistic** being, one who is capable of making rational moral judgments and acting on them. This individual is presumed to be free, and therefore responsible for those actions and choices. This view of the moral agent as **autonomous** and free of particular historical and social circumstances was given its most explicit formulation in the moral philosophy of **Immanuel Kant**. Given that women's agency is an essential component of their liberation, an analysis of moral agency has been an important part of feminist philosophy. Furthermore, female moral agency has traditionally been associated with the "good woman": a more limited picture of autonomy and range of choices for action.

Feminist philosophers have found two main problems with the traditional concept of moral agency. First, the standard framing of the concept assumes a problematic picture of the moral agent as an atomistic or abstract individual, one who judges from an **impartial** standpoint. It is this sort of picture that feminist philosophers see as evidence of the male bias in **canonical** philosophy. Second, questions need to be asked about the freedom of female moral agents. Feminist philosophers claim that the norms of **feminine** moral behavior serve to subordinate women by restricting their freedom for moral action and choice, whether through external pressures, or through internalization of these norms.

Some feminist philosophers have offered alternative theories of moral agency; these theories can be roughly categorized as **care**-based theories and oppositional theories. While there is no unitary theory of care-based moral agency, all care-based theories frame the self as relational. Moral choice is then reconceived within a framework that recognizes the existence of relationships and interdependencies and emphasizes the skills and capacities needed to act and judge within this framework. There is disagreement among feminist philosophers over whether this type of theory, as with all theories of the ethics of care, is subject to the criticism that it reinforces stereotypical notions of feminine self-sacrifice. Oppositional accounts of moral agency have their foundations in either **postmodernist** or **Marxist** thought. The thrust of both these types of accounts, in essence, is to critique the ways in which women are constructed by social forces; this means that the standard notion of agency, because it is based on a concept of an identifiable self, is dissolved. The possible problem with these accounts is that, with their emphasis on the ways that the self is socially constructed, the political potential for female moral agency may become lost. *See also* SUBJECTIVITY.

MORAL EPISTEMOLOGY. *See* EPISTEMOLOGY, MORAL.

MORAL PHILOSOPHY. *See* ANIMAL ETHICS; BIOETHICS; BLACK FEMINIST ETHICS; CARE, ETHICS OF; ECOFEMIN-ISM; EPISTEMOLOGY, MORAL; FEMININE ETHICS; FEMI-NIST ETHICS; LESBIAN ETHICS; MATERNAL ETHICS.

MOTHERHOOD. While the capacity to bear children is a fact of women's lives, the conceptualization and significance of motherhood has not been cross-culturally, or historically **universal**. Furthermore, there has not been any one reason that women have been culturally identified as the primary caretaker of children. Standard non-feminist justifications for this role have ranged from the belief that women are more childlike to the claim that they are innately nurturing. This latter conceptualization of mother-as-nurturer often played a central role in early **cultural feminist** speculations on the moral and social benefits of a "mother-ruled" society or on the ways that women's nurturing instincts were an essential component of moral and social progress. Despite the problematic **essentializing** of "woman's nature" that may underpin this type of thinking, the image of woman as nurturer is not necessarily bad in itself; rather, it is the meanings and uses of this image under **patriarchy** that have been a central target of feminist criticism.

The dominant image in the West of motherhood developed with the rise of the notion of a child-oriented, sentimental **family** in the eighteenth century. Motherhood was "institutionalized" in the sense that it became accepted that women are only fulfilled by motherhood and that there is a set of behaviors and characteristics that define the good mother. The earliest feminists of the **first wave** did not critique this institutional motherhood; indeed, the freedom of women to mother properly was often bound up with early calls for women's liberation.

From the 1970s onwards, feminists began to make a distinction between this problematic institutional motherhood and a potentially liberating motherhood understood in terms of a connection to children and the **body**. They also began to ask whether biological motherhood itself was a source of **oppression**, and whether true liberation for women can cóme only when they are free of the burden of their **reproductive** biology. There is no culturally universal form of this burden. While women in the West may see it as a limitation of their freedom for self-fulfillment and social advancement, the economic needs of women in the Third World may mean that they need to produce children as future economic support.

The current focus of feminist philosophers is to examine both the definition of motherhood and the value of motherhood. In the wake of new advances in technology, such as surrogacy, feminist philosophers have asked whether motherhood is a genetic, gestational, or caring relation to a child. In so doing, these philosophers are questioning the standard Western notion, often supported in courts of the law, that the biological relation is central. This standard notion is part of the institutional view of motherhood; its corollaries are the claims that the biological mother makes the best carer and that children need their biological mothers.

There is no agreement among feminist philosophers from any of the philosophical traditions on the issue of the value of motherhood. For some the strength of women may come literally from their ability to bear children, while others have asked whether a mother-daughter relationship—freed from patriarchy—can provide a new model of the **feminine**. Motherhood has sometimes been understood by **black feminist philosophers** as an empowering concept for black women. They argue that, through looking back at their own mothers, they can draw on a female-identified cultural tradition that evolved as a resource against **racism** and is also rooted in **African** tradition. Other feminist philosophers have turned to the **experiences** of women as mothers. Some have constructed a **maternal ethics** from these experiences that can provide an alternative to the dominant philosophical tradition of moral philosophy. Others have examined the way that the differences in experiences between mothers of color and white mothers can produce different understandings of the oppressive and empowering aspects of the institution of motherhood. *See also* POLITICAL AND SOCIAL PHILOSOPHY.

MULTICULTURAL FEMINISM. Multicultural **feminist theory** started in the 1980s as a critique of the theorizing of **first** and **second**

wave feminism. **Black feminists** in the United States are usually seen as being at the forefront of the multicultural feminist movement. Multicultural feminism shares with **global feminism** the notion that all women are not fundamentally the same and the recognition that there is a need for resistance to dominant groups of women speaking for marginalized groups. However, unlike global feminism, it focuses on examining differences within a particular nation.

Multicultural feminists argue that feminist theorizing of the first and second waves was not inclusive of all women; they hold that it only addressed the political needs and interests of white, middle-class European and American women. A central strategy of feminism, at this stage of its development, was to emphasize the sameness of the **sexes** in order to argue for **equality** of the sexes. Multicultural feminists criticize this orthodox account of feminism for its neglect of the differences in women's **experiences** of **oppression**, arguing that these differences are caused by women's subjection to other systems of oppression, such as **race** and class. Multicultural feminists claim that the fact that these systems interlock, and are mutually supportive, means that any attempt to analyze and remove women's oppression will fail unless there is a simultaneous analysis and removal of these other forms of oppression. Multicultural feminists claim, furthermore, that a neglect of difference constitutes its own form of oppression; women who are not part of the dominant group become invisible and their particular needs and interests become marginalized within both feminist theory and the movement itself.

This type of critique had a galvanizing effect on feminist thought, and most current feminists are committed to a recognition of the differences among women in their theorizing. For this reason, the use of the term multicultural feminism to identify a distinct type of feminist theory is falling out of use. Despite widespread agreement on the need for inclusivity, however, there is no one set view of how this is to be achieved. One central approach is to aim for a personal solidarity among women that comes from a friendship-based perception and understanding of the world of others; the other central approach is to aim for a political solidarity among different groups that is based on shared goals, although it may never be one of a shared understanding.

MURRAY, JUDITH SARGENT (1751–1820). American philosopher and writer Judith Sargent Murray was born into a wealthy Massachusetts family. Her parents allowed her to be educated alongside her brother. An able scholar, Murray recognized that she was deprived of the benefits of this education because of her **sex**: her brother went to Harvard; she married.

Murray is a notable early example of a thinker who went beyond merely raising feminist concerns; she offered a sustained and systematic feminist philosophy. The two works outlining her philosophy of feminism are *On the Equality of the Sexes*, written in 1779 and published in 1790, and *Desultory Thoughts upon the Utility of Encouraging Self-Complacency in the Female Bosom*, published in 1784. In *On the Equality of Sexes*, Murray outlines the **metaphysical** foundations of her philosophy. She holds that the spirit that animates the human **body** is sexless, which then means that the intellect is also sexless, and thus that the intellects of the two sexes must be **equal**. Based on these first principles, Murray develops in *Desultory Thoughts* an account of the main aim of female **education**: to teach young women to respect their own intellects. The practical usefulness of this development of intellectual self-esteem is clear, as she intends it to protect young women from making mistakes in their choice of husbands. In the four essays the make up *Observations on Female Abilities*, Murray aimed to prove, in the manner of a lawsuit, that women are as intellectually capable as men. Among the examples Murray lists as proof of her contention are the early feminist philosophers **Mary Astell** and **Catharine Macaulay**.

– N –

NATURE. Prior to the seventeenth century, nature was often conceived in the West as a living, organic whole, with humans as a part of that whole. A stock image for this conception of nature was a **mother** who must be treated with respect and care. The other image for nature during this period was the competing image of a capricious woman who could not be tamed or predicted.

With the advent of the **scientific** revolution, this second image of nature expanded: nature became a disorderly woman who needed to be dominated. A corollary of this feminization of nature is that it also becomes a passive object, with the scientific inquirer as the active subject. This imagery accompanied the new picture of scientific knowledge, which can be seen as originating with **Francis Bacon**. Feminist philosophers have claimed that Bacon does not simply hold that knowledge is gained through domination of nature; rather, he also conceives of knowledge itself as a control of a disorderly nature, a nature that may even need to be forced to give up its secrets. For underneath this disorder lies a mechanistic, regulated, inert nature whose movement is not self-generated but is instead the effect of being acted upon. This then means that nature is both potentially predictable and available to human control. For feminist philosophers, this new conception of the scientific project is a **gendered** conception: scientific knowledge is the process of the seduction and domination of a female nature by a male inquirer.

This mechanistic view of nature, and the role of the scientist, became the dominant paradigm for scientific and philosophical thinking. This change in thinking also correlated to a more general change in views of the earth spurred by the early beginnings of the industrialization of Europe; nature became something that was separate from humans, but was for their use for technological and economic progress. However, while the view of nature as inert and mechanistic has predominated since the seventeenth century, it was not the only available view. An organic view of nature was developed in the late seventeenth century by the Cambridge Platonists, as well as vitalists such as **Anne Finch Conway** and the seventeenth-century German philosopher Gottfried Leibniz, in part as a response to this mechanistic view.

Throughout his scientific writings, Bacon used gender imagery to describe the processes and goals of scientific inquiry, and this imagery continued to play out in later scientific and philosophical discourse. Feminist philosophers argue that this imagery reinforces both cultural attitudes toward women of that time and the normative **dualisms** of man/woman and culture/nature. Furthermore, this imagery also serves to identify the knower as male. Feminist philosophers have charged that this type of imagery has contributed to the legacy of the exclusion of women in scientific inquiry and has undermined women's **epistemic** authority.

Feminist philosophers of science have criticized the traditional paradigm of science for its ideals of **objectivity** and **value neutral-**

ity, ideals that some hold to be **masculine**. Some argue that if the traditional conception of science is to be altered, its accompanying view of nature must be changed, because the traditional conception of science is reinforced by, and reinforces, the notion of nature as inert and mechanistic.

Despite the often problematic metaphorical and cultural associations of nature with women, and the fact that these associations are not historically or culturally **universal**, there can be productive connections made between feminism and nature. **Ecofeminists**, for example, argue that the conceptual and literal connections between the **oppression** of women and the oppression of nature show that these oppressions are interlocked. Thus ecofeminists hold that an understanding of the relationship between sexism and naturism is the key to successful **feminist theory** and practice.

NATURE, WOMEN'S. *See* ESSENTIALISM.

NIETZSCHE, FRIEDRICH WILHELM (1844–1900). German philosopher Friedrich Nietzsche is an influential, if controversial, figure in **Continental philosophy**. Born in Röcken bei Lützen near Leipzig, Nietzsche entered the University of Bonn in 1864. He began teaching at the University of Basel in 1869 but lived an almost nomadic life from 1880 onward, his most creative period. He published his first book, *The Birth of Tragedy*, in 1872. Two of his best-known works are *Thus Spoke Zarathustra* (1883–1884) and *Beyond Good and Evil* (1886).

Like most feminist rereadings of the **history of philosophy**, critique and analysis of Nietzsche began in the 1980s. Feminist interest in his philosophy covers the whole spectrum of his different periods of writing. Work falls into the two categories of feminist historical analysis: investigation and critique of his comments on women and the **feminine**; and consideration of his potential as a resource for feminist philosophy.

Those who claim that Nietzsche has nothing to offer feminism point to his remarks on and attitudes toward women. Nietzsche is certainly notorious for his misogynist remarks, likening women to animals, or claiming that women need to be physically dominated. In *Thus Spoke Zarathustra*, Nietzsche reports a conversation in which his interlocuter says, "You are going to women? Don't forget your whip!" In *The Gay Science* (1882), Nietzsche writes: "When we love a woman, we easily conceive a hatred of nature on account of all the repulsive natural functions to which every woman is subject."

Based on his assessment of **gender** differences, Nietzsche holds that women should not take part in philosophy or politics; this is a significant claim, as he believes that these are among the most important social activities. He makes an even stronger anti-feminist claim when he argues that **equality** of the **sexes** should be rejected, as it would be disruptive of this difference. While there is nothing new in the assertion of these hyper-traditional notions of women, it is perhaps unexpected in a philosopher known for his critical stance toward cultural and philosophical tradition. However, it has also been claimed that Nietzsche's critiques of this tradition share ground with feminist philosophical thought, due to his claims that **objective** detachment cannot be attained, and that truth cannot be understood as separate from particular perspectives,

Thus far, the majority of work examining Nietzsche as a potential resource has focused on his gender **dualism**. Such work has tended to come out of contemporary French philosophy. On a closer examination, it can be seen that no one image or metaphor of women is at play in Nietzsche's work. For some feminist philosophers, these multiple and sometimes contradictory images can supply an implicit rejection of **essentialist** notions of women: notions that there is a fixed "woman's" nature. These images, in conjunction with the ambiguities and ironies of his style of writing, have also led some philosophers—most notably **Jacques Derrida**—to see Nietzsche as writing as woman. This may then mean that Nietzsche can provide a resource for those feminist philosophers who wish to interrogate the **masculinity** of the philosophical tradition from an alternative location: one that does not replicate the masculine positioning of this tradition. *See also* CANON, CRITIQUE OF.

NORMATIVE DUALISM. *See* DUALISM.

– O –

OBJECTIFICATION. Feminist philosophers' approach to the critique of the objectification of women is to produce an analysis of the concept itself. The starting point for this analysis is the understanding that the objectification of women is grounded in mistaken assumptions about women's **sexuality**. Thus the objectification of women is sexual objectification: women are sexual objects. At the heart of these assumptions about women's sexuality is a culturally reinforced, **essentialist** view of the actual nature of women: they are submissive. **Pornography** has been cited as the most obvious form of objectification.

Feminist philosophers have offered a variety of analyses of the phenomenon, ranging from the claim that objectification serves to reduce the social status of women, which undercuts claims for **equality**, to the claim that objectification serves to **alienate** women from their **bodies**. Some analyses examine the objectification of women in relation to other systems of **oppression**, such as capitalism or **racism**. Under capitalism, the lower socio-economic status of women—reinforced by objectification—serves to cloud male workers' understanding of their own status, as they feel empowered by the literal or implicit domination of women. The most radical type of analysis maintains that the separation of subject/object, generated by the philosophical ideal of **objectivity**, underpins sexual objectification.

Feminist philosophers have also analyzed the ways that women learn to self-objectify: for example, due to self-preservation, or to a **false consciousness** engineered through the "fashion-beauty complex." This does not mean, however, that all women find being treated as a sexual object to be oppressive. There is a distinction between being a thing and being an object of desire. This does not mean that the latter is always non-problematic; it is context driven, and thus some contexts may be less appropriate than others. *See also* SUBJECTIVITY.

OBJECTIVITY. Objectivity—detached thought from the world—is a central ideal for philosophical and **scientific** inquiry. Objectivity is seen in opposition to, and defined against, **subjectivity**. In the standard view, which is usually seen as having its first explicit formulation in **René Descartes**'s philosophy, the philosophical or scientific knower can only attain true knowledge free of her or his differences from other knowers, in particular the differences of **bodies** and values. Thus **value neutrality** and the ability to detach and remain separated from objects of knowledge are the accompanying requirements for objectivity. The strength of the ideal of objectivity is that, even though knowledge is attained by individual knowers, this knowledge can also be attained by other knowers; thus there is the possibility of **universal** truths for science or moral principles for ethics.

Feminist philosophers, in particular feminist philosophers of science, have questioned whether what Donna Haraway has termed the "god trick" is possible, and also whether objectivity is a useful ideal for the political goals of feminist philosophy. There have been different approaches to criticizing the possibility of objectivity. **Postmodernist feminists** reject the ideal knowing subject; they posit a multiplicity of subjects who are partially constituted by social and political forces that are often beyond their control. The postmodernist rejection of the traditional concept of the objective, knowing subject is also a rejection of the possibility of a privileged knowledge as well as of universal truths and moral principles.

Other approaches to the critique of the ideal of objectivity have been more explicitly feminist. Underpinning the different approaches is a shared position that objectivity is **gendered**, unattainable by women and conceptually confused, as it is itself the product of a male subjectivity. Feminist philosophers argue that, within the philosophical tradition, objectivity is a requirement for a symbolically male **reason**. They may also maintain that this ideal reflects a male **experience** of the world, in particular men's possibilities for **autonomy** and separation. Thus it is contrary to women's experiences, which are more grounded in the social and material world.

A further argument is that objectivity is an ideology that serves to reinforce the **oppression** of women, and other marginalized groups, as the ideal of objectivity either literally—or metaphorically—places (white) men in the position of a privileged access to knowledge. Knowledge and power are seen to be mutually reinforcing; thus a lack of access to knowledge for disadvantaged groups reinforces the power of dominant groups. In the case of science, this ideology reinforces the belief that the results of scientific inquiry are in actuality value neutral. In this way, scientific theories that reflect sexist attitudes are taken as objectively truthful, and thus can serve to reinforce problematic views of the nature and social status of women. One of the most radical critiques of objectivity as an ideal is that the separation of knower and object underpins the **objectification** of women by men.

The question for feminist philosophy is whether to reject or revise the ideal of objectivity for knowledge. **French feminists** have not interrogated the notion per se, but they implicitly reject the ideal through taking up a symbolic position of female (i.e., a subjective position) as a strategy to subvert the dichotomies of **masculine** thought and **language**. The notion of objectivity has been an important element of Anglo-American **analytic feminist** work in **epistemology** and science. Analytic feminists typically reject the formulation of the traditional ideal, for a wholesale rejection will destabilize other important ideals grounded upon it, such as **justice**. They usually aim, instead, for a revised notion of objectivity, one that will be able to support the political and epistemological goals of the feminist project.

Often underlying different feminist reconceptualizations of objectivity is the recognition that knowledge cannot be value free, and thus that it must begin from the right set of values: the removal of oppression and domination. The claim is that this explicitly value-laden position is not only realizable, but may in fact serve to achieve the goals of objectivity, as it will produce a more universal knowledge. The process of achieving knowledge must also include a recognition both of subjectivity and of the epistemic potential of different perspectives. However, there is a concern among both the supporters and critics of a revised objectivity that this latter claim may slip too easily into a problematic **relativism**: different knowledges or moralities are equally valid. If this is indeed the case, then this undercuts any claim that there is a feminist, and thus correct, position from which to critique and understand the subordination of women. *See also* DUALISM; IMPARTIALITY.

OBJECT RELATIONS THEORY. Object relations theory has become part of **psychoanalytic feminism**. However, feminist philosophers have also found it possible to use the explanatory framework provided by object relations theories without taking on wholesale the intricacies of psychoanalytic theorizing. Feminist philosophers have focused on the "social" relations school of thought, in particular the theories of Nancy Chodorow in her 1978 work *The Reproduction of*

Mothering: Psychoanalysis and the Sociology of Gender. There has been little interest in the other school of thought, based on the work of Melanie Klein, which focuses on psychical life.

Social object relations theory offers an explanation of the process of **gender** identification in children. This is the process of the internalization of their social relations to their parents. The specifics of the process are not **universal**; there can be variants depending on, for example, cultural variations in child-rearing practices. This psychological development occurs during the first three years of our life. Initially, the infant establishes a close relation ("symbiosis") with its primary caretaker, who is typically the **mother**. Next the infant develops a sense of self through "separation" from the mother, which is a process of differentiation and development of a sense of self, and through "individuation," which is a process of establishing a set of individual character traits. What is important for feminists is the fact that this sense of self is accompanied by a sense of gender. Moreover, this sense of oneself as gendered is also accompanied by an internalization of the higher or lower social value placed on that particular gender.

The process of separation and individuation is different for female and male children. The female does not separate completely from the mother, and thus she identifies with relationality and caring. The male, on the other hand, achieves separation through an identification with a (distant) father. The particulars of this process of male separation are a distancing through the devaluation of women, the suppression of identifiably "female" elements, and a reinforcement of this suppression through controlling them. In its turn this leads to a need to control their object: the mother/women. In this way, the child's identity as male is wrapped up with aggression, control, and **autonomy**.

Social object relations theory has been of interest to feminist philosophers, not just because of its contributions to an understanding of the construction of gender, but also because it can offer an explanatory framework within which to analyze the philosophical enterprise itself. For some feminist philosophers, object relations theory can offer an explanation of the dominant themes and ideals present in the **history of philosophy**, many of which remain in one form or another in current philosophy. They claim that, because philosophy is a traditionally male preserve, its definition and construction reflect male identity; thus philosophy is a male enterprise.

Some feminist philosophers argue that the need to control and devalue women plays out in the philosophical "need" of traditional Western philosophy to control "**feminine**" passions in order to achieve rationality and knowledge. Human passions or **emotions** are traditionally depicted as having a lesser value than human **reason**; sometimes they are even framed as being dangerous to rational thought and knowledge. It has also been claimed that this desire for control plays out in philosophical and **scientific** attitudes that see a feminized **nature** as an object to be dominated. Object relations theory has also been seen by some feminist philosophers to offer an explanation of why it has been so difficult to break out of the framework of **dualist** thinking of the Western tradition: it is part of our psyche.

The male self has also been seen as a central element of moral theorizing, both past and present. The traditional picture of the **moral agent** is notably male, according to object relations theory: **impartial**, autonomous, unemotional, and ultra-**individualist**. Similarly, the notion of a separated and isolated individual is often foundational to theorizing in the philosophy of **mind**, **political philosophy**, and liberal political theory. Feminist philosophers have also claimed that the distant, separated male self has underpinned the traditional ideal of the **objective**, separated knower of **epistemology** and science. Indeed, it has been claimed that there is an association of knowledge and science with "maleness," an association that functions to exclude women.

For some feminist philosophers, object relations theory does not simply explain what they see as the "maleness" of philosophical thinking; they hold that object relations theory can also help a critical understanding of how that thinking can be changed. The claim is that if the pattern of parenting, and thus human development, were different, then philosophical thinking would become more relational, contextual, and so forth. Other feminist philosophers hold the less radical view that philosophical thinking needs to be moderated through a revaluing of "feminine" thinking. Thus far the latter approach has had more influence on the philosophical enterprise; for example, the notion of **care** in ethics as providing an alternative, or a corrective, to traditional moral philosophy has become relatively mainstream.

Object relations theory, however, has also been the target of criticism from feminist philosophers. The theory is criticized because it accepts the problematic fact that the primary caretaker is the mother, a position that ultimately reinforces **patriarchy**. In a similar vein, it is also claimed that object relations theories cannot explain the existence of people who do not possess their assigned gender characteristics, nor can it explain how these characteristics can be changed. This means that object relations theory is open to a charge of **essentialism**: that there is a fixed "woman's" nature. Moreover, it has been challenged for its uncritical acceptance of **heterosexual** pair bonding as the norm. *See also* GILLIGAN, CAROL; SUBJECTIVITY.

ONTOLOGY. *See* METAPHYSICS.

OPPRESSION. Oppression is a central term in feminist discourse; however, it is generally agreed that there is no one shared way that different social groups are oppressed or **experience** oppression. Moreover, even though **feminist theory** is characterized by a commitment to the analysis and alleviation of the oppression of women, there is disagreement among theorists over the causes or roots of this oppression. Despite this, some feminist philosophers have shown that it is possible to produce analyses that identify certain characteristics of oppression, even though oppressed groups do not always experience all of them.

In this type of analysis, it is understood that oppression is not an experience of individuals as individuals; rather, it is experienced by an individual because of membership in a particular group or groups. Furthermore, oppression is not understood in terms of governmental or political repression but in terms of an interlocking system of disadvantage and injustice—in particular, economic, political, and ideological disadvantage and injustice. In terms of economics, women are, for example, often encouraged to enter traditionally female—and thus lower-paid—occupations. In terms of the political, certain **rights** or legal protections can be denied to women. Ideologically, stereotyping or **controlling images** serve both to control and marginalize women; women are not recognized as individuals but as representatives of a certain "type" of woman, and dismissed accordingly. These barriers of oppression need not be an external force. They can also be internalized by individuals of the oppressed group, who will then monitor and restrict their own behaviors. This interlocking system of disadvantage and injustice not only serves to disempower specific groups but also serves to make them more vulnerable to violence or the threat of violence.

One of two central reasons that institutional oppression has been hard to dismantle is the way that its interlocking nature leads to its invisibility. There appears, for example, to be no obvious reason why women cannot achieve the qualifications or promotions that would lead to **equality** of pay with men. This ignores the ways that cultural views of women's personalities play into their employment opportunities, or racial stereotypes lead to women of color being directed toward (lower-paid) service work. The other central reason for continued institutional oppression is that the restrictions placed on one group serve to privilege another group, which would be hesitant not only to give up such privilege but even to acknowledge its existence.

"OTHER" (THE "OTHER"). *See* BEAUVOIR, SIMONE DE; FRENCH FEMINISM.

– P –

PACIFISM. *See* CULTURAL FEMINISM; WAR AND PEACE.

PATRIARCHY. Radical feminists adopted the term patriarchy, literally "rule of the fathers," from the non-normative anthropological description of certain types of social organization. In the anthropological context, patriarchy refers to the structure of a **family** that is organized around one older man who has control over the family members. In the feminist context, patriarchy refers to a system of male power—economic, social, political, material, ideological and psychological—that produces the **oppression** of women. Not all men have equal power in relation to each other under patriarchy; however, many feminists argue that men as a group all have the power to dominate women. Thus it is ultimately in men's interests to maintain a patriarchal system, even if it means that men themselves are subject to the hierarchies (e.g., class) within that system.

Patriarchy for radical feminists is a universal and fixed system of male domination that affects all women in one way or another; other **feminist theorists** have argued that this position is oversimplistic. These latter theorists hold that patriarchy has different historical forms, and they typically focus on one particular element of the system of patriarchy as the central cause or basis of oppression. More controversially, some theorists argue that the patriarchal conceptual framework constructs reality itself through the use of **dualisms** and **value hierarchies**. Despite differences in how the system of patriarchy is understood, it remains a useful political concept for feminists to encapsulate the oppression of women.

PIZAN, CHRISTINE DE (DE PISAN) (1365–ca. 1430). Christine de Pizan was born in Venice but grew up in Paris. She is sometimes credited as being the first professional writer. Much of the information available about her life comes from her *Avision* written in 1405. Here she describes the way her father encouraged her intellectual growth and **education**, and her early forays into writing poetry, which were stimulated by financial need. Christine (which is how she is usually called) was married at the age of fifteen, a normal age for that period, and widowed ten years later. After her husband's death, she supported her family financially and dealt with the legal issues connected to his estate. In *La Mutacion de Fortune* (*The Mutation of Fortune*), she describes this period as one in which she had to "become a man," in that she took on traditionally male responsibilities and roles.

Christine wrote on a variety of subjects, including military ethics and government. Her most famous work, the 1405 *Le Livre de la Cité des Dames* (*The Book of the City of Ladies*), is also the work that allows her to be classified (although not without some dissent) as a proto-feminist. The title was inspired by **Augustine**'s *City of God*, and the work contains examples of virtuous women that were often drawn from Boccaccio's *De Mulieribus Claris* (*Concerning Famous Women*). These and other references to works of literature and philosophy in the *City of Ladies* not only show the breadth of Christine's own learning, but they also function as part of her argument: to demonstrate the possibility that women could be learned.

The *City of Ladies* is an allegorical work that describes the construction of a walled city (in essence a series of rebuttals and positive arguments) designed both to protect virtuous women of all social classes ("ladies") from the slanders of the misogynist literature of the time, as well as to alleviate the real-life **oppression** under which actual women lived. A second work, which is sometimes called *Le Trésor de la Cité des Dames* (*The Treasury of the City of Ladies*), is a more practical work aimed at teaching the virtues necessary to live in this city.

Modern feminist philosophers have shown some interest in Christine's work. Karen Green's examination of Christine's corpus has uncovered a not unproblematic **maternal ethics** and a maternalist political theory underpinning Christine's writings on ethics and government. Green argues that the latter is of interest for those working in feminist **political philosophy** on a non-**contractual** framing of political relations.

PLATO (ca. 428–347 BCE). The philosopher Plato, an Athenian Greek from an aristocratic family, was a follower of the philosopher Socrates (ca. 470–399 BCE). Plato founded the Academy in Athens, a place of intellectual study for young men (including **Aristotle**, who entered the Academy in 367 BCE). Almost every work by Plato takes the form of a dialogue, usually featuring Socrates among the protagonists. The philosophical relationship between Socrates and Plato in these dialogues has been the subject of much debate; works that feature Socrates as the main interlocutor are not usually taken as simply reports of the views of the historical Socrates.

Thus far, only a few of Plato's dialogues have been the subject of feminist discussion: the *Republic*, the *Symposium*, and the *Timaeus*. Discussion has centered on how to interpret Plato's explicit discussions of women, and how to interpret the way that the **feminine** plays out in Plato's philosophy. The former approach is more typical of feminist interpretations from the 1970s and 1980s, while the latter is more typical of current work. The vast majority of feminist philosophical work on Plato has tended to revolve around the question of whether Plato can be considered a feminist. The attribution of the label "feminist" to Plato is made complex, not only because it is a modern term, but also because of the different definitions of feminism held by commentators.

The focal dialogue for discussion of Plato's feminism has been the *Republic*, specifically *Republic V*. In this section, Socrates gives an account of the ideal or just state, one that, among other things, requires rulers—"guardians"—who have been taught wisdom and goodness: they are philosophers. For feminist philosophers, the crucial element in this section of the dialogue is that Socrates includes women among the guardians.

Considered the first argument of its kind, Plato advocates **equality** of **education** and opportunity for those women who have natures suitable for the role of guardian. In the dialogue, Socrates holds that the only natural differences between the **sexes** are the basic biological differences; he denies the existence of any further differences upon which it could be maintained that women lack the capacity to perform certain tasks or hold certain occupations. This component of the argument has been seen as anticipating modern feminist thinking, especially that of **liberal feminism**. For this reason, Plato has been commended for his progressive thinking and has been given the label of "first feminist." Some feminist philosophers have disputed this label on the grounds that Plato does not give all members of the ideal state education and opportunity; this type of social hierarchy is antithetical to feminism.

The central premise of the argument for inclusion of women among the guardians has proved to be a sticking point. In the dialogue, Socrates—most likely the mouthpiece for Plato at this period of Plato's writing, rather than the historical person—grounds his argument on the claim that men are typically better than women in *all* areas of activity, even those that are traditionally the role of women. The conclusion Socrates draws from this is that sex does not determine occupation or activity; the determiner is individual natures. Problematically, Socrates also has to draw the conclusion from this argument that, in any of these activities and occupations, women as a group are less able than men as a group.

A further element of guardian life is their communal living. Not only is private property abolished but, to all intents and purposes, so is the traditional **family** structure. The male and female guardians will be chosen by lot for temporary "**marriages**," while the children produced from these unions will be placed in a communal nursery and identified as the children of all those guardians who were "married" at the time of their conception. For some feminist interpreters, the question is then whether this abolition of the private family is related to Plato's inclusion of women in guardian occupations; some interpreters have asked whether this is simply a question of efficient use of resources. Other interpreters have questioned the implications of this minimizing of women's **reproductive** role by asking, for example, whether it serves to devalue women's function as child bearers and rearers.

Looking beyond the question of Plato's feminism, other feminist interpreters have considered the relationship between Platonic philosophy and the feminine. The *Timaeus* and the *Symposium* have been the focal dialogues for these latter discussions. In the *Timaeus*, Plato describes and explains the creation of the universe. The original humans were male, but those who cannot control their passions properly, by using their **reason**, were reborn as women. Feminist interpreters have pointed out that not only are women depicted as less perfect than men, but reason and **emotion** become both **gendered** and hierarchically ordered.

In the *Symposium*, the central protagonist is Socrates, who speaks of how love progresses from the human to the divine. He claims that we love beauty in other people, and from that physical love, we ultimately progress to knowing beauty itself. Crucially for feminist interpreters, Socrates reports his discussion with a Mantinean woman called **Diotima** on the subject of love, and he claims that it is from her that he learned his philosophy of love. The figure of Diotima, however, is ambiguous. Some feminist interpreters have asked if there is significance in the fact that she is not an actual participant in the dialogue, claiming that the feminine then becomes marginalized. Conversely, other interpreters have asked if there is significance in the fact that it is a woman who leads men to philosophical knowledge; it has been argued that Diotima could reflect an **ancient Greek** tradition of female wisdom, and an authority that is still present in the cultural life of Plato's contemporaries. *See also* CANON, CRITIQUE OF.

POLITICAL AND SOCIAL PHILOSOPHY. Within feminist philosophy there is no clear distinction between the fields of political and social philosophy, as feminist philosophy itself is both a social and a political philosophy. Feminist political and social philosophy can be divided into three main categories: the analysis of traditional political texts and theories; the critique and revision of traditional questions and concepts; and the introduction and development of new areas and lenses of analysis. Some feminist philosophers have focused on the analysis of the different types of **feminist theory** or on the requirements for theoretical adequacy within feminist theorizing. On the whole, however, this has not been a dominant strand in political analysis.

It is typical practice for non-feminist philosophers who examine both classical and contemporary political theories to ignore comments about, or the invisibility of, women. Feminist philosophers, however, consider a study of the ways that philosophers' theories about women interconnect with their political philosophies to be important to an understanding of these philosophies. Feminist philosophers criticize, in particular, the ways that the invisibility of women, of areas culturally associated with women (such as **education** of children), and of social and political relations between women and men affect theorizing about arrangements of political and social life. This type of analysis then leads to the ultimate question of whether these theories have the capacity to include women and issues associated with women, that is, whether these theories are **universal** enough to count as an adequate theory at all.

Feminist philosophers argue that the boundaries and concepts of traditional political thought are defined against the social realities of women's lives. Traditionally, the political life is identified with the life of men, defined as a life of **autonomous**, unrelated, **individualistic** beings, whereas the domestic life, the life culturally associated with women, is one of connection with dependent others. Confined to the domestic sphere, the contribution of women to political life is limited to such things as the production and education of future citizens. This conceptual and cultural division—the **public/private distinction**—of social life into the dichotomy of public and private spheres is at the heart of traditional political theorizing. Thus it has served both to write women out of theories of political life and to exclude them in reality from this life.

The central contribution of feminist thinkers to political philosophy is the rejection of this public/private distinction and its use in political philosophy. In addition, the erasure of this distinction allows feminist philosophers to explore new subject areas, concepts, and ways of building theory.

The breaking down of the public/private distinction has allowed feminist philosophers to theorize about social and political issues of particular interest to women, such as **reproductive** choice. However, some feminist philosophers have stated that this categorizing of certain issues as "women's issues" must be approached cautiously. Historically, the supposed differences between men's and women's political interests contributed to women's status as second-class citizens. Even if this were not the case, categorizing certain issues as "women's" may entail that differences among the needs and interests of women, as a group, become invisible.

The dismantling of the distinction has also meant that traditional divisions between social and political philosophy become blurred within feminist philosophy: there is little distinction between application (specific issues) and theory (how to organize political and social life). Analysis that is political in nature forms the groundwork for discussions of social issues, for feminist philosophy is, by definition, politicized. Conversely, social issues are part of feminist political theorizing, which is, by definition, contextual and practical.

The abandonment of the public/private distinction also leads to the abandonment of the traditional conception of the political subject, the conception that is still dominant today. This subject is an independent, freely choosing individual, whose political life is conducted solely in the public sphere among other such individuals. Thus the goal of traditional political arrangements is to regulate the interactions of these unrelated individuals and to maximize their involvement in political life. These are arrangements that are naturally grounded in the abstract concepts of **equality**, **justice**, **rights**, and citizenship.

For feminist philosophers, the political subject is not an abstract entity. This subject cannot be separated from a recognition of our relationships to others and the dependency that these produce. Thus some feminist philosophers argue that the goal of political arrangements is to protect and promote relationships among citizens; it is not to protect them from each other, or to promote their individual freedoms. Feminist philosophers also criticize the central concepts of the traditional model. A major criticism is that the abstractness and **gender** neutrality of these concepts may, in fact, work against the actual liberation of women, as they flatten the important differences between men and women. Thus these concepts make invisible the different requirements for female equality: for example, reproductive choice. Some feminists of color, in particular black Americans, have been at the forefront of the debate over the usefulness for political philosophy of both the notion of gender-neutral justice and the traditional concept of equality. They argue that the gender-neutral/gender-specific and equality/difference dichotomies are too universal, and that they thus fail to recognize the specific needs of women and men of different **races** and classes.

Feminist philosophers have offered a variety of different approaches to producing alternative or revised political theories. One central approach is the integration of the notion of **care** with justice. Its proponents claim that an approach based in the ethics of care allows for a more contextualized approach, one that can give equal priority to the relationships among individuals. This could then lead, for example, to the placing of the **family**, not the individual, as the political unit for which political arrangements are made. Another approach is to reject a universal model of citizenship and create a model or models that recognize gender difference as a means toward political and civil equality. There is some disagreement over the adequacy of both of these proposals. The former has been the subject of the standard criticisms for any ethic of care: for example, care is associated with women's traditional—subordinating—roles as wife and **mother**. The latter has been criticized because of its assumption that there is enough universality and identity among women to produce a gender-sensitive model of citizenship. *See also* BLACK FEMINIST PHILOSOPHY; POLITICAL SOLIPSISM; SUBJECTIVITY.

POLITICAL SOLIPSISM. Political solipsism is a term, used mainly by feminist philosophers, to describe the notion that humans are not only fundamentally solitary but also potentially in competition with others for resources and the satisfaction of needs. This notion of **human nature** is a foundational assumption of liberal political theory, and thus it is also a foundational assumption for **liberal feminism**.

Given this notion of human nature, one of the central questions for liberal political theory is how these solitary **individualistic** beings can form a civil society. This society will need to ensure the maximum amount of freedom and **autonomy** of these individuals—compatible with the freedom and autonomy of others—to pursue their own interests and needs. This question can be seen to play out in the way that mainstream liberal feminism aims to produce a society that guarantees **equality**, especially in the workplace, and freedom, especially **sexual** freedom, for women. Liberal feminists hold that, once barriers to their freedom of choice and equality of opportunity are removed, women will be able to achieve individual fulfillment.

Some feminist philosophers have claimed that this way of viewing human nature exhibits male bias, as it relies on a conception of the self as rational and autonomous—concepts that are identified with "maleness." Furthermore, this notion conflicts with lived human **experience** and human biology, in particular the fact that human children are necessarily dependent on others, and thus that social groups are formed in order to raise children. *See also* POLITICAL AND SOCIAL PHILOSOPHY; SUBJECTIVITY.

PORNOGRAPHY. The rise of **radical feminism** in the 1970s, and its critique of **heterosexual** relationships as relationships of male power, provided the intellectual background against which the contemporary feminist philosophical debate over pornography has taken shape. There are many different elements within the contemporary feminist debate over pornography. As models and actors are part of the production process, it can be seen as a form of sex work; thus it raises many of the same issues as the debate over **prostitution**. The pornography debate also includes questions about the representation of women and **sexuality** and the nature of freedom of expression. At the foundation of this debate lies the problem of the actual characterization of pornography itself. Feminist characterizations differ from non-feminist characterizations, in that they focus on the context in which pornography is produced and consumed, and the effects it may or may not have on women.

Typically, anti-pornography feminists claim that what is problematic about pornography is not its sexual content, but the connection of that sexual content with violence against or degradation of women. The task is then to show in what ways pornography harms women. One claim is that this connection is causal: that pornography leads to sexual violence against women. However, this has been hard to prove conclusively one way or the other. Another claim is that pornography tells lies about women, showing them not only to be sexually subordinate but to want this subordination; these lies contribute to a cultural and social environment that is harmful to women.

While this latter claim has strengths as an anti-pornography analysis, it conflicts with claims over the value and nature of the freedom of expression; this is an issue that resonates especially in the United States. There is not enough clear evidence of harm to warrant state interference with the **right** to freedom of speech claimed by the producers and the consumers of pornography. One response to this has been the argument that pornography is not just a form of expression but a particular discriminatory activity. In other words, pornography itself subordinates women. Not all feminist philosophers, however, endorse an anti-pornography position. Some philosophers are concerned that some kind of ban on pornography would lead to a dampening effect that would curtail the freedom of speech and restrict the freedom of women to explore forms of sexuality that have been labeled unacceptable by **patriarchal** culture. *See* OBJECTIFICATION; LANGUAGE, PHILOSOPHY OF; POLITICAL AND SOCIAL PHILOSOPHY.

POSTFEMINISM. The term postfeminism has two different meanings. Its primary use is to describe a conservative reaction, both in the media and in academia, toward **second wave feminism**. Typically, these postfeminists claim that feminism has achieved its goals or has outlived its usefulness and is no longer related to the needs of women. Its secondary use has been to describe the **feminist theorizing** that sees second wave feminism as untenable, because of its reliance on a problematically **essentialist** notion of "women": women have a fixed nature. *See also* FIRST WAVE FEMINISM; THIRD WAVE FEMINISM.

POSTMODERN (POSTMODERNIST) FEMINISM. There is no one unified or shared postmodern feminist position. Postmodern feminists characterize themselves as having taken on the postmodernist challenge to the Western intellectual tradition, but as using that challenge to theorize about the marginalization and domination of women within the dominant discourse of this tradition. Postmodern feminist philosophy shows influences of, among others, **Jacques Derrida**, **Michel Foucault**, Jean-François Lyotard, and **French feminists**, such as **Luce Irigaray**. The variations within postmodernist feminist theorizing are, in part, the reflection of the differing natures of these philosophical influences.

While it is generally agreed that the feminist philosophical project shares with postmodernism a desire to critique modernism—the thought of the Enlightenment—there is disagreement over what follows from this. Feminist philosophers disagree over whether they should align themselves with the postmodernist project in its entirety and thus reject modernism wholesale. They also disagree over whether it is possible to extract and appropriate postmodernist analyses of notions such as **self**, power, **gender**, **subjectivity**, difference, **body**, and **sexuality**. The third main disagreement is over whether the two projects are in an insoluble tension.

The postmodern critique shares with feminist philosophy a sweeping critique of the **epistemological** ideals and elements of the Enlightenment, specifically of the notion that there is a **universal** form of **human nature** characterized by **reason**. In this (rejected) picture, it is through the use of reason that humans can attain knowledge but, in order to utilize this capacity, the reasoning knower needs to be unsituated: free of particular social and bodily differences and subjective values. Freed from a subjective position in this way, this **individualistic** knower can attain a position of **objectivity**, and thus the possibility of reaching universal truths: knowledge that can be attained by all objective reasoning knowers.

Postmodernism and feminist philosophy share an understanding that the traditional epistemological project—and its goals, ideals, and characteristics—is not a true project or an objective project; rather, it comes out of a specific historical time, place, and politics: those of the Enlightenment. Part of the rejection of this picture is the understanding that knowledge is not objective and universal; rather, it is constructed within systems of power. Not only does this critique open up the possibility of a plurality of knowledges, but it entails a rejection of the modernist concept of the objects of knowledge on the grounds that it is **essentialist**, and thus fails to recognize difference. This critique plays out in specific criticisms of the possibility of absolutes, all-encompassing or totalizing theories, non-contextual theorizing, the ideal of objectivity, and the role of reason for knowledge.

Despite these shared perspectives, postmodernist feminists critique the standard feminist philosophical project, and non-postmodern feminists, in their turn, critique the postmodernist project. This tension ultimately comes from their different perspectives on the failure of modernism.

Feminist theory, in general, does not just demand description and analysis of women's **oppression** but also requires theories within which analysis can lead to solutions for this oppression; thus the feminist position is inherently political. The feminist theoretical project is seen by many postmodernists to attempt, mistakenly, to replace the "grand narrative" of the Enlightenment with another type of totalizing theory. Unlike Enlightenment theorizing, feminist theory is not grounded in abstract, objective, universal truths attained by non-situated knowers; instead, its starting point is the particular knowledge generated by women's **experiences**. This starting point, however, for postmodernists is problematically essentialist, as it relies on some kind of stable category of women that is somehow independent of discourse. Moreover, the goal of this knowledge is to find some universal cause or causes of the oppression of women, and thus some shared strategy of liberation. This is not just problematic in itself, according to postmodernist thought; it is also problematic because this knowledge is based on an assumed essentialism and universalism that is the hallmark of (rejected) Western thought.

Whereas the ultimate goal of the feminist project is problematic for postmodernists, for feminist philosophers this is the point at which postmodernism fails. They argue that the theorizing of postmodernism is inadequate because it cannot satisfy the political need for some kind of unified notion of "women": a social subject. Moreover, many feminist philosophers claim that this social subject is not some kind of essentialist notion of a female nature; rather, its construction is open to difference among women. They argue, furthermore, that an abandonment of the category of gender will mean that feminist politics can only be a personal politics of individuals; thus the feminist project ends before it has begun. This abandonment of the possibility of categorizing women into a group or groups is of particular concern to those groups of women, such as women of color or lesbians, who wish to combat their marginalization within feminist theory itself by asserting that—within the more general category of women—they have a distinct political identity of their own.

Non-postmodern feminist philosophers, moreover, hold that postmodernism may fail women. They argue that women are not yet in a position to share the postmodernist goal of complete rejection of Enlightenment notions of knowledge and reality, as women have not yet fully benefited from the political and social changes of the Enlightenment. Moreover, until feminists have fully analyzed whether modernist thought contributed to women's subordination, it will not be clear if it should be rejected. Thus postmodernism and its position of the decentered self may, in fact, be a position of privilege. This claim is further bolstered by the fact that male postmodernists, such as Derrida and Foucault, have not truly included a questioning of gender in their theorizing.

The fact that the rejection of the Western epistemological project leads to **relativism** is another contentious issue for feminist philosophy, as it entails that the discourse of feminism is simply one among others. Feminist philosophers require a position from which they can critique the value system of **patriarchy** as well as maintain that their own system is more valuable, holds more truth, and offers more accurate knowledge than other systems. A crucial element of the feminist epistemological project is the uncovering of male-biased reality; this then entails that there is another (feminist) reality that can be constructed. From a postmodernist perspective, however, this is a problematic totalizing and unitary theoretical position.

Despite these tensions, there are feminist philosophers who self-identify as postmodernist, and there is little doubt that postmodernist thought is increasingly influential on **analytic feminism**. Many feminist philosophers recognize that postmodern feminist philosophy is in a position to offer a radical resistance to the essentialism and **dualism** of patriarchal discourse and that it can do so without itself occupying a position within this discourse. Postmodernist feminist philosophers consciously take on **Simone de Beauvoir**'s notion of the "Other," a position that is outside the dominant discourse. From this position, they can critique patriarchal discourse and its dualist construction of reality, as well as create new systems of meaning, **language**, and knowledge. The strength of postmodern feminist philosophy is that it deconstructs the discourse of Western intellectual thought; it does not replace this thought with another—problematic—totalizing discourse, a trajectory that non-postmodernist feminists recognize as a risk of their own philosophical project. Postmodern feminists reject the charge of relativism, arguing that it is only within Western intellectual discourse that the oppositional categories of personal/political and objective/subjective have meaning, and thus the tension between feminist politics and postmodernism is illusory.

The influence of postmodernist thought on feminist philosophy, in general, is hard to measure, as it has not entered feminist philosophy wholesale, but rather surfaces in general concerns about unitary categories, difference, and totalizing theories. The central contribution made by feminist philosophers who are either influenced by or hold the postmodernist perspective is a critique of the fundamental lens of feminist analysis: the category of gender. Postmodernist critiques of essentialism have moved the gender debate from the overly simple **sex**/gender distinction to a more nuanced and politically productive analysis, one that has allowed discussion of the multiple experiences of women and the differences among them. This type of critique has helped feminist philosophers become aware of the risks of the processes and goals of theorizing: feminist theories may, in their turn, be totalizing and thus marginalize, for example, non-Western women. *See also* CONTINENTAL PHILOSOPHY; SUBJECTIVITY.

POWER. *See* BACON, FRANCIS; FOUCAULT, MICHEL; MILL, JOHN STUART; PATRIARCHY.

PRAGMATISM. Feminist philosophers have shown little interest in the American tradition of pragmatist philosophy; rather, the project of critiquing and appropriating the Anglo-American and European philosophical traditions dominates feminist **history of philosophy**. This neglect may be mutual, as traditional pragmatism and its more modern versions appear to have little to say directly about the situation of women.

For these reasons, feminist work on pragmatism has tended to remain focused on the task of showing why this marginalized tradition has significance for the feminist philosophical project, in particular through showing the similar relations of these two philosophies to the mainstream tradition. One possible reason for the marginalization of pragmatism within the mainstream tradition is that it does not share the tradition's **masculine** nature. If this is indeed the case, then there could be some significant shared ground between pragmatism and feminist philosophy. Moreover, pragmatism appears to take a more **feminine** approach to theorizing: it is grounded in particulars not abstractions, on human relations, and the individual philosophizes out of his or her own personal and social **experiences**. This is in contrast to the traditional ideal of the **objective**, **individualist** philosopher who relies solely on **reason** to attain knowledge, a picture that feminist philosophers claim only reflects men's experience or is wrapped up with male **gender** identity.

Moreover, like much of feminist philosophy, the goal of pragmatist theorizing is not to solve abstract philosophical problems but to attain knowledge of a concrete, social reality and to focus on the problems of actual experience. This knowledge and experience will then direct political action and social change: theory and practice are interrelated. Based on this experiential and practical foundation, pragmatists hold, among other things, that there is a plurality of values and meanings, that human action can better the human condition, and that there is a relationality between the experiencing **subject** and the experienced **object**. All these elements parallel, or could be of use to, the feminist philosophical enterprise. Future use of the pragmatist tradition for feminist philosophy will be contingent on showing how it did not, and need not, exclude women and their needs and interests.

PREGNANCY. *See* REPRODUCTION, SEXUAL.

PRIVACY. There are three ways of categorizing the **right** to privacy. The first is that there is a fundamental right to physical privacy that places limitations on governmental control over people and their property. This general notion of privacy is not merely the privilege of Western democracies but is more or less recognized globally. The second is that there is a right to informational privacy. This has been significant for Western women, in particular, because it preserves the confidentiality of medical records of their **reproductive** histories. The third category is decisional privacy. This is the liberty of the individual to make and act on decisions without undue interference from other individuals or the state. This third category of decisional privacy underpins women's rights to birth control and **abortion** in the United States.

The actual concept of decisional privacy, however, has been the subject of critical analysis by feminist philosophers because of its foundation on an assumption of the division of social life into two separate spheres: public and private. Historically the cultural and conceptual association of women with the private sphere has served to justify the exclusion of women from public life. *See also* FAMILY; JUSTICE; POLITICAL AND SOCIAL PHILOSOPHY; PUBLIC/ PRIVATE DISTINCTION.

PROSTITUTION. The majority of feminists who have written on prostitution have voiced disapproval of it and of other forms of sex work. The central criticism of prostitution and other forms of sex work is that they subordinate women: either directly through the ex-plicit control of sex workers by their pimps, or indirectly through the reinforcement of the cultural message that women should be avail-able to men. Feminists point to the fact that sex work is rarely freely chosen; it is instead a consequence of the wider problem of **gender** discrimination in employment. This discrimination either keeps women out of the workforce or keeps them from earning a living wage.

Feminists do not just focus on the problem of prostitution within Western societies. They also investigate the way that prostitution has become a part of the tourist industry in some non-Western nations, and they critique the role that Western societies play in the establish-ment and growth of this industry in other countries.

Some feminists argue that sex work can and should be framed within a feminist context. They claim that sex work fits a feminist model, as sex workers make a free choice to take up what can be defined as a skilled profession, and have far more **autonomy** within this work than female workers in other professions. In response, it can be argued that the level of freedom offered by sex work is not recognized, because the **sexual** values of **patriarchal** society dictate the monogamy of women, and thus exclude the possibility that sex work can be an empowering or valid choice for women. This type of analysis leads to the call for the legalization and formalization of sex work as a way of protecting and enhancing women's freedom of choice. *See also* PORNOGRAPHY; POLITICAL AND SOCIAL PHILOSOPHY.

PSYCHOANALYTIC FEMINISM. Psychoanalytic **feminist theory** developed in the 1970s as an outgrowth of Sigmund Freud's psychoanalytic theory. Freud (1856–1939) is considered the "father" of psychoanalysis. In his 1905 work, *Three Essays on the Theory of Sexuality*, he offers his (still controversial) theory of infant sexuality in which he identifies the different stages of psychosexual development, including the formation of the Oedipus complex.

The term psychoanalytic feminism covers a broad spectrum of positions, ranging from those of **French feminist** philosophers—such as **Luce Irigaray** and Julia Kristeva—who have been influenced by the psychoanalyst Jacques Lacan's radical reinterpretation of Freudian theory, to theorists who aim to develop Freudian theory itself for use for feminist analysis. A typical approach of the latter group is to focus on the pre-Oedipal stage of the Freudian framework of psychosexual development. They argue that it is during this stage that women's socially assigned role as primary caretaker serves to construct **gender**. Having identified this particular stage of the development of the female psyche as the root cause of women's **oppression**, psychoanalytic feminists offer different explanations of the relation of the role of the **mother** to the construction of female gender identity.

Some psychoanalytic feminists place more of an emphasis on the constructions of **sexuality**, and sexual relationships, that come out of the mother-infant relations. Others offer a social **object relations theory**: they examine the process of gender identification in children produced through the internalization of a child's social relations to his or her parents. Of these two approaches to Freudian theory, only object relations theory has been of interest for feminist philosophers.

In essence, object relations theory states that the female child never separates completely from the mother. Thus gender identity for the female child is formed from connection to, and similarity with, the mother and becomes identified with "female" characteristics such as caring and the need for relationships. The male child achieves separation from the mother both through a rejection or devaluation of the "female" and through an identification with a distant father. Thus gender identity for men is bound up with, for example, **autonomy** and the suppression of these female characteristics.

Object relations theory has generated interest among feminist philosophers because of the way that the ideals of the male-dominated philosophical tradition, such as **objectivity** (detached thought), can be identified as the characteristics of male gender identity. Moreover, in the traditional picture, philosophical knowledge is hindered by the presence of "female" characteristics such as the **emotions**. Thus the philosophical enterprise itself is not gender neutral; rather, it is **masculine** and excludes the **feminine**. In addition, feminist philosophers have shown interest in psychoanalytic feminism because it recognizes relationality as a central aspect of human life and identifies the role of the **family** as a central institution for the maintenance of **patriarchy**.

On the whole, however, psychoanalytic feminism has been the target of criticism by feminist philosophers for two main reasons. First, it is not seen by feminist philosophers as a true **political philosophy**. Psychoanalytic feminism offers an analysis of women's oppression that is limited to the psychological realm. In so doing, it neglects factors outside the psychological, such as economic structures, that are central components of any complete feminist analysis of women's oppression. Moreover, the strategies that can be offered by psychoanalytic feminism for the eradication of gender injustice remain limited to changing parent-infant relations: for example, through the introduction of dual parenting. Some feminist philosophers argue that this strategy is overly simplistic, as it fails to recognize the way that women's traditional role as primary caretaker supports patriarchy; this role serves to give men the freedom to spend more time in the workplace and, therefore, contributes to the maintenance of male

182 • PSYCHOLOGY, PHILOSOPHY OF

economic and social superiority. Thus psychoanalytic feminism has explanatory strength in that it can give an analysis of gender formation, but it is not complete as a theory because it cannot offer any incisive solutions for eliminating the oppressive construct of gender.

The second reason feminist philosophers tend to criticize psychoanalytic feminism is because of its foundation in Freudian theory itself. Freud holds that the lack of a penis in girls is the ultimate source of psychological differences, and thus he holds that this lack or inferiority of female biology is the source of the inferiority of their psychological characteristics. This **biological deterministic** position limits the possibility of women's liberation and is antithetical to a central feminist claim that psychological differences between the **sexes** are the result of **socialization**. For these reasons, Freud's conclusions about the female **body** and the female psyche appear to be irretrievably misogynistic, and thus unsuitable for feminist revision.

PSYCHOLOGY, PHILOSOPHY OF. *See* MIND, PHILOSOPHY OF.

PUBLIC/PRIVATE DISTINCTION. The term public/private distinction refers to the conceptual and cultural division of social life into the dichotomy of public and private spheres. The public is the sphere of ownership and citizenship and is identified as the province of men. The private is the sphere of the home and **family** and is identified as the province of women. This type of organization of social life has a long history, stretching at least as far back as the distinction between the *polis* (city-state) and the *oikos* (household) in ancient Greece. The specific conceptualization of this division that remains today has been seen either as the product of the rise of capitalism or of the hierarchical **reason/emotion** dichotomy of the Enlightenment. This conceptualization has also been reinforced by **biological determinism**: the view that physiological differences between the **sexes** determine their different social and cultural roles.

Feminist theorists have not agreed on whether female liberation can best be achieved through dissolving the split (advocated by **socialist feminists**), through its revaluing (advocated by **cultural feminists**), or through creating ways in which women can enter the public sphere (advocated by **liberal feminists**). Feminist philosophers, on the whole, have tended to focus specifically on an analysis of the concept and its formulation. An analysis of the distinction shows that it is normative, not descriptive, and thus serves to justify the separation and exclusion of women from public life. This normativity is further reinforced by the values that are drawn from this distinction: for example, that "good" women are naturally maternal. Feminist philosophers have also challenged the notion that the private sphere is truly separate. They claim that the private sphere is not free of government control of its organization and members; for example, most state and federal laws in the United States make **marriage** an exclusively **heterosexual** institution. *See also* DUALISM; POLITICAL AND SOCIAL PHILOSOPHY; PRIVACY.

PYTHAGOREANISM. *See* ANCIENT GREEK PHILOSOPHY.

– R –

RACE AND RACISM. Many authorities now agree that race itself does not exist as a natural kind; the view that there are common physical characteristics that form natural separations among people is false. Instead, like **gender**, race is a social construction. The categorizing of individuals into different racial groups is not **value neutral**; rather, race is about political domination through the creation of "superior" and "inferior" groups. The construction of race creates systems of global socio-economic privilege for the dominant white "superior" group; it also creates an ideology that reinforces this privilege and produces a framework within which racialized social identities (and even an ontology of race) are formed.

The earliest philosophical discussions of race from the Western tradition come from the eighteenth century. Although a few philosophers of this period, such as Comte de Buffon, hypothesized that skin color was the result of climate, the dominant view was that people could be divided into races by skin color, a characteristic that was considered hereditary. During the nineteenth century, rather than just marking racial differences, **scientists** attempted to produced a biologically grounded account of these differences. Despite the failure of these attempts, the ideology that comes from the belief that there are essential differences between the races remains.

Feminist philosophical work on race burgeoned in the 1980s. Some feminist philosophers work in the areas of critical race theory, focusing on showing that revision of laws can remove only the surface manifestations of white domination, because this domination is written into the social, political, and economic framework itself. Others focus on giving analyses of what it means to talk about race, once it has been established that it is not a genetic category.

The study of racism has been of importance to **feminist theorists** because of its similarities with sexism. Racism, like sexism, is grounded in the initial assumption that people can be categorized into different groups based on a fundamental or **essential** set of shared physical and psychological characteristics, and on the further assumption that these characteristics entail the physical and intellectual superiority or inferiority of a particular group. Once these two assumptions are accepted as true, discrimination against a particular group appears to be justified. Some feminist theorists claim that a comparative analysis of the similarities of sexism and racism can help identify the foundations, justifications, and effects common to any system of **oppression**.

Despite the fact that an analysis of the similarities between racism and sexism can illuminate the discrimination of women, feminist philosophers have tended to criticize this analysis. The comparison of racism and sexism is grounded in the assumption that there is a **universal**, comparable **experience** of each system. This assumption is not only a false essentialism but also serves to keep the two interlocking systems separate. This separation hides the way in which racism has served to privilege white women economically and socially, and the way in which white privilege means that white women are more likely to achieve **equality** with (white) men. Furthermore, the separation of the systems has meant that, because of the intertwined nature of racism and sexism, there is no theoretical space within which to examine the particular **oppressions** that are experienced by women of color.

Despite the recognition by many feminist philosophers that gender is raced, only a few feminist philosophers work explicitly on race and racism. There appear to be two main reasons for this. Feminist philosophers often concentrate on providing critiques and alternatives to an intellectual tradition that has largely ignored race, and there is also a tendency to see work on race as the particular province of feminists of color, a group underrepresented in academia. *See also* BLACK FEMINIST PHILOSOPHY; COOPER, ANNA JULIA; GOUGES, OLYMPE DE; POLITICAL AND SOCIAL PHILOSOPHY.

RADICAL FEMINISM. Radical feminist thought originated in the United States in the 1960s and became an identifiable **feminist theory** by the 1970s. Even though there has been radical feminist work in both Europe and **Latin America**, it has been most closely associated with the feminist movement in the United States. Radical feminists not only identify **patriarchy** as the sole and **universal** cause of women's subordination but also hold that male domination is the most wide-ranging and fundamental form of human **oppression**. Radical feminists adopted the term patriarchy from the non-normative anthropological description of certain types of social organization. Beyond this single shared focus on the system of patriarchy, there is no one theory that is radical feminism.

Given that patriarchy is identified as the cause of women's subordination, the central commitment of radical feminism is an analysis of male domination and strategies for women's liberation from men. For radical feminists, this male domination is so universal that it has become almost invisible. Thus the goal of radical feminism is to unmask the different forms that women's subordination to men can take and to prescribe ways of overturning or resisting patriarchy. The subordination of women is typically attributed to male control of three things: women's **reproductive** capacities, women's **sexuality**, and the ideology of **femininity**.

In the case of women's reproductive capacities, early radical feminists often argued that these biological differences are the root cause of male dominance as, for example, they make women more vulnerable in terms of not being able to take care of their own physical needs during pregnancy. For some radical feminists, the solution is for women to take control of their **bodies** through the use of artificial technologies. Others claim that women's reproductive capacities are, in themselves, the potential solution. They claim that, rather than making women vulnerable, the ability to produce life is the source of value and power.

In the case of women's sexuality, radical feminists reject the patriarchal definition of women's sexuality as being for men's needs and desires. One controversial strategy for resistance has been the rejection of **heterosexuality** outright and the championing of lesbianism as the true expression of female sexuality.

For many radical feminists, one of the various ways that the construction of femininity serves to oppress women is the way that femininity is identified with women's fulfillment of male-dictated sexual and reproductive roles. Radical feminists therefore aim to resist femininity, for example, through the rejection of typical ideals of feminine beauty.

Radical feminists do not see all "women's **experiences**" as negative or without value: women can create and produce their own positive and liberating experiences. Participation in, and creation of, what is often termed as "womanculture" can also be a key to liberation. Womanculture, in essence, is separated from the general culture of a society, which radical feminists claim is nothing more than a guise for male culture. Womanculture can be achieved in a variety of ways, ranging from the creation of female-oriented **religions**, to cooperative women-owned business enterprises.

Feminist philosophical interest in radical feminism covers a wide range of approaches. Some philosophers write as radical feminists, the best-known being **Mary Daly**. Others examine standard philosophical fields such as **epistemology** and reality through a radical feminist lens. There are also those who argue for the introduction of new areas into the philosophical enterprise, such as lesbianism or the construction of femininity. When radical feminist philosophy is interpreted loosely to mean a separation from the male, **French feminism** comes under its umbrella, due not only to its critique of the maleness of the Western intellectual tradition but also to its creation of "female" ways of thought and writing.

Some feminist philosophers have also offered a variety of critiques of both the theoretical and the conceptual adequacy of radical feminist theory. Some have criticized the way that radical feminism is a double-edged sword for the liberation of women. On the one hand, it valorizes female qualities such as nurturing that comes out of their supposedly separate nature. On the other hand, this seems little different from the ideal "good" woman of the nineteenth century, a woman who was simultaneously valued for her different womanly characteristics and disempowered by them.

Radical feminist thought is generated by the experience of women, rather than from any specific notion of social **justice**. Thus it offers little that can be counted as thorough-going political theorizing. Moreover, the political analyses that radical feminists offer of women's subordination have been open to criticism. In particular, radical feminist theorizing has been criticized for its dependency on a problematic claim that there is a universality of women's experiences of oppression and of womanhood. This universalism rests on what is seen as the questionable assumption that all women have something in common—a female nature—and thus radical feminism has been criticized for its **essentialism**. For this reason, among others, it has been claimed that radical feminist theorizing neglects the way that class, **race**, and nationality affect women's experiences of oppression. Thus, for its critics, radical feminism is politically problematic and conceptually incoherent: there is no such thing as the "woman" identified by radical feminists to be liberated.

RAND, AYN (1905–1982). Philosopher and novelist Ayn Rand was born Alice Rosenbaum in St. Petersburg, Russia; she emigrated to the United States in 1926 and worked as a screenwriter in Hollywood. Rand's philosophy—Objectivism—is presented not only in essay form but also in her novels *The Fountainhead* (1943) and *Atlas Shrugged* (1957). For Rand, art was a method of communicating moral ideals; indeed, she was critical of academic philosophy, holding instead that philosophy should be written to inform the lay person. Central to Rand's Objectivist philosophy is the notion of the rational self-interest of the individual, and she valorizes the creative, productive, free-thinking individual focused on her or his own happiness. For Rand, the free market of capitalism is the only political system that can allow for the personal development and success of this individual.

Rand is a highly controversial figure for feminist philosophy; indeed, many Objectivists reject the validity of feminism. Certainly Objectivism's commitment to capitalism, individualism, and an extreme rationalism would seem to place a gulf between Rand's philosophy and feminism. However, some commentators have considered the possibilities of whether Rand's philosophy can be a part of feminist discussion, rather than merely a target of criticism. For example, Rand's philosophy may be seen as compatible with a type of feminism that has its roots in the nineteenth-century women's movement for **equality** of **rights**, one that points to the restrictive nature of government as the real "enemy" of women (rather than capitalism or men). Moreover, in her novels, Rand depicts women as **autonomous**, self-assertive individuals—with her philosophy providing the *moral* justification for such behavior—thus offering a fruitful counterimage to the self-sacrificing behavior traditionally expected of women.

RATIONALITY. *See* REASON.

RAWLS, JOHN. *See* CONTRACTARIANISM.

REALITY. *See* METAPHYSICS.

REASON. Although there has not been agreement on its specific role in philosophizing, or its particular characteristics, reason lies at the heart of Western philosophical thinking. Traditionally it has been considered the faculty through which knowledge is acquired and moral judgments are made.

Historically women have not been associated with the full possession of reason as traditionally conceived, or they have been prevented from exercising this faculty. Philosophers in the Western tradition have typically held that reason is a **universal** human faculty, yet many have simultaneously maintained, implicitly or explicitly, that there are degrees of rationality based on **gender** and **race**. **Aristotle** offers the most explicit setting out of this way of thinking, arguing that women possess the capacity for rationality but without "authority": their judgments have no standing or cannot be relied on. Women were also literally excluded from reason in the sense that they were barred from the physical sites of the development and exercise of reason, such as universities. For these reasons, early feminist philosophers, such as **Mary Astell** and **Mary Wollstonecraft**, tended to focus on women's **equal** capacity to reason. They held that the existence of an equal capacity for reason would support claims for the equal **education** for women as well as for their civil, economic, and political equality.

An examination of reason is still a major component of current feminist philosophy. However, unlike their predecessors, they are not responding to sexist claims about the lack of rationality in women. Instead, the role that reason plays in philosophical theorizing is now the object of intensive scrutiny. Feminist philosophers are now examining, among other things, the moral ideals that valorize reason, and the philosophical **methodologies** and practices that are grounded in traditional notions of rationality. Feminist critics of reason do not constitute an identifiable group; they can come from both the **analytic** and the **Continental** schools of thought, and can be engaged in work, for example, on **canon critique**, **epistemology**, philosophy of **science**, or philosophy of **language**.

The central feminist criticism is that reason—within the philosophical tradition—has covertly been identified with "maleness" and thus is only superficially gender neutral. The central target of this type of criticism is the binary opposition, prevalent in the Western philosophical tradition, of reason and **emotion**, or reason and **body**. Not only is the category of emotion/body opposite to reason, but for some philosophers in the tradition, it is a hindrance to reason and thus the attainment of knowledge. Given that women are culturally associated with the body, this **dualistic** framework means that women are excluded from the realm of reason. This exclusion can be literal, as when a philosopher declares that women's bodies or emotions make them unfit for reason, or metaphorical, through the representation of the body and emotion as **feminine**. Feminist criticism of reason often involves the examination of specific philosophers from the canon, especially **René Descartes**, given his position in the history of reason. This is not to say, however, that all feminist work on canonical philosophers is solely critical; some examines canonical philosophers as a potential resource for feminist philosophical work on reason.

One important approach to the critique of the traditional concept of reason has been influenced by **French feminist** philosophy. This approach examines the symbols and metaphors associated with reason, as well as the concepts, such as emotion or the body, that are framed as its opposites. In examining the meanings of these symbols and metaphors, and the way they function, these philosophers aim to demonstrate how the variety of philosophical conceptions of reason all rely in some way on the devaluation, control, or transcendence of the "feminine."

Anglo-American analytic approaches have also influenced feminist philosophical analyses of reason. One central strand is the revaluation of the aspects of human life, such as emotion and desire, that have been devalued in the traditional dualism of reason and the passions. Another important strand is the examination of the connections between the ideal of rationality and the social construction of "maleness" in the light of recent analyses of gender categories. *See also* IRIGARAY, LUCE; OBJECTIVITY; SUBJECTIVITY.

RELATIVISM. The philosophical position of relativism not only precludes but denies the possibility of uncovering **objective** and **universal** truths that are independent of a human understanding or perspective; indeed, relativism and universalism have traditionally been framed as mutually exclusive opposites.

There have been two intertwined feminist analyses of the question of relativism: a conceptual analysis, and an examination of its political implications. A conceptual analysis of the traditional picture of knowledge shows that it specifically and explicitly precludes relativism. In this picture, individuals attain knowledge through the use of **reason**, the universal characteristic of humans. The knowledge attained by the individual knower is not relative to that individual; it is available to others through the use of their reason. This interchangeability of knowers ensures the universality and objectivity of knowledge. Moreover, the assumption that these knowers are capable of discovering the true nature of reality adds further insurance against a vulnerability to relativism. This traditional picture of knowledge has been the target of criticisms that have ranged from the more radical critique of universalism by **postmodern feminists**, to claims that the ideals of the traditional picture reflect only the **experiences** of a particular subset of humanity: middle-class Western males.

However, the critique of the universalism of the traditional picture of knowledge does not mean that feminist philosophy is committed to an untenable relativism. The universalism/relativism dichotomy itself has been questioned, and thus the standard conceptualizations of the philosophical position of relativism have also been brought into question. Some feminist philosophers have maintained that a sophisticated position of **epistemological** relativism can have important political strengths. It can be claimed that truth is relative to a particular group (such as a particular grouping of women), and that the truths of the group's experiences can be discovered by employing traditional ideals and procedures, such as **impartial** examination of empirical evidence. In this way a relativist view of truth need not fall into a problematic subjectivism. However, it does not close off the possibility that some truths are universal; for example, the falsity of sexist stereotypes is not something that would be described as relative. A feminist relativism of this kind allows a political recognition of the truths of different women's lives and offers a way of examining the supposed facts about the world that are in tension with their experiences.

Feminist philosophical discussions of relativism have focused not only on facts but also on values: moral truths. Some varieties of **feminist ethics** hold that moral knowledge is not abstract and objective but contextual and concrete. This then means that there is no one moral knowledge; rather, there are different moral perspectives generated by different experiences. In this view, there is no reason to suppose that these different perspectives cannot work together productively, nor that, in the absence of a monolithic and universal morality, there cannot be any criteria for judging among different moral actions and choices. Indeed, the ability to apply different moral knowledges to different situations may offer a more flexible and finer-grained analysis than universally applicable abstract rules or formulas.

RELIGION, PHILOSOPHY OF. Feminist theology, as a general field, is burgeoning. The specific field of philosophy of religion, however, is a marginal one in philosophy within the **Christian** tradition, and there is hardly any work being done within the **Judaic** and **Islamic** traditions. A few philosophers of religion may be politically feminist, but their philosophical work does not typically reflect this.

This neglect is explained by a variety of reasons. First, the work of feminist philosophers of religion tends to be categorized as purely theology or religious studies. This marginalization reflects the status of early feminist philosophy in general before it became established as a field in its own right. Second, the philosophy of religion is perceived as male biased. It has historically been dominated by men, and the religious texts and theology that form part of its foundations are seen as misogynist. This male bias is not recognized by mainstream philosophers, as it appears that the standard philosophical issues, such as the existence of God, appear to be **gender** neutral. However, following the innovative post-Christian work of **Mary Daly**, feminist philosophers have claimed that the traditional concept of a transcendent male God—a being who is separate from **nature**—is a concept of a being with "power over," a relationship that is replayed and reaffirmed in **patriarchal** society. Finally, the philosophy of religion as a specific field is seen as fundamentally Eurocentric.

Feminist critiques of the philosophy of religion tend to focus on critiquing its acceptance of the traditional division of spirit and **body**, in which the latter is seen as the source of hindrance to or disruption of human spirituality. Within the Christian tradition, women have been culturally associated with lust, carnality, and other sins of the flesh. Moreover, the Christian philosophical tradition accepted the **Aristotelian** account of **reproduction**, in which women are passive vessels for reception of a male-made soul: their central function is biological. In these ways, women have been excluded from the spiritual life.

The little feminist work that has been done on the revision of the field of philosophy of religion rarely engages with the traditional questions about religion. The most radical of these revisions are proposals for a goddess-centered religion, one that invokes the power of the symbol of "goddess." The symbol of the goddess allows women to move outside the traditional religious paradigms that have required the obedience of women to men and to a patriarchal divine ruler. The goddess also functions as a symbol of the power of women and as a revaluing of women's association with the physical, specifically their connections with life giving and nurturing. Moreover, as the symbol of the goddess usually draws on ancient global traditions, it provides an alternative to Western religion. In these ways, a feminine religion can be part of a feminist struggle: it is political action.

However, feminist philosophy of religion does not often move outside the traditional framework to develop an alternative religion; rather, philosophers of religion aim toward revision of the elements, such as the notion of spirituality, of a particular religious tradition. A traditional notion has been that the spiritual life is one of asceticism and prayer. A revision proposed by Toinette M. Eugene is that the transcendent nature of spirituality should be seen as potentially liberating. The spiritual life would be seen as one of freedom and an understanding of human unity. The relationship with God would be one of friendship, rather than a power relation with a father or ruler. Thus this account forms an alternative paradigm for relationships among humans. *See also* AQUINAS, THOMAS; AUGUSTINE OF HIPPO.

REPRODUCTION, SEXUAL. Prior to the rise of feminist philosophy in the 1970s, little feminist philosophical work dealt explicitly with procreative issues; rather, feminist philosophers tended to focus on the effects of child-bearing on women. The one exception is **Emma Goldman**, whose belief that female political liberation required **sexual** liberation led her to argue for the dissemination of birth control information in her 1916 essay "The Social Aspects of Birth Control."

For contemporary feminists, procreative issues cover a wide range: in particular, contraception, **abortion**, surrogacy, genetic testing, new reproductive technologies, and population control. A central question is whether reproductive technologies and interventions serve to liberate or **oppress** women. The answers vary depending on the type of feminist political analysis that is employed. **Liberal feminists** typically support the development of technologies and interventions that increase women's reproductive choices. **Socialist feminists** tend to argue that reproductive freedom is best produced by a restructuring of the institutions of the social and business worlds, rather than through the development of high-tech interventions that are available only to the few who can afford them. Some feminists, Angela Davis in particular, have emphasized the need to examine procreative issues through the lenses of **race** and class, stressing the historical connections of the birth control movement to the eugenics movement, and pointing to the sterilization abuse of women of color.

From the early beginnings of **radical feminism**, the debate over procreative issues has focused on whether reproduction itself is the key to women's liberation or oppression. Some radical feminists claim that liberation from reproduction would be liberation from **patriarchal** control. Others argue that artificial reproductive technologies will serve to reduce still further the "usefulness" of women in patriarchal society. Some radical feminists, who also see reproduction as connected in some way to women's social value, may instead argue that reproduction can be a positive source of women's power and value in an otherwise male-dominated society. *See also* BEAUVOIR, SIMONE DE; ESSENTIALISM; FAMILY; MATERNAL ETHICS; MOTHERHOOD; POLITICAL AND SOCIAL PHILOSOPHY; PRIVACY.

RIGHTS. The call for the **equal** rights of women has been a central part of the feminist movement. Given that the capacity for **reason** was the specific human characteristic that endowed rights, feminist philosophers of the eighteenth and nineteenth centuries typically aimed to show women's equal intellectual capacities in order to argue for equality in civil rights, such as the rights to vote and own property. The development of the **second wave** of feminism in the 1960s and 1970s was spurred, in part, by the recognition that—even though American and European women had achieved equal civil rights—the goal of full equality for women had not been achieved. One of the characteristics of feminism of this era was, therefore, the view that equal rights could be attained through reform of those policies and laws that were discriminatory.

Feminist philosophers have recently begun to question the usefulness of the concept of rights for social **justice**. On the whole, this has been a concern only for feminists in the United States, given its particular constitution and legal system. This concern, however, is not necessarily shared by all U.S. feminist philosophers. Some U.S. feminist philosophers of color, and some Third World feminists working in the United States, have argued for a need for the rhetorical and political power of rights talk.

One line of questioning that has grown out of the ethics of **care** focuses on the moral issues related to rights. The ethics of care forms both a criticism of and alternative to the dominant moral tradition that views **moral agents** as **impartial**, **autonomous**, and abstract individuals. The typical goals of the traditional moral project are to direct the actions of these individuals and, through the device of rights, protect these individuals from the harmful actions of others. Thus rights holders in the traditional picture are isolated individuals who require protection from potential conflict with other individuals. In contrast, the ethics of care is based on and responsive to the connections and relations between contextualized moral agents. In this picture, the traditional notion of rights is inadequate to deal with the interactions and relationships of these agents.

A second line of questioning of the usefulness of rights discourse comes from the claim that the concept of rights reflects only male **experience**. Rights discourse applies best to interactions among strangers in the traditionally male public sphere, whereas women have traditionally been confined to the domestic sphere, and to interactions with a small group of related others. The practical result of this conceptualization is that women have few real rights to protect them from known (or unknown) others in the home or in the **family**. Moreover, it can be argued that legal rights, far from creating equality, serve to reinforce **patriarchy**. The assumption is that before the law all persons are equal. This "formal" equality also assumes that all persons are the same; however, the resulting **gender**-neutral legal rights may produce discriminatory results for women, in particular in their marital, family, or **reproductive** rights.

These criticisms need not entail a denial of the usefulness of rights. Instead, these criticisms are often seen as the initial step toward a reframing of rights as pragmatic, contextualized strategies to produce liberation and social justice. *See also* ABORTION; ANIMAL ETHICS; INDIVIDUALISM, ABSTRACT; LIBERAL FEMINISM; POLITICAL AND SOCIAL PHILOSOPHY; PRIVACY; PUBLIC/PRIVATE DISTINCTION.

ROUSSEAU, JEAN-JACQUES (1712–1778). The philosopher, essayist, and novelist Jean-Jacques Rousseau was born in Geneva. He was one of the premier intellectuals of the eighteenth-century French Enlightenment. His first publication was the 1750 essay *Discourse* *on the Sciences and Arts.* Rousseau wrote novels, operas, and auto-biographical works; however, he is best known for his moral and political philosophy, his most famous work being *The Social Contract* (1762). Central to Rousseau's moral and political philosophy is the opposition he sees between the corruption of contemporary society and the true—morally good—nature of man. Much of his philosophical work is then devoted to theorizing about the type of morally true political system and education that can provide an antidote to this corruption of man's nature in the modern age.

Rousseau's specific discussions of women and the private sphere have been of interest to present-day feminist philosophers; this is despite the inherent sexism in Rousseau's discussions of women and their role in civil society. Feminist philosophers have been interested in his work because his **political philosophy** offers an analysis of the **family** and the role of women that locates these two things as central elements of civil society. Rousseau's analysis is also of historical interest because these spheres had been neglected by most other political philosophers of the modern period.

Much of feminist interpretation to date has focused on identifying the ways in which Rousseau produced an early political philosophy that raises questions and issues still present in current feminist philosophy, and on considering the potential for appropriation of Rousseau's work. As yet, there has not been much actual appropriation of Rousseau's political thought for feminist political philosophy. Rousseau's main writings covering the areas of women and the family are *Julie, ou la nouvelle Héloïse, Lettre à M. d'Alembert,* and *Émile.* These have been the main focus of feminist philosophical analysis, with *Émile* as the central text.

The reception of Rousseau's work by his female or feminist contemporaries was mixed. Rousseau was sharply criticized by the eighteenth-century feminist philosopher **Mary Wollstonecraft** for the way that his **sex complementarian** views promoted and justified the subordination of women. However, many of his female contemporaries, such as Madame de Staël, also found his sex complementarian ideals for **feminine** behavior and social roles to be empowering. Women of the upper social classes at that time typically left their children to the care of servants and tutors, whereas Rousseau's philosophy emphasized the social necessity of the traditional female role of child-rearing. For Rousseau's female followers, this not only made their lives more "natural" but gave them a social value that was theirs by virtue of their **sex**.

The *Lettre à M. d'Alembert* is a public letter criticizing Jean le Rond d'Alembert, the editor of *l'Encyclopédie*, for his suggestion that there should be a theatre in Geneva. Among the central reasons Rousseau gives for the morally deleterious effect a theatre would have on the Genevan citizens is the claim that a theatre would encourage a desire for finery and competition among the female audience. Rousseau claimed that this sort of behavior would distract them from their duties to their family life. The connection that Rousseau makes between the virtues, behavior, and roles of women and the morality—or lack thereof—of society is a central theme in his philosophy of women.

In *Émile*, ostensibly a work on **education**, Rousseau gives the most fully developed account of his philosophy of women. Rousseau hypothesizes the form of education necessary for the boy Émile, the primary subject of the work, to develop according to his nature, free of the corrupting influences of society. The perfect helpmate for Émile is his female counterpart, the "natural" woman Sophy. The two sexes are seen as different but complementary, and through **marriage** they form a whole. While Rousseau is eager to show Émile's true nature free of societal influence, he accepts many of the stereotypical notions of women prevalent at that time. Thus Sophy's education is to be directed toward the development of what Rousseau perceives as her natural docility and her natural function of being pleasing to men.

The philosophical roots of Rousseau's views of the different "natures" of men and women, and his endorsement of sex complementarity, are clear in his earlier work on political philosophy, *Discourse on the Origin of Inequality* (1755). In Rousseau's hypothetical picture of the early stage of the development of humans, both men and women are initially isolated and **equal** beings. Independent of others, these pre-social individuals are free of the problematic egoism and competition that are the natural consequences of the civilized society Rousseau wishes to criticize. Rousseau identifies a stage in humanity's hypothetical development that lies between these two extremes: the nuclear "sentimental" family. For Rousseau, this social grouping of humans will play a central role in producing a cooperative, non-egoistic, civil society.

For feminist philosophers, the problem with the hypothetical development of the nuclear family from individuals who were initially equal and independent is that it is seen by Rousseau to require the sexual **division of labor**. Moreover, even though Rousseau's view of "natural" woman is often left unclear, apparently this social stage of human development is "natural" to women, not the initial truly pre-social stage. Thus it is ambiguous whether the societal roles for women identified by Rousseau are derived purely from women's "nature," or whether they are also derived from the perceived needs of civil society. If the latter is indeed the case, then Rousseau's philosophical vision of the good civil society cannot be achieved without the subordination of women.

On the surface, therefore, Rousseau's views of the "natural" for women appear problematic for the feminist reader. Rousseau's sex complementarianism not only clearly dictates the proper roles for women, but its foundational role for civil society entails that women must not break out of these roles. However, it would be a mistake to assume that these clearly delineated roles for women are generated purely by sexist thinking. Rousseau argues that the differences between the sexes are so radical that it makes little sense to ask if one is superior or equal to the other. Moreover, even though the role of women is restrictive, it is consistent with Rousseau's critique of the liberal view that champions the freedom of individuals to pursue their own (egoistic) interests.

Despite the problematic conclusions drawn by Rousseau about the "natural" roles of the two sexes, Rousseau's aim to create roles that were the product of **nature**, not society, is a shared goal with the feminist enterprise. Again, despite Rousseau's introduction of a problematic sexual division of labor, the political importance of the family unit—rather than the individual—for society in general is another shared area of interest. For some feminist political philosophers, the traditional notion of the political subject—one who is an isolated, abstract individual—needs to be replaced by an understanding that individuals are interconnected. This more contextualized approach gives priority to the protection of the relationships among individuals, rather than the protection of unconnected individuals from each other. This type of approach can then lead to the family becoming the political unit for which political arrangements are made. Finally, Rousseau depicts his heroines Sophy and Julie as suffering precisely because they embody his ideals of the good woman. This has provided feminist philosophers with ammunition against such ideals of femininity, and has led some philosophers to question whether Rousseau was aware on some level of the fragile underpinning of his political system. *See also* CANON, CRITIQUE OF; CONTRACTARIANISM; ESSENTIALISM.

RUDDICK, SARA. *See* MATERNAL ETHICS.

– S –

SARTRE, JEAN-PAUL (1905–1980). French philosopher Jean-Paul Sartre is a central figure in **existentialist** philosophy. Sartre studied at the École Normale Supérieure and then began a career as a philosophy teacher. He wrote philosophical novels and plays as well as academic works; eventually he left teaching to became an author full-time. His earlier work, for which he is best known, contains an examination of the concept of human freedom. For Sartre, freedom is understood against, and begins from, the background of our individual situation. The pivotal work from this period is *L'Être et le Néant* (*Being and Nothingness*), published in French in 1943. His later works focused on social responsibility.

Thus far, little work has identified Sartre's philosophy as a resource for feminist philosophy. The three central reasons for this are his intellectual relationship with **Simone de Beauvoir**, the apparent sexism in his work, and the competing influences of other French philosophers. It is possible that, in an effort to include Beauvoir in the philosophical **canon**, it has been necessary to deemphasize Sartre's philosophical contributions, despite such prominent works as *Being and Nothingness*, in order to assert Beauvoir's originality in her foundational text for feminist thought: *The Second Sex* (1949).

Feminist work on Sartre is often, but not exclusively, grounded in an initial consideration of the relationship of his work to that of Beauvoir. Earlier work on Sartre tended just to ask how much his philosophy was influenced by hers; the most recent work examines whether his versions of the notion of freedom—and **objectification** through "the look"—may ultimately offer more for feminist philosophy because of their greater complexity. The charge of sexism leveled against Sartre often relies on his use of women as illustrative examples for his critical examination of certain types of negative behavior, in particular self-deception. The final reason that can be identified for the neglect of Sartre is the fruitfulness for feminist philosophy of French philosophers such as **Michel Foucault** and **Jacques Derrida**, who explicitly rejected Sartre's thought because of its modernist elements.

SCHURMAN, ANNA MARIA VAN (1607–1679). Anna Maria van Schurman was born of Dutch parentage in Germany. She was given a home **education** that was grounded in the classics, and she became known throughout Europe for her learning. Van Schurman was in contact with other feminist philosophers of the time, including **Marie de Gournay** and **Bathsua Pell Makin,** and it would appear that she influenced the work of the latter.

Van Schurman wrote on a range of philosophical and non-philosophical topics. Her 1641 work *De ingenii muliebris ad doctrinam et meliores litteras aptitudine* (published in English in 1659 as *The Learned Maid; or, Whether a Maid May Be a Scholar*) was well known in its time. Van Schurman's argument for the education of women is composed of a series of syllogisms designed to prove the proposition that "a maid may be a scholar" and to reply to potential objections to this proposition. Van Schurman anticipates Virginia Woolf in her claim that, in order to study, women need sufficient money and time.

SCIENCE, PHILOSOPHY OF. Given that throughout the **history of philosophy**, science and philosophy have influenced and informed each other, the philosophy of science is a significant field for feminist philosophers. Feminist philosophers have expanded the boundaries of the subject area of philosophy of science, in particular by incorporating some of the more general feminist criticisms of science; these general criticisms challenge both the exclusion of women from science and the **gender** bias in scientific ideals and **methodology.**

Women have not always been excluded from the study of science, either literally or metaphorically. One strand of thinking in early modern culture symbolized science as a woman; this image faded away during the eighteenth century. This symbolism brought with it the association of women leading the male scientist to truth and knowledge. The notion of the "scientific lady" developed during the scientific revolution, and noble women of the seventeenth and eighteenth centuries were often encouraged to know something of science. Despite this, no feminist philosophers prior to the late twentieth century could, strictly speaking, be called philosophers of science; a rare few could be considered as offering some kind of feminist science: **Anne Finch Conway**, **Charlotte Perkins Gilman**, and **Antoinette Brown Blackwell**.

Feminist philosophers began to question the sciences and technology in the late 1970s. The main thrust of their criticism is that science has traditionally been based on the **experience** of men and has focused on the needs of men. Thus science is not **value neutral** but rather contains biases against, or entails the exclusion of, women. While earlier criticisms tended to focus on the "softer" social sciences, more recent criticisms have also been made of "harder" natural science.

Feminist philosophers tend to connect **epistemology** with feminist philosophy of science; they do not view them as two separate fields within philosophical inquiry. Feminist philosophy of science, like feminist epistemology, is engaged in examining how gender does and should affect knowledge, in particular in our practices of inquiry and justification. Feminist discussions of science and philosophy of science also follow patterns of critique and revision similar to those of epistemology: there is a feminist critique of **androcentric** bias in science and the philosophy of science, as well as attempts to develop a specifically feminist philosophy of science.

Feminist philosophers vary in their criticisms of the androcentric bias in science. The majority of work thus far falls under the umbrella of **analytic** philosophy. On the most basic level, it is claimed that this bias comes from the fact that science is primarily done by men. The dominance of men in the sciences has been seen to lead to biases not only in which areas are considered important to pursue, but also in the design of scientific experiments and the interpretation of their results. This criticism is typically made of scientific fields that have humans as the focus of their study, such as the social sciences. The work of **Carol Gilligan** in the field of psychology is often cited as an example of this type of criticism; in addition, Gilligan's work is seen as offering possibilities for the elimination of such biases.

However, even the hard sciences, as well as the ideals of scientific theorizing, have been criticized for their androcentric bias. This criticism can draw on **object relations theory** or on feminist studies of the history and philosophy of science. The latter type of criticism argues that the enterprise of science is not conducted free of its social and political context. The criteria that scientists use to chose one theory over another, for example, reflect our cultural framework; indeed, even scientific "facts" are hard to separate from the values of Western culture. Object relations theory points to the way that scientific ideals of **objectivity** and rationality reflect (white Western) males' gender ideals of **emotional** detachment, objectivity, and control.

The **language**, metaphors, and symbols of scientific discourse have also been the focus of feminist attention. Indeed, scientific theories themselves are read as "texts" or "narratives" in order to tease out their covert biases and ideologies. Since the scientific revolution, science is often depicted by male philosophers and scientists as symbolically male; part of its goal is to "penetrate" the mysteries of a symbolically female **nature** or to control and manipulate that nature. **Luce Irigaray** argues that the gender bias of science has its roots in the "male" language of science itself, as this language is grounded in symbolically male **logical** relations, such as disjunction or conjunction. Within this **patriarchal** language, the symbolically female relations of, for example, reciprocity or fluidity are not logical relations, and thus are not part of scientific discourse. Irigaray argues that these types of female-identified relations can only find expression in a differently **sexed** language: a **feminine** language and writing. The creation of this language works to resist male scientific discourse.

Feminist philosophy of science is also a reconstructive project aimed at defining, and ultimately producing, a feminist science, and much of the current work is being done in this area. The aim of this project is not to create some kind of new science, but rather one that avoids the failures of the traditional model of science while working for social change. There has been some work in developing "feminine" methodologies that reflect "feminine" cognitive styles; thus, for example, scientific research methods could include intuition or some kind of emotional connection with the subject matter. For some philosophers, the move from the Newtonian paradigm in twentieth-century science to the more contextual and relational way of thinking in quantum physics reflects a feminine way of thinking. Another strand in this reconstructive project has been to include overtly feminist politics in the philosophy of science and the scientific enterprise. It has been asked, for example, whether a politically grounded and motivated approach, despite being in tension with traditional notions of scientific inquiry, could lead to more reliable hypotheses about the natural and the social world. *See also* BACON, FRANCIS.

SECOND SEX, THE (LE DEUXIÈME SEXE). Originally published in 1949, French philosopher **Simone de Beauvoir's** *The Second Sex* is heralded for setting the framework within which contemporary **feminist theorizing** has taken place. Beauvoir's work is also recognized for its influence on the actual lives of women. *The Second Sex* offers a comprehensive demonstration and analysis of the historical and contemporary **oppression** of women, explanations of how this oppression is produced, and recommendations for women's liberation. Beauvoir's central theoretical concepts employed for this analysis are her claims that **femininity** is socially constructed and that women are constructed as "Other": the second **sex**.

The Second Sex is divided into seven parts, each part offering an analysis of a particular aspect of women's oppression. In the first part, Beauvoir critiques the explanations of women's condition offered by biology, psychoanalysis, and **Marxism**. For Beauvoir, biology can identify physical differences between the sexes; however, she argues that this does not provide an adequate explanation for the social values placed on these differences: why woman is Other. In the case of Sigmund Freud's **psychoanalytic** explanations, the condition of women is grounded in the differences between male and female **sexuality**, in particular in women's lack of male sexual characteristics. For Beauvoir, this explanation is too simplistic; the greater social power of men cannot be due to their sexuality alone. Finally, Beauvoir counters Friedrich Engels's claim that the dismantling of capitalism will automatically raise the status of women. She argues that capital would not have led to the othering of women if the desire for domination did not exist first.

In the second part of the book, Beauvoir traces the history of sexual hierarchy, starting with its origins in primitive forms of human society. In primitive societies, men were active subjects, working to support the group, both as inventors and warriors. As both creator and risk taker, man had reasons for being; as risk taker, he had an end more valuable than preserving his own life. In these ways, man differentiated himself from, and raised himself above, animals. Women, however, could not participate properly in these activities, as they were incapacitated by the physical demands of **reproduction**. Moreover, reproduction only produces life; it does not actively risk it. Thus the life of women became more closely connected to animal life.

In these early nomadic groups, women were simply materially disadvantaged; Beauvoir claims that it was during the following period of early agricultural communities that the oppression of women became established. In moving from a nomadic existence to a life supported by agriculture, man became dependent on **nature**, and in these early communities, men believed that the success of the harvest had magical connections with the reproductive power of women. In this way, women and nature became symbolically connected; moreover, both were necessary for the material and social needs of men. However, women and nature were also now something man needed to control in order to lose his dependence on them; man needed to assert himself as independent subject, and he achieved this through the framing of nature—and thus woman—as Other. Beauvoir claims that a central part of this shift toward control of earth-woman was the concept of property; with the ownership of land, men began to need to own women and children who could work and inherit the land.

Beauvoir claims that the notion of Other is a fundamental category of human thought, such as sun/moon, day/night, and so on. She argues that for a group to be or identify as the One—to form a sense of self—it needs the Other to define itself against. For each group there is no one permanently designated Other, except in the case of women, who are the historically fixed Other. Thus, in the relation between male and female, men are constructed as the positive norm;

they are defined against women, who are then constructed as the negative or second sex.

Here Beauvoir relies on G. W. F. Hegel's concept of the master-slave dialectic for her analysis, substituting the terms Subject and Other for master and slave. Like the Hegelian master, man is the absolute human type; like the Hegelian slave, woman is measured against this standard and is found wanting. For Beauvoir, the first moment of the development of the relations between men and women in primitive society—risk taker versus passive reproducer—is at the foundation of women's subordination. She argues that it is reproduction that makes women, if not exactly slaves, the possessors of a slave consciousness produced by their relationship with men. Thus, for her, it is ultimately reproduction that is the central hindrance to women's liberation.

This notion of a woman as constructed Other provided the framework for the most influential **second wave feminist** theorizing in the United Kingdom and the United States, such as that of Betty Friedan, Kate Millett, and Shulamith Firestone. Woman as constructed Other is also at the heart of the linguistic and cultural analyses of sexual **difference** within **French feminist** thought, such as that of **Luce Irigaray**, that began to emerge in the 1970s.

In the third part of *The Second Sex*, Beauvoir demonstrates how part of the domination of women is produced through controlling myths and images of the ideal woman. Ultimately, the ideal woman in all her different guises is the woman who sacrifices her own self for the self of the man. Beauvoir explains that the reason women do not resist this **controlling image** of the feminine ideal is they have learned to internalize it: women as well as men accept that this ideal defines woman.

In parts four to six, Beauvoir offers a detailed analysis of the life of the contemporary woman from childhood to old age. This analysis is aimed at demonstrating her famous dictum at the beginning of part four: "One is not born, but rather becomes, a woman." Her discussions of the different aspects of the social construct of femininity have been central to subsequent feminist thought on childhood, **marriage**, and **motherhood**.

In her discussion of childhood, Beauvoir shows how the internalization of femininity, and thus the acceptance and internalization of inferiority, is part of the passage to adulthood for young girls. The identification of the forms of this internalization, and the way that internalization works both to control women and to block their political awakening, were central tenets of the feminist theorizing of the 1960s and 1970s.

For Beauvoir, becoming a woman is not simply a question of age or maturity, but a more literal "becoming": a construction. Beauvoir thus sets the framework for the use of the distinction between sex and **gender** that has been pivotal for feminist thought. From the 1960s onward, feminists have argued that biological differences between the sexes are fixed, but that the psychological differences used to justify the inequality of women are not natural: they are the product of gender **socialization**. In the 1980s, the sex/gender debate shifted toward a discussion of whether the concept of woman has an **essential** meaning, and Beauvoir's claim that there is no such thing as "woman" can be seen to underpin this debate as well.

For Beauvoir, women's Otherness is further reinforced through the institutions of marriage and motherhood. She argues that marriage not only makes women economically dependent on men but also blocks their possibilities for independence. Unlike men, women cannot find self-realization that comes through work and activity; these things can only be achieved physically outside the home and psychically outside the self-sacrifice of marriage. Her analysis of motherhood is even harsher. Given that she locates the origins of women's oppression in the limitations of being able only to give life, she holds that restricting women to mother maintains this oppression. For the contemporary woman, the role of motherhood is one of self-sacrifice and self-limitation, as she becomes merely an object to fulfill the needs of the child.

Here Beauvoir sets the framework for the notion that wife and mother are roles that women play, rather than something that is required to fulfill their special nature. This notion underpinned feminist claims of the 1960s that marriage and motherhood are only part of women's lives, while frustration and a sense of meaninglessness are caused by the social restrictions that keep women bound to home and **family**. Whereas these early theorists often argued that **equality** for women could be achieved by meaningful work outside the home, Beauvoir anticipated later criticisms of this view with her claim that a career does not provide an escape for women. She argues that career women are still expected to preserve their femininity through their appearance and behavior, and that this ultimately detracts from their careers in terms of time spent both on preserving this femininity and in affirming their inferiority for their co-workers.

Beauvoir also claims that women are partly to blame for internalizing their inferior status, and are thus complicit in its maintenance; in so doing, women avoid their duty as individuals to strive for transcendence. Beauvoir argues that the reasons for this compliance are twofold: women prefer the advantages they gain from being the protected Other, and they have no sense of themselves as having a political identity or unity. Beauvoir was the first to raise this question of women's complicity in their own oppression, and it is a question that remains a controversial one for feminist theorizing.

In the final part of *The Second Sex*, Beauvoir offers her solution for the liberation of women: liberation must be collective and can only begin with economic change. For Beauvoir, women escape oppression through transcendence—an understanding of themselves as subject—achieved through productive work, intellectual activity, and socialism. The **existentialist** framework of this liberation was not adopted by mainstream feminist theorists, even though the goals of freedom, choice, and self-determination are central to the feminist project. Ultimately, with or without this framework, Beauvoir set the terms of the feminist theoretical project: the uncovering and analysis of the oppression of women; the location of its causes; and the formulation of solutions for its removal. *See also* DUALISM; SARTRE, JEAN-PAUL; SUBJECTIVITY.

SECOND WAVE FEMINISM. The term second wave feminism was first used by Marsha Lear in 1968 to describe the emergence of women's political movements in the 1960s. Second wave is now used to describe the feminist movement of the 1960s and the 1970s in both Europe and the United States. A central reason that the second wave arose in the United States was the recognition that, despite improvements in the legal and civil **rights** of women, women had not yet achieved true **equality**. This second wave feminist movement was not a unified movement; however, two major approaches can be identified: a primarily **liberal feminist** approach and a more **radical feminist** one.

The liberal approach can be seen as grounded in the theory of political liberalism, and it is typified by the National Organization for Women (NOW), which was founded in 1966 to campaign for the equal rights of women in all areas of society, such as employment, **education**, and **family**. The women's liberation movement was a more radical movement composed of a variety of connected groups. Often the members of this movement were women who had been part of other protest movements of the 1960s but who had recognized that even these movements were sexist or male dominated.

In 1968, a feminist activist movement developed in the United Kingdom that had its roots in socialism and class struggle, and thus an emphasis on employment issues such as equality in pay, child care, and the availability of **abortion**. The feminist movement in France that began in 1968 grew out of a rejection of the sexism within the student movements of that time. Like the movement in the United Kingdom, the French movement was grounded in socialist political thought.

The activist work of the second wave feminist movement is reflected in feminist philosophical work of the 1970s: for example, in work on issues within the "personal" or private realm, such as the family and abortion, as well as in discussions of rights and the notion of equality. *See also* FIRST WAVE FEMINISM; POSTFEMINISM; THIRD WAVE FEMINISM.

SELF. *See* SUBJECTIVITY.

SEPARATISM. The origins of separatist thought lie in the feminist thought of the **first wave** of feminism. **Cultural feminist** Margaret Fuller, in her 1845 work *Woman in the 19th Century*, was the first to discuss the value to women of separation from **patriarchal** culture. Fuller envisions women's self-development as not only an individual process, but as occurring within a woman-only community retired from the world. Fuller's vision was one of social reform; recent versions of separatism are now viewed as a political strategy. Separatism can mean organizing for the liberation of women apart from men, a separation from **oppressive** institutions, or a psychological break from patriarchal culture as a form of empowerment. Work within feminist philosophy has been done by Marilyn Frye, who understands separation as an activity of the exclusion of men: depriving men of the usual access they have to women. Separatism—this controlling of access—is thus an act of power for women.

SEX. During the 1960s, feminists began to distinguish sex, "male" and "female," from **gender**, "men" and "women." The sex of an individual was seen as determined by a set of fixed biological characteristics, whereas gender was seen as a set of mutable social characteristics that were the result of **socialization**. This distinction challenged **biological determinism**, the dominant **scientific** and popular view that the biological differences between the sexes determined the different social and cultural roles of men and women, as well as the relations between them.

The political success of the sex/gender distinction for the feminist movement is not under question, but more recently the distinction itself has been challenged. Some feminist philosophers argue that biological characteristics are not immutable, as they can be affected by social practices. In some cultures where there are food shortages, for example, women are often of a smaller stature than men. This would appear to be the result of the lower social value of women, as the practice in times of shortage is to give the food to men. It is also possible, moreover, that cultural ideals of desirable characteristics of women may affect the actual amount of these characteristics within a given population, as women with these characteristics may be more likely to be selected as **reproductive** partners. Some feminist philosophers also point to the fact that the way that male and female biological differences are seen is the result of social interpretation. The current notion that there are two different sexes is fairly recent. In eighteenth-century Europe, male and female were not framed as opposites; rather, women were understood as inferior or less-developed versions of men.

The notion that there are two distinct sexes, and only two, is also being challenged from two different positions: one comes from the existence of intersexed persons; one draws on the work of **Michel Foucault** on sex. The existence of intersexed persons raises the question of whether there are only two sexes. In fact, five sexes can be identified: male, female, and three "intersex" groups who have both male and female characteristics. The current medical practice is for a particular sex to be surgically assigned to an individual from an intersex group, and indeed this is considered a medical imperative. Philosophers have questioned what underlies this pressing and unquestioned need for sex assignment. They argue that the existence of an intersexed individual challenges the assumption that there are only two sexes, an assumption that is part of our ordering of reality, and thus our social system.

For Foucault, sex functions as a way to artificially group biological and behavioral elements. Thus sex is the product of material discursive practices that construct individuals; it is enacted on the **body**. Some feminist philosophers have extended this analysis; they claim that the concept that the body is some natural, fixed structure is dangerous, as this underpins the assumptions about the natural, fixed structure of sex difference that justify and form the domination of women. Moreover, the subsequent naturalness of the existence of two oppositional unitary sexes, and thus the assumption of a **sexual** attraction between complementary opposites, supports the **heterosexist** social system. *See also* FEMININITY; FRENCH FEMINISM; MASCULINITY.

SEX COMPLEMENTARITY (SEX COMPLEMENTARIANISM). Also known as natural complement theory, **sex** complementarity is a theory about the natures of the two sexes and the relations between them. The theory developed in the eighteenth century and was the foundation of dominant philosophical views during that time of the nature and social roles of the sexes. The theory states, in essence, that the biological differences between the sexes produce psychological, intellectual, and moral differences, and that these various differences define the appropriate behavior and roles for men and women. Most importantly, the natures of the two sexes, and their attendant behaviors and roles, are held to be natural complements of each other. Each nature actually needs the other to complete itself; this then entails that **heterosexual** relationships are seen as both normal and beneficial for humans of both sexes.

The theory of the complementary natures of the sexes need not carry with it the automatic assumption that one sex is inferior to the other, and many thinkers, pro-feminist and non-feminist alike, held that it offered an **equality** between the sexes. Feminist philosophers, however, argue that this is unlikely, as the "different" characteristics of women are their historically "inferior" characteristics, such as **emotionality**. *See also* HILDEGARD OF BINGEN; KANT, IMMANUEL; ROUSSEAU, JEAN-JACQUES.

SEX WORK. *See* PORNOGRAPHY; PROSTITUTION.

SEXUAL HARASSMENT. What constitutes harassment covers a wide range of actions, from jokes to physical assault. Harassment is not restricted to sexist behavior; it also includes, among other things, **racist** and **heterosexist** behaviors. The focus of analyses of harassment is usually on behaviors in the workplace but also includes, for instance, the use of American Indian names and images for sports teams in the United States. Feminist philosophers have argued that any analysis of sexual harassment requires the recognition of the way that, for example, racism and classism intersect with sexism. Thus black women, for instance, can be harassed because of their membership in this specific group (not simply because they are women); in addition, membership in a marginalized group means that these women's complaints are less likely to be heard.

Feminist philosophers have focused on explaining how exactly sexual harassment constitutes **sex** discrimination, arguing that sexual harassment is about men using their social and economic power to dominate women in a particular situation: it is not about **sexual** attraction. Moreover, it is not just one individual dominating another; rather, the crucial harm of sexual harassment is the harm that it causes women as a group. This is because unwanted sexual attention reinforces perceptions of women as sex objects or as subordinates more generally. *See also* POLITICAL AND SOCIAL PHILOSOPHY.

SEXUALITY. For feminist philosophers, sexuality covers sexual identity, desire, and **experience**. Feminist philosophical work on sexuality examines the realities of women's experiences, a rejection of the ideology of human sexuality, and an analysis of the **oppressive** nature of this ideology. This work reflects a variety of approaches that come from **radical feminist** thought, **analytic** philosophy, and **post-modern** philosophy. All of these approaches have, as part of their foundations, the recognition that Western philosophers have seen human sexuality as dangerous or threatening. Contemporary non-feminist philosophers tend to avoid discussions of sexuality; when the subject is discussed by non-feminists, it tends to be grounded in the assumption that **heterosexuality** is the norm.

Radical feminism holds that much of the oppression experienced by women stems from male control of female **reproduction** and sexuality. There are culturally approved definitions of both male and female sexuality, but only the definition of the latter has been seen as a form of oppression; this is because, within **patriarchal** society, female sexuality is supposed to be directed solely toward the pleasure of men. Thus one way to resist patriarchy is for women to control and explore their own sexuality and sexual pleasure. For some radical feminists, lesbianism is the model for this control. Other radical feminists have argued that women's sexual liberation, and its necessary accompaniment of improved contraceptive measures, ultimately benefits men, not women.

Analytic feminists tend to focus on **logical** and linguistic analyses of sexual desire and sexual practices, such as **prostitution**. Those **lesbian philosophers** who are influenced by the analytic approach argue that the definition of sexual activity as heterosexual intercourse between a dominant male and a passive female means that gay and lesbian sexualities cannot be accounted for: there is no **language** to describe their sexuality.

The influence of postmodern philosophy on analytic analysis is increasing, and the postmodern philosophical analysis of sexuality has been the dominant approach in Western philosophy since the 1990s. Postmodern feminist philosophers typically draw on **Michel Foucault**'s work on the history of sexuality to claim that sexuality is not innate; rather, definitions of sexuality are political creations and, as such, are the objects of knowledge and control. **Judith Butler** takes this approach, holding that the construction of men and women in opposition to each other supports the system of heterosexuality, because this construction defines sexual desire as a desire between opposites.

The work of **Luce Irigaray**, the **French feminist**, has also had an influence on discourse on women's sexuality, in particular for the way she offers new, non-patriarchal ways of writing this discourse. Irigaray critiques the clitoral/vaginal conception of female sexuality as a phallocentric conceptualization. Woman's sexuality has been represented as either vaginal, a passive receptacle for a penis, or clitoral, the activity of a little penis. Thus female sexuality does not have an existence, as it has no cultural representation. Irigaray does not offer an alternative conception of female sexuality—of what this sexuality is in reality—as this replays the maleness of the concept that sexuality is one thing. She holds, instead, that female sexuality is unstructured, fluid, and multiple. This is expressed through Irigaray's counter-representation of female sexuality using the metaphor of the "two lips" of women's genitals: they are both one and two.

Most of the work on female sexuality has been done by white Western feminists. Feminists from non-Western cultures who discuss the issue of female sexuality tend to see the more theoretical interests of Western feminists as lacking relevance to the realities of women's lives. They focus, instead, on the way that many sexual practices, such as genital surgery, are actually dangerous for women. For Western feminists of color, discussion of the sexuality of non-white women requires an understanding of a different set of cultural stereotypes; for example, both men and women of color, black people in particular, are seen within the dominant white culture as hypersexual. This image projects the problematic element of the animal nature, and thus the sexual nature, of humans onto people of color; in this way, it serves to reinforce assumptions of white superiority. *See also* BODY: GENDER; SEX.

SHIVA, VANDANA (1952–). The Indian physicist and **ecofeminist** activist Vandana Shiva can be credited with the first successful development of a specifically **Indian feminist philosophy**. As an ecofeminist, Shiva grounds her philosophy on a theoretical analysis of the traditional connections of women and **nature**, and the way that these connections play out in practice within Indian women's grassroots movements for the protection of the environment. Her best-known book is *Staying Alive: Women, Ecology, and Development* (1998).

The central foundation for Shiva's philosophy is the **feminine** principle of *prakriti*, and respect for this principle. These are part of written philosophy and oral spiritual traditions. *Prakriti* is part of the ontological framework of traditional Hindu thought in which the individual soul (*atman*) and the divine spirit (*brahman*) are not separate but unified. *Prakriti* is conceived of as an energy that pervades all matter, both human and non-human. It is a living, conscious energy that, because of this monist ontology, is part of the material as well as the spiritual world. Thus it is not a principle of opposites but of both difference and oneness.

Even though *prakriti* is understood as feminine, it does not contain the characteristics traditionally associated with women and the feminine. It is an active, not passive, principle. It is not simply about the power of female **reproduction**, which many feminists regard as a reductionist view of women, but about production: it is a creative principle. Respect for this principle involves a recognition that both nature and humans have consciousness. Thus nature is not an inanimate object that needs technological development in order to be fully productive; it is not to be used solely as a resource for humans.

An understanding of this ontology is interconnected with a need for political change, a shift in ethical thinking, and the development of a new (feminine) **epistemology**. For Shiva, the imposition of Western capitalist economic values is grounded in a separation of humans from nature; indeed, this separation is fundamental to this system's way of seeing nature as nothing more than a resource, one that can have value only once it has been subject to capitalist development.

Shiva calls this "maldevelopment," and argues that it is the direct cause of environmental destruction as well as the socio-economic inequalities between those who are part of the process of production and those who are not. Environmental destruction and the reconception of work as capitalist production are especially problematic for women, as their work has traditionally been work on the land. Women's connection to nature is one of cooperation with a source of life that is expressed in practice: for example, through the replanting of trees that can be used for firewood. Women's traditional use of nature is, therefore, devalued, and their use of the land is dismissed because it is not real "production": it does not contribute to the gross national product.

Shiva also argues that the technology/nature dichotomy underpins the Western dichotomy of development/backwardness, a conceptual framework that allows only two opposing alternatives for the society and economy of India. Even though Shiva is not denying the real existence of material poverty, she claims that this **dualist** way of thinking results in the labeling of a subsistence lifestyle—one that satisfies human needs without recourse to consumer goods—as a life of poverty.

In contrast, respect for the feminine principle leads to the revaluing of a subsistence lifestyle. This is both a political and an ethical change in thinking and acting. In terms of political change Shiva argues, for example, that humans must reject the consumerist culture and economy, and recognize that natural resources must be understood as common goods, not the private property of a few. In order to achieve such sweeping changes, women and men need to cultivate traditional—feminine—ways of moral thinking about our relationship with nature. In this way, the importance of women's roles in sustaining life will be made visible, and their knowledge of the activities needed for sustainability will be epistemically necessary. This is beneficial for women as well as the environment, as it will also raise women's social status. This change in thinking and its practical results are not simply for the liberation of women; Shiva holds that both **sexes** will be freed as humans, in the sense that they will have returned to their rightful place in nature. *See also* DUAL SYSTEMS THEORY; FEMININE ETHICS; FEMINIST ETHICS.

SOCIAL CONTRACT. *See* CONTRACTARIANISM.

SOCIAL PHILOSOPHY. *See* POLITICAL AND SOCIAL PHILOSOPHY.

SOCIALIST FEMINISM. The **political philosophy** of socialist feminism began in the 1970s and shares much with both **radical** and **Marxist feminist** thought. Some philosophers consider it an extension of one of these theories, rather than a distinct political philosophy, but socialist philosophers attribute that impression to the fact that socialist feminist political philosophy is still in the process of development. Moreover, they argue that work thus far in socialist feminism is partially grounded in a critique of the theoretical and practical inadequacies of radical and Marxist explanations of the **oppression** of women. Thus, they argue, socialist feminism is not an extension of these other forms of political feminism, but rather a new theory developed to addresses the inadequacies of earlier theories. On the whole, the development of a socialist feminism that is positioned as distinct from Marxist feminism has tended to remain confined to the United States.

Socialist feminism takes from radical feminism the understanding that there is a political need to address women's oppression in the private sphere. However, socialist feminists employ a historical materialist approach to analyzing this oppression, rejecting the radical feminist view of the **universality** across culture and time of the forms that this oppression takes. Socialist feminism shares with Marxist feminism the view that **human nature** is not fixed; rather, it is the creation of a particular set of historical social circumstances. Socialist feminists, however, do not share the Marxist view that class is the sole source of women's subordination, nor do they accept the radical feminist claim that male domination is the only source of this subordination. They analyze, instead, the interconnection of the systems of class and **gender**. For socialist feminists, radical feminism fails to recognize that the oppression of women is not just the product of male dominance, while Marxist feminism fails to recognize the import of women's labor in the private sphere. Socialist feminism was criticized by feminists of color in the 1980s for the failure to recognize **race** as another system of domination. More recent socialist theorizing has moved toward the understanding that sexism and capitalism cannot be separated from racism, imperialism, and **heterosexism**, and that to dismantle one system requires dismantling them all.

As with other feminist theories, no one position defines socialist feminism; however, there is a shared goal of demonstrating the connections of the sexual **division of labor** with the domination of women. One connection that is often the subject of analysis is the construction of gendered characteristics through the organization of the division of labor in child-rearing, although socialist feminists do not claim that these characteristics are universal. **Mothers** are usually the primary caretakers in the traditional **family**, and this social practice serves both to impose a rigid binary distinction between the

sexes and to identify **femininity** with characteristics, such as nurturing, as well as with a lower social status.

The sexual division of labor in the private sphere reinforces male dominance over individual women, and it also serves to free men as a group to spend more time earning money. In contrast, the division of labor is an economic disadvantage for women. It translates into the public sphere in the way that their paid work often involves caring and serving; moreover, such work is seen as the province of women. In its turn, this may encourage women to use their **sexuality** to get **married** and have children: to have economic advancement and security. Thus, in a socialist feminist analysis, **reproduction**, child-rearing, and sexuality can be understood in economic terms.

Socialist feminists advocate dismantling the economic and power differences between men and women that rest on the division of labor. They also target the root of these differences, calling for the rejection of the organization of social life into public and private spheres. A primary element of this prescription includes the reproductive freedom of women. This can mean economic freedom through systems of state support for child-rearing, and women's control over their own **bodies** through easy access to contraception and **abortion**. One concern for socialist feminists is that these changes are primarily for the privileged women of industrialized "developed" nations; the economic freedom they produce may be enhanced by the exploitation of both women and men from less-developed nations as workers for the production of cheap commodities. *See also* ALIENATION; PUBLIC/PRIVATE DISTINCTION.

SOCIALIZATION. The standard account of the phenomenon of socialization is that the apparent psychological and intellectual differences between the **sexes** is the result of a social conditioning that begins at birth; thus **gender** roles and characteristics are not fixed or the product of biology. In order to demonstrate this, **feminist theorists** have typically pointed to the fact that these characteristics are not **universal** across cultures or through history. The first feminist philosopher to identify this phenomenon was **Mary Wollstonecraft**, who argued that the social conditioning of her eighteenth-century contemporaries to be compliant and pleasing was specifically designed to benefit men. The first in-depth examination of the phenomenon was Juliet Mitchell's *Women: The Longest Revolution* (1966).

The concept of socialization is premised on the distinction between sex and gender. With the challenges to this distinction in the 1980s, the standard concept of socialization is no longer prominent in feminist philosophical discussions, having given way to more complex accounts of the relation between society and gender. *See also* BIOLOGICAL DETERMINISM; ESSENTIALISM.

SOCIETY FOR WOMEN IN PHILOSOPHY (SWIP). SWIP is a professional society with the goal of promoting and supporting women in philosophy. There are branches of the society in the United States, United Kingdom (SWIP [UK]), and Canada (CSWIP).

SOCIETY FOR WOMEN'S ADVANCEMENT IN PHILOSOPHY (SWAP). SWAP is a graduate student organization in the United States that was formed to support women graduate students in philosophy.

SOCRATES. *See* PLATO.

SOMATOPHOBIA. Philosopher Elizabeth Spelman coined the term somatophobia to describe the rejection of the importance of—or even the disgust at—the **body** that is prevalent throughout the Western philosophical tradition. The accompanying view within this tradition is that the **mind**, and its capacity for **reason**, is superior to the body, and may even require transcendence from the body. The historical and cultural association of women with the body has led to the implicit or explicit exclusion of women from the philosophical project, understood as a project of the search through reason for truth and knowledge.

Some feminist philosophers argue that somatophobia plays out covertly in present-day feminist theory, particularly in **liberal feminism**. The identification of women's liberation with the freedom and opportunity to develop mentally leads to an accompanying neglect of the physical or bodily aspects of women's lives. Also neglected is the reality that different bodies, for example, through a **disability**, can dictate the amount of freedom and opportunity **experienced** by different women. *See also* DUALISM.

SOPHIA [pseud.] (fl. 1739). The 1739 tract *Woman Not Inferior to Man or, A Short and Modest Vindication of the Natural Right of the Fair Sex to a Perfect Equality of Power, Dignity, and Esteem*, written under the pseudonym "Sophia, a Person of Quality," is an early English argument for female **equality**. Some commentators have claimed that it was influenced by **François Poullain de la Barre**'s 1673 work *On the Equality of the Two Sexes: A Physical and Moral Discourse Which Shows the Importance of Overcoming Prejudice*.

The unidentified Sophia makes use of Enlightenment discourse of the superiority of **reason** over passion to critique the arguments for the inferiority of women made by male Enlightenment philosophers. Sophia points out that, as human beings, women possess reason just like men. Moreover, she says, men cannot lay claim to a superior reason for they are so controlled by their own passions that there is nothing in their behavior that can justify such a claim. Sophia further states that the arguments offered by men for women's inferiority are rooted in male prejudice and self-interest. She appeals, instead, to what she calls "rectified reason" as an **impartial** judge of the true nature of the **sexes**. Sophia claims that any difference between the intelligence or reason of the sexes can be traced to the inferior **education** of women. Her arguments are not just theoretical; they also have practical corollaries. She claims that, once women are properly educated, they will be capable of taking part in government and even holding some military roles.

SPINOZA, BENEDICT (BARUCH) DE. *See* AUSTRALIA, FEMINIST PHILOSOPHY IN.

STANDPOINT THEORY. *See* EPISTEMOLOGY.

STEREOTYPES. *See* CONTROLLING IMAGES.

SUBJECTIVITY. The traditional philosophical concept of self is a contentious one for feminist philosophy. This concept has its roots in **René Descartes**'s notion of the individual knowing "I," an individual who is a thinking thing. It is through the use of its **reason** that this conceptually disembodied, solitary self attains knowledge of the world. During the Enlightenment, this self was conceptualized as an **autonomous**, self-determining agent, a reasoning self who was usually disembedded and disembodied. This self could not only attain knowledge but had the capacity for its individual self-fulfillment. Moreover, as each self was unsituated, and characterized only by a capacity for reason, these selves were fundamentally **equal**.

This notion of a **gender**-neutral, core identity has been appealing for some feminist philosophers. A denial of selfhood to women has traditionally provided justification for their social and philosophical exclusion. Thus it has been argued by some feminist philosophers that women's equality can be achieved through claiming this self and its attendant benefits and characteristics.

However, this approach may be in tension with the feminist philosophical enterprise. Part of this enterprise is to examine traditional philosophy for its male bias. At its core, the Western philosophical concept of the autonomous, **individualist**, unsituated self may be nothing more than the reflection of the **experience** of privileged, white Western males. As a result, some feminist philosophers have claimed that the notion of the self must be revised to become a situated self: one that is gendered, **embodied**, and formed through its relations, both positive and negative, with others. Ultimately, however, a complete rejection of some notion of a core self may be in tension with feminist goals, for it would seem that there needs to be a bearer of **rights**, a recipient of **justice**, and a knower who can uncover truths behind the **patriarchal** framework of reality.

Postmodern feminist philosophers argue that only a complete rejection of the self can disentangle contemporary intellectual thought from the failures of Enlightenment thought. They hold that the self is not the source of its determination; the self is, instead, the product of discursive practices. In this view, the term "subject" is more appropriate, as the whole notion of self is being rejected. However, the postmodern subject does not function as a replacement concept for the single model of the self; rather, there is a multiplicity of subjects. This rejection entails a rejection of a gender identity, an innate **sexuality**, and the conception of the **body** as some kind of "natural" fixed structure. *See also* EPISTEMOLOGY; PHILOSOPHY OF MIND.

– T –

TAYLOR MILL, HARRIET (1807–1858). English philosopher Harriet Taylor began a lifelong friendship with **John Stuart Mill** when they were both in their twenties; they married in 1851, two years after the death of her first husband, John Taylor.

Taylor began writing philosophy in 1830. Sometime during 1831 or 1832, Taylor and Mill wrote essays for each other on **marriage** and divorce. Taylor took a more radical stance than Mill in her untitled essay on marriage, not only arguing that women should be given civil and political **equality**, but claiming that there should be no laws at all related to marriage. Once this was achieved, she argued, women would be the one responsible for the children, and thus, by the same token, women would decide how many children to have, as this would no longer be a way of binding her husband to her. As Taylor only mentions briefly the necessary corollary of the employment of women in this early essay, it is not clear whether she is referring just to divorced women or whether she includes married women as well. She states that in order to be in a position to support their children, women would need to be both properly **educated** and free to take up any occupation they wanted. To deny all of this to women is essentially to require them "to barter person for bread."

In the past there has been some dispute about the authorship of the 1851 work *The Enfranchisement of Women*, but it is now generally agreed that Taylor—not John Stuart Mill—was the author. This is based on both the evidence of correspondence between the two philosophers and the differences in the content of these works. The overall thrust of *The Enfranchisement* is the political, civil, and social equality of women. A central point of divergence between *The Enfranchisement* and Mill's 1869 work *The Subjection of Women* is the claim that married women should continue to work outside the home after marriage as a way of ensuring both their independence and equality within that marriage, as well as their general social equality.

While Taylor is now recognized as a philosopher in her own right, her influence on Mill's work is still unresolved. Mill claimed that *The Principles of Political Economy* (1848) and *On Liberty* (1859) were collaborative efforts with Taylor. Some argue that, because these two works were published naming Mill as the sole author, this claim was essentially a courtesy for her editorial work. For others, the fact that Taylor is not credited with authorship is seen as a casualty of social conventions that kept women from the public sphere of publishing and accorded them little intellectual authority.

THEOLOGY. *See* RELIGION, PHILOSOPHY OF.

THIRD WAVE FEMINISM. Third wave feminism is sometimes termed postfeminism, but this term is contested by some self-defined third wave feminists because of its use to describe the conservative reaction to **second wave** feminism that began in the mid-1980s. Third wave feminism is an activist movement mainly in the United States. It can be traced back to the 1980s and is still in its infancy. While its proponents continue to aim for the liberation of women, they do not see this as a separate task from the liberation of other subordinate groups. In terms of theory, this third wave of feminism draws on the work of Third World feminists and feminists of color that has emphasized the differences in women's **experiences** of **oppression** due to **race**, class, nationality, and so forth. Third wave feminism is inclusive; it is a coalition politics formed from a diverse community. For these reasons, third wave feminism resists easy definition; it is a collective voice, not a single unified voice. *See also* FIRST WAVE FEMINISM.

TRANSSEXUALITY. *See* GENDER; SEX.

– U –

UNIVERSALISM. The term universalism has two types of use within feminist philosophy. The first use of the term is sometimes called "**metaphysical** feminism" and is part of feminist thought, usually **radical feminism**, more generally. It is the claim that all women have something fundamentally in common—biological, psychological, and/or social—that is the same across culture and history. The term universalism is sometimes used interchangeably with the term **essentialism**, but universalism does not necessarily entail the further claim of essentialism that these shared characteristics are an innate, fixed part of female nature. Universalist claims often formed an important part of early feminist arguments; however, since the 1980s, universalism has been criticized for marginalizing, or making invisible, differences (such as **race** and class) among women.

Within feminist philosophy, the second use of the term universalism has a more specific use. Feminist philosophers have questioned both the notion of a universal **human nature** and the notion of universality as a necessary characteristic of knowledge claims and moral judgments. In the former case, even if they accept that there is a universal human nature, some feminist philosophers have criticized traditional philosophical characterizations of human nature as **gender** biased; this is because these characterizations reflect traits and ideals that are culturally associated with "maleness."

While the belief that universality is a necessary component of knowledge claims and moral judgments has a long philosophical history, current understanding of its importance owes much to Enlightenment thought. **Reason**, the characteristic of humans, leads (alone or with the senses) to the acquisition of universal knowledge and a correct understanding of morality. However, this universal rational agreement is attained, in part, through an abstraction from the particulars of situated reality.

For these reasons, some feminist philosophers have charged that the characteristic of universality is grounded in the assumption of the knowing self as disembodied and disembedded, thus ignoring the way that such things as **experience** and the **body** can affect both access to knowledge and the conceptualization of morality. For some feminist philosophers, this self is not gender neutral, as it only reflects male experience. For others, the actual universal agreements generated by these supposedly abstract selves only reflect the particular experience or perspective of dominant social groups. Ultimately these criticisms mean that, at best, the use of the concept of universalism is approached with caution by most feminist philosophers. *See also* EPISTEMOLOGY; IMPARTIALITY; INDIVIDUALISM, ABSTRACT; OBJECTIVITY; RELATIVISM; SUBJECTIVITY.

UTILITARIANISM. *See* MILL, JOHN STUART; WHEELER, ANNA DOYLE.

– V –

VALUE HIERARCHICAL THINKING. In a similar way to normative **dualism**, value hierarchical thinking is a key feature in the conceptual frameworks that justify the **oppression** of women and other groups. Value hierarchical thinking frames the difference or diversity between groups, for example, the **sexes**, as a difference of value organized vertically: lower value (women) and higher value (men). This way of organizing the world then functions to sustain oppressive conceptual frameworks, such as sexism. In itself, hierarchical thinking, and even value hierarchical thinking in certain contexts, may not be problematic. For example, it is not problematic to claim that particular species are better at adapting to changes in their environment than others. However, one problem is that the perceived superiority of one group over another sanctions the subordination of the inferior group. Moreover, oppressive social systems dictate the identification of the groups that are to be organized and valued hierarchically.

VALUE NEUTRALITY. Feminist philosophers have begun to question the attainability—and the desirability—of the ideal of value neutrality for philosophical and **scientific** investigation, description, and explanation. The formalization of this ideal is often seen as rooted in the Cartesian project, with this project's development of the concept of a disembodied and disembedded knower attaining and evaluating knowledge through use of her or his **reason**. Freed from their values, **emotions**, and particular social contexts, knowers are fundamentally the same. A rigid dichotomy is thus formed between **objective** facts and subjective values. This fact/value distinction has been central to twentieth-century Anglo-American **analytic** philosophy, in particular to ethical theorizing.

Feminist philosophers argue that, even though the goal of value neutrality can eliminate the particular values of individuals engaged in scientific and philosophical investigation, what are taken as the facts generated by this investigation often reflect general social values. These general values underpin the choices of research subjects and the hypotheses to be tested. Feminist philosophers argue that this is not just a question of theoretical adequacy, but that scientific and philosophical theories have reflected male-biased cultural assumptions about **human nature** and **sex** difference. Thus the knowledge generated by these theories has served to reinforce the subordination of women. Moreover, some feminist philosophers have also maintained that the grounding of the ideal itself is male biased, as it reflects the male **experience** of the world, which has traditionally been unrestricted by the concrete demands of home and **family**.

A typical approach to this problem, offered by Anglo-American analytic feminist philosophers, has been to hold that the situatedness of knowers is of **epistemic** significance, and to argue that one of the requirements of feminist philosophy is that it must be consciously value laden in order to achieve the goal of political change. *See also* DESCARTES, RENÉ; FEMINIST ETHICS; LANGUAGE, PHILOSOPHY OF.

VEGETARIANISM. Within mainstream philosophy, vegetarianism is part of the subject field of **animal ethics**. In the case of feminist vegetarianism, it is not just an ethical issue, but one that is informed by **gender** politics. Even as early as the nineteenth century, writers and activists were linking women and vegetarianism. Based on the fact that meat eating was historically associated with power/wealth and **masculinity**, early feminist arguments drew connections between vegetarianism and gentleness in women versus meat eating and dominance in men. **Charlotte Perkins Gilman**'s 1915 novel *Herland*, which depicts a utopian community of women, was the first work to connect vegetarianism explicitly with the political movements of feminism and pacifism. This vegetarianism-feminism-pacifism connection was brought to the fore for some feminists during World War I, when violence and **war** became a politically charged reality. The killing of humans was seen as an outgrowth of the killing of animals, while the presence of war was seen as an outgrowth of **patriarchy**.

The central arguments of current feminist philosophers have not changed much from those of the nineteenth and early twentieth centuries, although their work offers more explicitly politicized and detailed analyses of feminist vegetarianism. In particular, feminist philosophers have examined the ways that meat eating both supports and is supported by patriarchal culture, how violence against women reflects violence against animals, and how women are treated, particularly in **pornography**, as "meat." *See also* ECOFEMINISM.

VINDICATION OF THE RIGHTS OF WOMAN, **A. Mary Woll-stonecraft**'s 1792 polemical treatise *A Vindication of the Rights of Woman* is usually seen as the first sustained philosophical argument for the **equality** of women. An early **liberal feminist**, Wollstonecraft founded her demand for the **rights** of women on her theories of **human nature** and morality.

Wollstonecraft wrote *A Vindication of the Rights of Woman* at a time when economically privileged women were undereducated and discouraged from developing their rational capacities. She recognized that the resulting mental and moral inferiority of these women was not due to a supposed female nature. She claimed, instead, that their rationality and morality had been weakened by bad or no **education** as well as by a social environment that groomed them to play the role of pleasing mistress, not responsible wife or **mother**. Rather than being trained to develop their capacities for **reason**, these women were encouraged to develop an ultra-refined **emotionality** that was identified with **femininity**. Wollstonecraft supports her claim that the **sex** differences observed in females are the result of social conditioning and education by pointing to the "feminine" character of males in the upper ranks of the military. These military men pay particular attention to their dress and behavior and live a life dedicated to pleasing others through their gallantry and social accomplishments.

Wollstonecraft rejects the notion that the sexes have different natures that require different courses of education and different standards of social behavior. She holds, instead, that there is a **universal** human nature, with the distinguishing characteristic of reason. It is because of reason that humans, unlike animals, have the capacity for the development of virtue. Given this supposition, Wollstonecraft argues that women—due to their social conditioning and lack of education—were being denied their human rights to develop their innate capacities for reason and virtue. Moreover, because Wollstonecraft also held that the development of reason and virtue forms the basis of society itself, she claimed that women were also being denied their rights to become contributing members of society. Wollstonecraft's emphasis on reason as the defining characteristic of human beings has led some current feminist philosophers to question whether she devalued, or even rejected, the emotions: the elements of human life that have traditionally been associated with women or the feminine.

There are some problematic classist elements in Wollstonecraft's call for the equality of women. She takes it as understood that women, once liberated, will still require household servants to assist them, so that they can fulfill properly their roles as mother, wife, and citizen. Thus it would appear that she is only interested in the liberation of women of the middle classes. *See also* ROUSSEAU, JEAN-JACQUES; SOCIALIZATION.

VIOLENCE. *See* WAR AND PEACE.

– W –

WAR AND PEACE. There has not been much feminist work on the traditional philosophical questions associated with war, such as "just war" theory. The one notable exception from the **history of philosophy** is **Christine de Pizan**, who wrote on military ethics in *The Book of Feats of Arms and Chivalry* (*Le Livre des Fais d'Armes et de Chevalerie*). This work covers a variety of topics beyond the just war, including a discussion of the ideal military commander. Aimed at military men, rather than theorists, the book was intended to encourage and establish appropriate behavior in the relations between commanders and soldiers and between warring countries.

Contemporary feminist philosophers have typically criticized the standard approach to discussions of war: just war theory. Just war theory has been criticized because it is overly abstract, because it fails to recognize that war involves individual humans and concrete harms, and because an emphasis on **justice** and **rights** serves to overshadow the needs and interests of those affected by war. Underlying these criticisms is the more general criticism of the foundational assumption of just war theory: the assumption that war is ultimately necessary. There have been very few attempts by feminist philosophers to offer an alternative to just war theory. Typically these attempts have aimed to modify the theory in relation to how it would actually be practiced.

Feminist philosophers have not limited their discussions to the violence of **war**; they have also focused on the concept and practice of peace. In these discussions, peace is not understood as simply a state of non-war. Discussions of peace range from analyses of the abuse of one individual by another to the violence of social injustice and environmental damage. Moreover, given that violence of all kinds often affects disempowered groups the most, the central feminist goal of social justice would appear to incorporate a goal of peace. In addition, feminist philosophers tend to focus on analyzing such things as the contexts in which war takes place, the specific concrete elements of war, and the symbolic or cultural connection between war and **masculinity**. The latter connection is played out in a variety of ways, such as through the prizing of male aggression, through the depiction of men as protectors and women as victims in need of saving, through images of **feminine** loyalty, and through female roles within wartime as caretakers.

This connection can also serve to disguise the fact that war does have a specific effect on women as women; military spending, for example, can take away funding from social welfare programs. Some feminist philosophers argue that, as historically and culturally there are connections between militarism and citizenship, the connection between militarism and masculinity needs to be ruptured through the **equal** inclusion of women in the military; this way women can achieve full political agency. Others wish to maintain this connection in some way and typically argue for the need to revalue and reframe the "feminine" side—not as mere passivity—but as a part of active political peace-making or non-violent resistance.

One major area of interest is the analysis of the ethical and political thinking that lies behind women's non-violent peace movements, as well as the reasons for the success of these movements. There are concerns, however, that these analyses may be a double-edged sword. They may invoke the traditional images of women as peace-makers or as somehow more connected to peaceful behavior. One criticism of this notion of women as non-violent carers is that it reinforces questionable traditional female roles and characteristics; it also ignores the fact that women have contributed to violence and war, typically through caring for those involved in the fighting.

WHEELER, ANNA DOYLE (1785–1848). Irish philosopher and activist Anna Doyle was born in County Tipperary, Ireland, to an Anglican family. Married at fifteen to Frances Massey Wheeler, she left her husband in 1812, taking their two children with her. Wheeler then spent much of her life moving between England, Ireland, and France. She was part of the socialist circles in France and England of that time, and she wanted to combine the socialist philosophies of Charles Fourier, Robert Owen, and Henri de Saint-Simon. Wheeler was also connected to the English Utilitarians, in particular Jeremy Bentham.

Wheeler achieved recognition as a speaker on women's **rights**, but she is best known for the work she co-authored with William Thompson: *The Appeal of One Half the Human Race, Women, Against the Pretensions of the Other Half, Men to Restrain Them in Political and Thence in Civil and Domestic Slavery* (1825). The distinctive contribution of *The Appeal* to feminist philosophy, as well to as the women's movement, lies in the fact that it was the first sustained argument for women's suffrage.

The Appeal was written as a response to James Mill's *Encyclopedia Britannica* entry on government. In this entry, Mill claims that political rights could be denied to women because their interests were "covered" (coverture) by those of their husbands or fathers. Wheeler and Thomson see this as conflicting with the moral principle of utility. They understand the utilitarian goal of the overall greatest happiness in terms of the collective happiness of each individual in society, rather than the happiness of some people being subsumed under a mythical "public good." Wheeler and Thompson argue that, in order to achieve the greatest happiness of the greatest number, women must be given **equal** political and civil rights with men. They make it clear that they are not asking whether giving political rights to women would lead to the happiness of men; rather, they claim that, as women constitute half of the human race, women's happiness deserves consideration in itself.

WITTGENSTEIN, LUDWIG JOSEF JOHANN (1889–1951). Philosopher Ludwig Wittgenstein was born in Vienna, Austria. He produced his first major work, the *Tractatus Logico-Philosophicus*, in 1921. In 1929, he went to Cambridge, England, to teach; his writing from this period culminated in his other major book, *Philosophical Investigations* (published posthumously in 1953). In essence, Wittgenstein argues in this work that there is no "thing"—either in objective space or inside the mind—that gives words their meaning. **Language** is not one thing but a collection of different activities or practices, which he terms "language games." This does not commit him to the view that the meanings of words are radically unfixed or arbitrary. Language games cannot be examined in isolation from what he calls their "forms of life": our interactions, the human world, and so forth. It is only within these "forms of life" that we can make judgments about the correct or incorrect use of language, for meaning comes from the agreement in judgments and use within the linguistic community itself.

At present, there is philosophical work on Ludwig Wittgenstein that has feminist implications, and feminist work that has Wittgensteinian influences, but there is little work explicitly exploring the potential of connections between Wittgenstein's philosophy and feminist philosophy. This would seem to be due to a fundamental tension between Wittgensteinian philosophy and **feminist theorizing**. Whereas Wittgenstein held that agreement in judgments and shared forms of life provide the background for intelligibility (and thus cannot be challenged as a whole), feminist philosophers aim to challenge what we take for granted, arguing that the world that frames our understandings and actions is problematically **androcentric**.

The two approaches, however, do share significant common ground: a questioning of the traditional philosophical enterprise itself. Philosophers of both types wish to interrogate why certain questions have been deemed the central questions of philosophy, why these questions have been framed only in certain ways, and why only certain methods are considered philosophically appropriate for doing philosophy. Where feminist philosophers and Wittgensteinian philosophers differ, however, is that the questioning by the former of the traditional philosophical enterprise is directed toward uncovering the way that **gender** plays out in and constructs this enterprise.

Thus far, the few feminist investigations of Wittgenstein's philosophy break down into two basic categories: those that explore Wittgenstein in relation to the development of feminist theorizing itself, and those that utilize his work to answer specific problems within that theorizing. The first has been the predominant category. One of its central elements is the examination of the shared desire to reject

epistemologies that are **objectivist** and realist **metaphysics**, albeit for differing reasons. It has been acknowledged by feminist philosophers that this kind of challenge to the traditional epistemology and metaphysics is potentially dangerous, as it can lead to **relativist** claims about truth and knowledge. Such relativism has been seen as problematic, as it would appear that it cannot offer any firm ground for either the theoretical or the practical component of the feminist philosophical project. Wittgenstein's work has been seen to offer a third way of grounding truth and knowledge that provides an alternative to the objectivism-relativism dichotomy. *See also* CANON, CRITIQUE OF.

WOLLSTONECRAFT, MARY (1759–1797). The early English **liberal feminist** Mary Wollstonecraft is known for her 1792 work *A Vindication of the Rights of Woman*. Wollstonecraft spent her early adult years working variously as a companion, a governess, and a teacher at a day school that she established in 1783. After the failure of the school, one of Wollstonecraft's friends suggested that she support herself financially through writing. Her first published work was *Thoughts on the Education of Daughters: with Reflections on Female Conduct, in the More Important Duties of Life* (1787). Though the content of this work appears little different from other female conduct books of this period, it is still possible to see the presence of many of the subjects that became part of her later feminist works: for example, her discussion of the fate of women who are left without money or an **education**. Strictly speaking, *A Vindication of the Rights of Woman* is Wollstonecraft's only work of feminist philosophy. Her two other feminist works, the autobiographical *Mary* (1788) and the unpublished *Maria, or the Wrongs of Women*, both present her philosophical thoughts in the form of fiction.

WOMAN/WOMEN. *See* ESSENTIALISM; GENDER; SEX.

WOMANIST/WOMANISM. *See* GLOBAL FEMINISM.

WOMEN PHILOSOPHERS, HISTORY OF. One aspect of the **canon critique** by feminist philosophers is the recovery of forgotten or undervalued women philosophers from the **history of philosophy**.

Mary Ellen Waithe's *A History of Women Philosophers* provides the most inclusive survey, documenting women philosophers from 600 BCE to the twentieth century. This type of canon critique rewrites the history of philosophy by showing that it has not been solely a male enterprise, and thus provides feminist philosophers with potential "foremothers," while interrogating the way that philosophy in the present still rests on assumptions that it is a male enterprise.

A central priority for the inclusion of these women philosophers in the history of philosophy has been to identify the ways that they have been excluded. Social conditions have kept women out of the places of public philosophical discourse, such as universities, or have led to pressures to write anonymously, because writing philosophy was seen as a **masculine** preserve. This lack of presence within the standard locations of philosophy then means that women philosophers have often been invisible to the writers of histories of philosophy.

Moreover, philosophy as a discipline has been defined in contrast to the symbolically **feminine**: the **emotions**, certain styles of writing, the practical. Despite the fact that female philosophers may not have shown any more tendencies than male philosophers to write and think in ways that are symbolically feminine, non-feminist interpreters have been ready to emphasize these elements in the work of female philosophers, and thus to dismiss or devalue their work. This has occurred even though similar elements in the work of male philosophers have just as readily been ignored or explained away.

The recovery of women philosophers has brought with it discussions of the ways their work can inform present-day philosophizing, as well as questions about the actual research and classification involved in the process of recovery. The recovery of these women philosophers also raises more general philosophical questions about the way the history of philosophy is approached: whether women in fact philosophize differently and whether the nature of contemporary philosophy would have been different with a greater inclusion of these women philosophers.

While the project of retrieval of women philosophers is a feminist project in itself, few of the philosophers recovered can be easily described as feminist. However, assuming that women philosophers can only be interested in feminist topics may serve to ghettoize historical women philosophers. Instead it is essential to recognize the wide variety of philosophical areas in which women philosophers have written; this is necessary in order both to value their work itself and also to produce a complete history of philosophy through the inclusion of this work.

Based on the secondary literature, a standard list of women philosophers from the history of philosophy who have been seen as writing feminist or proto-feminist work is as follows: **Mary Astell, Simone de Beauvoir, Antoinette Brown Blackwell, Christine de Pizan, Anna Julia Cooper, Sor Juana Inés de la Cruz, Charlotte Perkins Gilman, Emma Goldman, Olympe de Gouges, Marie de Gournay, Catharine Macaulay, Bathsua Pell Makin, Damaris Cudworth Masham, Anna van Schurman, Sophia, Harriet Taylor Mill, Anna Doyle Wheeler**, and **Mary Wollstonecraft**.

At present, this list contains only two women of color: the Mexican de la Cruz and the African American Cooper. There is little work that can be identified as a feminist tradition within **Latin American** philosophy. A **black feminist** intellectual tradition in the United States stretching as far back as the early 1800s can be identified, but the actual products of this tradition are often lost or fragmented. Moreover, in part as a result of the explicit or implicit exclusion of these thinkers from the intellectual and academic worlds of their contemporaries, this tradition merged intellectual and activist work. Given standard definitions of philosophical theorizing, this merger then further serves to keep nineteenth-century African American feminist thinkers located outside the history of philosophy. Recently there have been signs that this trend may be reversed; one particular example is a renewed interest in the work of the nineteenth-century African American philosopher Cooper.

"WOMEN'S WORK." *See* DIVISION OF LABOR, SEXUAL.

Bibliography

The bibliography is separated into four main sections. The first section includes general works in feminist philosophy and theory. The second deals with concepts and terms in current use in feminist philosophy. The titles listed in this section should be fairly self-explanatory. The third section covers the various fields within feminist philosophy. The number of included works varies for these fields according to the newness of or level of interest in a particular field. The fourth section lists works of individual philosophers and is predominantly a bibliography of feminist interpretations of canonical philosophers and early feminist philosophers. It is substantially longer than the others; in philosophy—perhaps more than in many other disciplines—we study the history of our discipline itself. Relatively few works on individual contemporary feminist philosophers are included. The reason for this is that most feminist philosophers are engaged in a collective enterprise; thus the contributions of each individual are best seen as subsumed into the larger political and intellectual enterprise.

A comprehensive collection of articles on feminist philosophy can be found in *A Companion to Feminist Philosophy*, edited by Alison Jaggar and Iris Marion Young. The volume contains articles written by experts in their particular subject areas within feminist philosophy. The general categories are the history of Western philosophy; feminist philosophy from outside the West; knowledge and nature; religion; subjectivity and embodiment, art; ethics; society; politics. Within each of these categories, there are a number of articles on the important issues of each subfield. The collection is not committed to any particular school of thought or methodology; its commitment is to an understanding of feminist philosophy as an identifiable and distinct branch of philosophy. It is the most thorough collection of articles on feminist philosophy thus far.

The Cambridge Companion to Feminism in Philosophy, edited by Miranda Fricker and Jennifer Hornsby, contains a series of articles that cover the history of philosophy; epistemology; language; metaphysics; psychoanalysis; philosophy of mind; philosophy of science; political philosophy; ethics. The articles on philosophy of mind and metaphysics are particularly useful, as these subjects are rarely covered in other collections. The general philosophical approach of this collection is Anglo-American analytic philosophy. One weakness of the collection is that it does not treat feminist philosophy as an identifiable and distinct philosophy; rather, the contributors aim to explore the role of feminism *in* philosophy: how feminist concerns can illuminate mainstream philosophy.

There is a useful collection of articles in the journal *Metaphilosophy* that discuss the state of feminist philosophy in the 1990s. These articles are by the American feminist philosophers Claudia Card, Ruth Ginzberg, Naomi Scheman, Nancy Tuana, and Margaret Urban Walker.

The different approaches to feminist philosophical thought are postmodernist, French feminist, and analytic. In works written in English, analytic philosophy is the dominant philosophical approach. The result of this is that feminist philosophers from the analytic tradition rarely explain this tradition or how their work is a part of it. For the novice reader, therefore, an overview of the analytic tradition and the approach of feminist philosophy from this tradition can be helpful. The clearest account of the subject field of analytic feminism and its methodology is the series of articles in a special issue of *Hypatia* edited by Ann Cudd and Virginia Klenk.

Luce Irigaray is usually seen as the central figure of French feminist philosophy; her work has also influenced some of the recent developments in Anglophone analytic philosophy. However, Irigaray's work is deliberately ambiguous, and it is hard to read even for the professional philosopher. The best way of approaching her thought is by reading the fairly lucid account of it in Elizabeth Grosz's *Sexual Subversions: Three French Feminists*.

There is still not much published on postmodernist feminism in English. Moreover, what there is tends to be monographs on the subject rather than introductions to the subject field. Two works that function reasonably well to provide an introduction are Jane Flax's *Thinking Fragments: Psychoanalysis, Feminism, and Postmodernism in the Con-*

temporary West, and *Feminism/Postmodernism*, edited by Linda Nicholson.

Pragmatist feminism is still in the early stages of development; thus there is relatively little work in this field. The central resource for the explanation of the importance of the American pragmatist tradition for feminist philosophy is the work of Charlene Haddock Seigfried.

Thus far, feminist philosophers have tended to be white women. The major works by black feminist philosophers, or social critics who have influenced feminist philosophy, are Angela Davis, *Women, Race & Class*; bell hooks, *Ain't I A Woman? Black Women and Feminism*, and *Feminist Theory from Margin to Center*; Patricia Hill Collins, *Black Feminist Thought: Knowledge, Consciousness, and the Politics of Empowerment*.

Very little work is available on feminist philosophy outside the West. The main resources are in the section of Jaggar and Young's *A Companion to Feminist Philosophy* on Africa, Asia, Latin America, and Eastern Europe. Nanette Funk has edited a "special cluster" in European feminist philosophy for *Hypatia*, and O. Vorinina has written on East European philosophy. Xiao Jiang Li has written monographs on Chinese feminism that are of interest to philosophers. Ofelia Schutte, D. H. Maffia, and M. Santa Cruz have written on Latin American feminist philosophy.

In terms of feminist theory more generally, Alison Jaggar's *Feminist Politics and Human Nature* is the central contribution to discussion of the different feminist theories defined as political philosophy. Although it contains a rather dense account of feminist political philosophy, it is rewarding for readers at all levels. It is important to note, however, that Jaggar does not intend to remain neutral on the merits of each theory: she argues for socialist feminism as the most adequate form of feminist theory at the present time.

In the subject field of aesthetics, the recommended title for the most comprehensive and accessible overview of this field is the edited collection by Hilde Hein and Carolyn Korsmeyer, *Aesthetics in Feminist Perspective*. The editors' introduction offers a clear overview of the subject field; the collection itself covers questions of the nature of art and its interpretation, as well as analyses of traditional philosophical aesthetics. This collection is from 1993, and the general reader may find books and articles from the late 1980s and the early 1990s the most accessible.

There is a tendency for the most recent works to be written for the professional philosopher.

There is very little work in feminist philosophy of education. The main work is being done by Jane Roland Martin, who writes on the tradition of philosophy of education, and on a feminist rethinking of contemporary educational practices. Martin's work is appropriate for the reader without a philosophical background.

The subject area of the environment and nature is dominated by ecofeminist thought. The best introduction to ecofeminism is Ynestra King's article "The Ecology of Feminism and the Feminism of Ecology"; King's article is clear and covers all the central elements of ecofeminist thought. For the reader who has some knowledge of ecofeminist thought, works by Vandana Shiva are important, as she provides analyses of both theory and practice. The reader should also consider the titles listed for Francis Bacon, as he is credited with the development of our modern concepts of nature.

Epistemology and philosophy of science make up one of the central subject fields in feminist philosophy, and the number of titles listed in this section reflect this. The most accessible introduction to this field is Lorraine Code's *What Can She Know? Feminist Theory and the Construction of Knowledge*, where she sets up the central issue for feminist theory of knowledge: is the sex of the knower epistemologically significant? Sandra Harding's earlier works and Lynn Nelson's *Who Knows: From Quine to a Feminist Empiricism* provide accounts of the two main positions within analytic feminist philosophy. These works are important in the field but may require the reader to have some background in philosophy. Elizabeth Anderson offers a concise overview of postmodern feminist approaches to questions of knowledge in *The Stanford Encyclopedia of Philosophy* (http://plato.stanford.edu/archives/sum2004/entries/feminism-epistemology/).

Phyllis Rooney's articles on contemporary work on the concept of reason and Genevieve Lloyd's account of the history of the concept, *The Man of Reason: "Male" and "Female" in Western Philosophy*, provide useful accompaniments for a reader's introduction to the fields of epistemology and philosophy of science.

Patricia Hill Collins offers the only systematic account of black feminist epistemology in her book *Black Feminist Thought: Knowledge,*

Consciousness, and the Politics of Empowerment. This is a central reading for its contribution to the more specific area of black feminist philosophy, as well as to epistemological thought more generally. This work is easily accessible to the novice. An engaging account of non-Western feminist epistemology is Jane Duran's *Worlds of Knowing: Global Feminist Epistemologies.*

Feminist ethics is the major subject field of feminist philosophy, as the number of titles listed in this section attest. Rosmarie Tong's introduction to the subject field of feminist ethics, *Feminine and Feminist Ethics*, is indispensable, and it should be of interest for readers at all levels. The collection edited by Claudia Card, *Feminist Ethics*, and the collection edited by Eva Kittay and Diana Tietjens Meyers, *Feminist Morality: Transforming Culture, Society, and Politics*, both contain a series of informative and interesting articles on specific feminist ethical issues. Susan Sherwin is the leader in the subfield of bioethics, and her work is vital for any exploration of this area. The psychologist Carol Gilligan's work on the ethics of care is important for the reader who wishes to explore this area in depth. The more casual reader need not have this background and will find the work of Virginia Held and Joan Tronto on the ethics of care useful as an introduction to and an examination of this type of ethical theory. Patricia Hill Collins offers the most comprehensive and persuasive account of black feminist ethics. Katie G. Cannon's *Black Womanist Ethics* is considerably narrower in its scope and tends to offer more of a personal account of black feminist ethics. Sarah Lucia Hoagland's work on lesbian ethics provides a solid reconceptualizing of ethical theory that is accessible for both the casual and the professional reader.

In the field of feminist history of philosophy, Beverly Clack's *Misogyny in the Western Philosophical Tradition* can provide an introduction to the issue of sexism in the canon for the reader new to philosophy. On the whole, Clack does not offer an account that goes much beyond this single issue. Nancy Tuana's *Woman and the History of Philosophy* requires some knowledge of philosophy on the part of the reader; however, it is significantly rewarding as an introduction to male bias in the philosophical tradition. For readers at all levels, Charlotte Witt's "Feminist History of Philosophy" is the recommended reading on this subject; it provides a clear and comprehensive guide to all the different approaches in this subject area. It can be found in *The Stanford Encyclopedia of Philosophy* (http://plato.stanford.edu/archives/sum2004/entries/feminism-femhist). For work that is representative of French philosophical thinking, Penelope Deutscher's *Yielding Gender: Feminism, Deconstruction and the History of Philosophy* and Michèle Le Doeuff's *The Philosophical Imaginary* are interesting works; however, the latter's work is more accessible to the professional philosopher with knowledge of both the history of philosophy and French feminism. For information about women philosophers from the history of philosophy, Mary Ellen Waithe's edited history, *A History of Women Philosophy*, is incomparably the best. The reader should also consider titles that are listed for individual philosophers in the fourth section of the bibliography; these works are typically aimed at canon revision.

Work in logic and philosophy of language in the analytic tradition tends to be very technical; work grounded in postmodern thought (such as the work of Luce Irigaray and Judith Butler) can be complicated. The casual or novice reader is advised not to read such works. The most accessible title for this reader is the special issue on philosophy of language in *Hypatia* edited by Dale Bauer and Kelly Oliver. For the professional reader, most of the titles listed in the bibliography are important for an examination of philosophy of language.

In the field of metaphysics, Charlotte Witt's "Feminist Metaphysics" is the central reading for all levels. On the whole most of the other titles listed for this subject area require an understanding of the major questions in this field. Marilyn Frye's *The Politics of Reality: Essays in Feminist Theory* is accessible but may only be of interest for the reader who is politically feminist.

Janice Moulton's "A Paradigm of Philosophy: The Adversary Method" is an important text that examines standard analytic methodology; it should be of interest to any reader with a passing knowledge of philosophy. Joyce Trebilcot's "Ethics of Method" is of interest as it offers new, feminist ways of thinking about methodology; it is accessible to the novice reader but may be controversial for the non-feminist professional philosopher.

The best introductions to feminist work in the philosophy of mind are Susan James's "Feminism in Philosophy of Mind: The Question of Personal Identity" and Naomi Scheman's "Feminism in Philosophy of Mind: Against Physicalism." However, the reader should note that these articles are part of a collection, *The Cambridge Companion to Feminism in Philosophy*, that examines what feminism can provide for philosophy, rather than constructing a specifically feminist philosophy of mind. The authors assume that their readers will have a thorough knowledge of the subject area. Maria Lugones's "Playfulness, 'World'-Traveling, and Loving Perception" offers a non-technical revisionist account of the classic issue in the philosophy of mind: personal identity.

Thought in feminist philosophy of religion is dominated by the work of Mary Daly. *Beyond God the Father: Toward a Theory of Women's Liberation* is the germinal work in this field. Most of this work should be accessible to any reader who has some knowledge of both the Christian tradition and feminism. The reader should note that a collection of a comprehensive selection of articles on Mary Daly, *Feminist Interpretations of Mary Daly*, is listed in the individual philosophers' section of the bibliography. There is very little work on religions other than Christianity; recommended articles are Baccarat Tanya's "Islam" and Rachel Adler's "Judaism." There is also very little work by feminists of color on philosophy of religion. Toilette Eugene offers the most systemized account of a revisionist black feminist philosophy of religion; her work is accessible for readers at all levels.

Many of the titles listed in the section on political and social philosophy are works on specific applied issues in this subject area; these titles should be self explanatory. Two useful collections that cover theoretical aspects of political philosophy are *Feminist Interpretations and Political Theory*, edited by Mary Lyndon Stanley and Carole Pateman, and *Reconstructing Political Theory: Feminist Perspectives*, edited by Mary Lyndon and Uma Narayan. Carole Pateman's *The Sexual Contract* is seen as one of the germinal works in feminist critique of classical political theory; it is necessary reading for the professional philosopher, and should be both accessible and of interest to the new reader.

A central, excellent source on the Internet for overviews of the various fields of feminist philosophy is *The Stanford Encyclopedia of Philosophy* (Summer 2004 edition), edited by Edward N. Zalta. The *Encyclopedia* can be found at http://plato.stanford.edu/. All the entries are written by experts in the field. Some of the professional organizations for women feminist philosophers maintain websites. The Society for Women in Philosophy (SWIP) can be found at www.uh.edu/~cfreelan/SWIP/. The site for the Canadian Society of Women in Philosophy

(CSWIP) is http://sbrennan.philosophy.arts.uwo.ca/cswip/. The Society for the Study of Women Philosophers (SSWP) is located at http://ksumail.kennesaw.edu/~ldamico/sswp.htm. The Society for Women's advancement in Philosophy (SWAP) is located at www.swapusa.org/. Thewebsite for the Association for Feminist Ethics and Social Theory (FEAST) is www.afeast.org.

GENERAL WORKS ON FEMINIST PHILOSOPHY AND FEMINIST THEORY

Addelson, Kathryn Pyne. *Impure Thoughts: Essays on Philosophy, Feminism, and Ethics*. Philadelphia: Temple University Press, 1992.
———. "Feminist Philosophy and the Women's Movement." *Hypatia* 9, no. 3 (1994): 216–24.
Al-Hibri, Azizah Y., and Margaret A. Simons, eds. *Hypatia Reborn: Essays in Feminist Philosophy*. Bloomington: Indiana University Press, 1990.
Anzaldúa, Gloria. *Borderlands/La Frontera*. San Francisco: Spinsters/Aunt Lute, 1987.
Battersby, Christine. "Recent Work in Feminist Philosophy." *Philosophical Books* (October 1991): 193–201.
Battersby, Christine, et al., eds. "Going Australian: Reconfiguring Feminism and Philosophy." Special issue, *Hypatia* 15, no. 2 (2000).
Beauvoir, Simone de. *The Second Sex*. New York: Knopf, 1953.
Braidotti, R. *Patterns of Dissonance: A Study of Women in Contemporary Philosophy*. Cambridge, Mass.: Polity Press, 1991.
Butler, Judith. *Gender Trouble: Feminism and the Subversion of Identity*. New York: Routledge, 1990.
———. *Bodies That Matter: On the Discursive Limits of "Sex."* New York: Routledge, 1993.
Card, Claudia, ed. *Adventures in Lesbian Philosophy*. Bloomington: Indiana University Press, 1994.
———. "Feminism and Philosophy in the Mid-Nineties: Taking Stock." *Metaphilosophy* 27, nos. 1–2 (1996): 193–96.
Chodorow, Nancy. *The Reproduction of Mothering: Psychoanalysis and the Sociology of Gender*. Berkeley: University of California Press, 1978.
Cixous, Hélène. "The Laugh of the Medusa." Trans. K. Cohen and P. Cohen. *Signs* 1, no. 4 (1979): 875–93.
Collins, Patricia Hill. *Black Feminist Thought: Knowledge, Consciousness, and the Politics of Empowerment*. New York: Routledge, 1990.
Cudd, Ann, and Virginia Klenk, eds. Special issue on Analytic Feminism. *Hypatia* 10, no. 3 (1995).

Davis, Angela. *Women, Race, and Class*. New York: Random House, 1981.

Deutscher, Penelope, ed. Special issue on Contemporary French Women Philosophers. *Hypatia* 15, no. 4 (2000).

Ferguson, Ann. "Twenty Years of Feminist Philosophy." *Hypatia* 9, no. 3 (1994): 197–215.

Flax, Jane. *Thinking Fragments: Psychoanalysis, Feminism, and Postmodernism in the Contemporary West*. Berkeley: University of California Press, 1990.

Fricker, Miranda, and Jennifer Hornsby, eds. *The Cambridge Companion to Feminism in Philosophy*. Cambridge: Cambridge University Press, 2000.

Funk, Nanette, ed. Special cluster on Eastern European Feminism. *Hypatia* 8, no. 4 (1993).

Funk, Nanette, and M. Mueller, eds. *Gender Politics and Post-Communism*. New York: Routledge, 1993.

Garry, Ann, and Marilyn Pearsall, eds. *Women, Knowledge, and Reality*. Boston: Unwin Hyman, 1989.

Ginzberg, Ruth. "The Future of Feminist Philosophy." *Metaphilosophy* 27, nos. 1–2 (1996): 197–201.

Gould, Carol, ed. *Beyond Domination: New Perspectives on Women and Philosophy*. Totowa, N.J.: Rowman and Allanheld, 1984.

Gould, Carol, and Marx X. Wartofsky, eds. *Women and Philosophy: Toward a Theory of Liberation*. New York: G. P. Putnam's Sons, 1976.

Griffiths, Morwenna, and Margaret Whitford, eds. *Feminist Perspectives in Philosophy*. Bloomington: Indiana University Press, 1988.

Grimshaw, Jane. *Philosophy and Feminist Thinking*. Minneapolis: University of Minnesota Press, 1986.

Grosz, Elizabeth. *Sexual Subversions: Three French Feminists*. Sydney: Allen and Unwin, 1989.

Havelkova, Hana. "Who Is Afraid of Feminist Philosophy?" *Filosoficky-Casopis* 40, no. 5 (1992): 729–41.

Hekman, Susan. *Gender and Knowledge: Elements of a Postmodern Feminism*. Boston: Northeastern University Press, 1990.

Hoagland, Sarah Lucia. *Lesbian Ethics*. Palo Alto, Calif.: Institute of Lesbian Studies, 1988.

hooks, bell. *Ain't I a Woman? Black Women and Feminism*. Boston: Southend Press, 1981.

———. *Feminist Theory from Margin to Center*. Boston: Southend Press, 1984.

Hudson-Weems, C. *African Womanism: Reclaiming Ourselves*. London: Bedford Publications, 1996.

Irigaray, Luce. *The Speculum of the Other Woman*. Trans. G. Gill. Ithaca, N.Y.: Cornell University Press, 1985.

———. *The Sex Which Is Not One*. Trans. C. Porter and C. Burke. Ithaca, N.Y.: Cornell University Press, 1985.

———. *An Ethics of Sexual Difference*. Trans. C. Burke and G. Gill. Ithaca, N.Y.: Cornell University Press, 1993.

Jaggar, Alison M. *Feminist Politics and Human Nature*. Totowa, N.J.: Rowman and Littlefield, 1998.

Jaggar, Alison M., and Susan R. Bordo, eds. *Gender/Body/Knowledge*. New Brunswick, N.J.: Rutgers University Press, 1989.

Jaggar, Alison, and Iris Marion Young, eds. *A Companion to Feminist Philosophy*. Oxford: Blackwell, 1998.

Li, Xiao Jiang. *Gender Gap*. Beijing: Sanlian Publishing House, 1989.

———. *Toward the Woman*. Zhengzhou: Henan People's Publishing House, 1993.

Lugones, Maria, and Elizabeth Spelman. "Have We Got a Theory for You!" In *Women and Values*, ed. Marilyn Pearsall. Belmont, Calif.: Wadsworth, 1986. 19–31.

Maffia, D. H. "De los Derechos Humanos a Los Derechos de las Humanas." In *Capacitación Politica Para Mujeres: Género y Cambio Social en la Argentina Actual*, ed. D. H. Maffia and C. Kuschnir. Buenos Aires: Feminaria Editora, 1994. 63–75.

Mahowald, Mary. *Philosophy and Women*. Indianapolis, Ind.: Hackett, 1983.

McAlister, Linda Lopez. "On the Possibility of Feminist Philosophy." *Hypatia* 9, no. 3 (1994): 188–96.

Mendus, Susan. "Recent Work in Feminist Philosophy." *Philosophical Quarterly* 43 (1993): 513–19.

Nagl-Docekalova, Herta. "What Is Feminist Philosophy?" *Filosoficky-Casopis* 40, no. 5 (1992): 742–56.

Nagl-Docekal, Herta, and Cornelia Klinger, eds. *Continental Philosophy in Feminist Perspective*. University Park: Pennsylvania State University Press, 2000.

Nicholson, Linda, ed. *Feminism/Postmodernism*. New York: Routledge, 1990.

Nye, Andrea. *Feminist Theory and the Philosophies of Man*. London: Croom Helm, 1988.

———. "It's Not Philosophy." *Hypatia* 13, no. 2 (1998): 107–15.

Richards, Janet Radcliffe. *The Skeptical Feminist: A Philosophical Enquiry*. London: Routledge and Kegan Paul, 1980.

Santa Cruz, M., et al. *Mujeres y Filosofia (I): Teoriá filos óficia de Género*. Buenos Aires: Centro Editor de América Latina, 1994.

Scheman, Naomi. "Panel on Feminist Philosophy in the 90s." *Metaphilosophy* 27, nos. 1–2 (1996): 209–13.

Schutte, Ofelia, ed. "Spanish and Latin American Feminist Philosophy." *Hypatia* 9, no. 1 (1994): 142–94.

Seigfried, Charlene Haddock. *Pragmatism and Feminism*. Chicago: University of Chicago Press, 1996.

———, ed. Special issue on Feminism and Pragmatism. *Hypatia* 8, no. 2 (1993).

Shiva, Vandana. *Staying Alive: Women, Ecology, and Development*. New Delhi: Kali for Women, 1998. Reprinted London: Zed Books, 1988.

Smith, B., ed. *Philosophy and Political Change in Eastern Europe*. La Salle, Ill.: Hegler Institute, 1993.

Tong, Rosmarie. *Feminist Thought: A More Comprehensive Introduction*. Boulder, Colo.: Westview Press, 1998.

Tuana, Nancy. "A Roundtable on Feminism and Philosophy in the Mid-1990s." *Metaphilosophy* 27, nos. 1–2 (1996): 218–21.

Tuana, Nancy, and Rosemarie Tong, eds. *Feminism and Philosophy: Essential Readings*. Boulder, Colo.: Westview Press, 1995.

Vetterling-Braggin, Mary, et al., eds. *Feminism and Philosophy*. Totowa, N.J.: Rowman and Littlefield, 1977.

Voronina, O. "Soviet Patriarchy: Past and Present." *Hypatia* 8, no. 4 (1993): 97–112.

Walker, Margaret Urban. "Some Thoughts on Feminists, Philosophy, and Feminist Philosophy." *Metaphilosophy* 27, nos. 1–2 (1996): 222–25.

Wylie, Alison. "Contemporary Feminist Philosophy." *Eidos* 6 (1987): 215–29.

Young, Iris Marion. *Throwing Like a Girl and Other Essays in Feminist Philosophy and Social Theory*. Princeton, N.J.: Princeton University Press, 1990.

CONCEPTS AND TERMS

Allen, Prudence. *The Concept of Woman: The Aristotelian Revolution 750 BC–AD 1250*. Montreal: Eden Press, 1985.

Bartky, Sandra Lee. "Body Politics." In *A Companion to Feminist Philosophy*, ed. Alison Jaggar and Iris Marion Young. Oxford: Blackwell, 1998: 321–29.

———. "Narcissism, Femininity, and Alienation." *Social Theory and Practice* 8, no. 2 (1982): 127–43.

Beauvoir, Simone de. *La Force de l'Age* (*The Coming of Age*). Trans. Peter Green. Cleveland: World Publishing, 1962.

Collins, Patricia Hill. *Black Feminist Thought: Knowledge, Consciousness, and the Politics of Empowerment*. New York: Routledge, 1990.

Faludi, Susan. *Backlash: The Undeclared War against Women*. New York: Crown, 1991.

Ferguson, Ann. "Androgyny as an Ideal for Human Development." In *Feminism and Philosophy*, ed. Mary Vetterling-Braggin, Frederick A. Elliston, and Jane English. Totowa, N.J.: Rowman and Littlefield, 1977.

Flax, Jane. "Political Philosophy and the Patriarchal Unconscious: A Psychoanalytic Perspective on Epistemology and Metaphysics." In *Discovering Reality: Feminist Perspectives on Epistemology, Metaphysics, Methodology, and Philosophy of Science*, ed. Sandra Harding and Merrill B. Hintikka. Dordrecht: Reidel, 1983. 245–79.

Foreman, Ann. *Femininity as Alienation: Women and the Family in Marxism and Psychoanalysis*. London: Pluto Press, 1977.

Frye, Marilyn. *The Politics of Reality: Essays in Feminist Theory*. Freedom, Calif.: Crossing Press, 1983.

Gamble, Sarah, ed. *The Routledge Critical Dictionary of Feminism and Postfeminism*. New York: Routledge, 2000.

Gilman, Charlotte Perkins. *The Man Made World or Our Androcentric Culture*. London: Fisher Unwin, 1911.

Jaggar, Alison M. *Feminist Politics and Human Nature*. Totowa, N.J.: Rowman and Littlefield, 1983.

Keller, Evelyn Fox. "Gender and Science." In *Discovering Reality: Feminist Perspectives on Epistemology, Metaphysics, Methodology, and Philosophy of Science*, ed. Sandra Harding and Merrill B. Hintikka. Dordrecht: Reidel, 1983. 187–205.

Lear, Marsha. "The Second Feminist Wave." *New York Times Magazine*, March, 10, 1968.

Lloyd, Genevieve. *The Man of Reason: "Male" and "Female" in Western Philosophy*. Minneapolis: University of Minnesota Press, 1984.

Marx, Karl. *Economic and Philosophic Manuscripts of 1844*. Ed. and intro. Dirk J. Struik. New York: International Publishers, 1964.

———. *Capital: A Critique of Political Economy*, vol. 1. New York: International Publishers, 1967.

Mumm, Maggie, ed. *The Dictionary of Feminist Theory*. Columbus: Ohio State University Press, 1989.

O' Brien, Mary. *The Politics of Reproduction*. Boston: Routledge and Kegan Paul, 1981.

Rich, Adrienne. "Compulsory Heterosexuality and Lesbian Existence." *Signs* 5, no. 4 (1980): 631–60.

Scheman, Naomi. "Individualism and the Objects of Psychology." In *Discovering Reality: Feminist Perspectives on Epistemology, Metaphysics, Methodology, and Philosophy of Science*, ed. Sandra Harding and Merrill B. Hintikka. Dordrecht: Reidel, 1983. 225–44.

Spelman, Elizabeth V. *Inessential Woman: Problems of Exclusion in Feminist Thought*. Boston: Beacon Press, 1988.

———. "Anger and Insubordination." In *Women, Knowledge, and Reality*, ed. Ann Garry and Marilyn Pearsall. Boston: Unwin Hyman, 1989. 263–73.

Trebilcot, Joyce. "Two Forms of Androgynism." *Journal of Social Philosophy* 8 (January 1977): 4–8.

Tuana, Nancy. *Woman and the History of Philosophy*. St. Paul, Minn.: Paragon, 1992.

Vetterling-Braggin, Mary, ed. *"Femininity," "Masculinity," and "Androgyny": A Modern Philosophical Discussion*. Totowa, N.J.: Littlefield, Adams, 1982.

Vetterling-Braggin, Mary, Frederick A. Elliston, and Jane English, eds. *Feminism and Philosophy*. Totowa, N.J.: Rowman and Littlefield, 1977.

Young, Iris Marion. "Socialist Feminism and the Limits of the Dual Systems Theory." *Socialist Review* 50–51 (1980): 169–88.

FIELDS WITHIN FEMINIST PHILOSOPHY

Aesthetics

Battersby, Christine. *Gender and Genius*. London: Women's Press, 1989.

Brand, Peg, and Mary Devereaux, eds. Special issue on Women, Art, and Aesthetics *Hypatia* 18, no. 4 (2003).

Brand, Peg, and Carolyn Korsmeyer, eds. *Feminism and Tradition in Aesthetics*. University Park: Pennsylvania State University Press, 1995.

Freeland, Cynthia. "Film Theory." In *A Companion to Feminist Philosophy*, ed. Alison Jaggar and Iris Marion Young. Oxford: Blackwell, 1998. 353–60.

Hein, Hilde, and Carolyn Korsmeyer, eds. *Aesthetics in Feminist Perspective*. Bloomington: Indiana University Press, 1993.

Klinger, Cornelia. "Aesthetics." In *A Companion to Feminist Philosophy*, ed. Alison Jaggar and Iris Marion Young. Oxford: Blackwell, 1998. 343–52.

Nochlin, Linda. "Why Have There Been No Great Women Artists?" In *Art and Sexual Politics*, ed. T. B. Hess and E. C. Baker. New York: Collier Books, 1971. 145–78.

Pearsall, Marilyn, ed. *Women and Values*, chap. 7. Belmont, Calif.: Wadsworth, 1986.

Education

Laird, S. "Reforming 'Women's True Profession': A Case for 'Feminist Pedagogy' in Teacher Education?" *Harvard Educational Review* 58, no. 4 (1988): 449–63.

Leach, Mary. "Mothers of Intervention: Women's Writing in the Philosophy of Education." *Educational Theory* 41, no. 3 (1991): 287–300.

Martin, Jane Roland. "Bringing Women into Educational Thought." *Educational Theory* 34, no. 4 (1984): 341–53.

———. "Education." In *A Companion to Feminist Philosophy*, ed. Alison Jaggar and Iris Marion Young. Oxford: Blackwell, 1998. 441–47.

———. *Reclaiming a Conversation: The Ideal of the Educated Woman*. New Haven, Conn.: Yale University Press, 1985.

Nicholson, Linda. "Women and Schooling." *Educational Theory* 30, no. 3 (1980): 225–34.

Noddings, Nel. *The Challenge to Care in Schools*. New York: Teacher's College Press, 1992.

Environment and Nature

Adams, Carol J. *The Sexual Politics of Meat: A Feminist-Vegetarian Critical Theory*. New York: Continuum, 1990.

d'Eaubonne, Françoise. *Le Feminisme ou La Mort*. Paris: Pierre-Horay, 1974.

Kheel, Marti. "The Liberation of Nature: A Circular Affair." *Environmental Ethics* 7 (1985): 135–49.

King, Ynestra. "The Ecology of Feminism and the Feminism of Ecology." In *Healing the Wounds*, ed. J. Plant. Philadelphia: New Society Publishers, 1989. 18–28.

Merchant, Carolyn. *The Death of Nature: Women, Ecology, and the Scientific Revolution.* San Francisco: Harper and Row, 1980.

Mies, Maria, and Vandana Shiva. *Ecofeminism.* New Delhi: Kali for Women, 1993.

Plumwood, Val. "Ecofeminism: An Overview and Discussion of Positions and Arguments." *Australasian Journal of Philosophy* 64 (1986): 120–38.

———. "Nature, Self, and Gender: Feminism, Environmental Philosophy, and the Critique of Rationalism." *Hypatia* 6, no. 1 (1991): 3–27.

Shiva, Vandana. *Staying Alive: Women, Ecology, and Development.* New Delhi: Kali for Women, 1998. Reprinted London: Zed Books, 1988.

Slicer, Deborah. "Your Daughter or Your Dog?" *Hypatia* 6, no. 1 (1991): 108–24.

Warren, Karen. "The Power and Promise of Ecological Feminism." *Environmental Ethics* 12, no. 2 (1990): 121–46.

———. ed. *Ecological Feminist Philosophies.* London: Routledge, 1994.

Epistemology and Philosophy of Science

Alcoff, Linda. *Real Knowing: New Versions of Coherence Epistemology.* Ithaca, N.Y.: Cornell University Press, 1996.

Alcoff, Linda, and Elizabeth Potter, eds. *Feminist Epistemologies.* New York: Routledge, 1993.

Antony, Louise, and Charlotte Witt, eds. *A Mind of One's Own: Feminist Essays on Reason and Objectivity.* Boulder, Colo.: Westview Press, 1993.

Benhabib, Seyla, Judith Butler, Drucilla Cornell, and Nancy Fraser. *Feminist Contentions: A Philosophical Exchange.* New York: Routledge, 1995.

Blenky, Mary Field, Blythe McVicker Clinchy, Nancy Rule Goldberger, and Jill Mattuck Tarule. *Women's Ways of Knowing: The Development of Self, Voice, and Mind.* New York: Basic Books, 1986.

Bordo, Susan. *The Flight to Objectivity.* Albany: State University of New York Press, 1987.

Braidotti, Rosi. *Patterns of Dissonance: A Study of Women in Contemporary Philosophy.* Cambridge, Mass.: Polity Press, 1991.

Code, Lorraine. *What Can She Know? Feminist Theory and the Construction of Knowledge.* Ithaca, N.Y.: Cornell University Press, 1991.

———. "Epistemology." In *A Companion to Feminist Philosophy*, ed. Alison Jaggar and Iris Marion Young. Oxford: Blackwell, 1998.

Collins, Patricia Hill. *Black Feminist Thought: Knowledge, Consciousness, and the Politics of Empowerment.* New York: Routledge, 1990.

Duran, Jane. *Worlds of Knowing: Global Feminist Epistemologies.* New York: Routledge, 2001.

Fricker, Miranda. "Epistemic Oppression and Epistemic Privilege." In "Civilization and Oppression," ed. Catherine Wilson. *Canadian Journal of Philosophy*, supp. vol. (1999): 191–210.

———. "Feminism in Epistemology: Pluralism without Postmodernism." In *The Cambridge Companion to Feminism in Philosophy*, ed. Miranda Fricker and Jennifer Hornsby. Cambridge: Cambridge University Press, 2000.

Garry, Ann, and Marilyn Pearsall, eds. *Women, Knowledge, and Reality*. Boston: Unwin Hyman, 1989.

Haack, Susan, ed. *Feminist Epistemology: For and Against*. Special issue, *Monist* 77, no. 4 (1994).

Harding, Sandra. *Is Science Multicultural? Postcolonialisms, Feminisms, and Epistemologies*. Bloomington: Indiana University Press, 1998.

———. *The Science Question in Feminism*. Ithaca, N.Y.: Cornell University Press, 1986.

———. *Whose Science? Whose Knowledge?* Ithaca, N.Y.: Cornell University Press, 1991.

Harding, Sandra, and Merrill B. Hintikka, eds. *Discovering Reality: Feminist Perspectives on Epistemology, Metaphysics, Methodology, and Philosophy of Science*. Dordrecht: Reidel, 1983.

Hartsock, Nancy. *The Feminist Standpoint Revisited and Other Essays*. Boulder, Colo.: Westview Press, 1998.

Haslanger, Sally. "On Being Objective and Being Objectified." In *A Mind of One's Own: Feminist Essays on Reason and Objectivity*, ed. Louise Antony and Charlotte Witt. Boulder, Colo.: Westview Press, 1993.

———, ed. "Feminist Perspectives on Language, Knowledge, and Reality." Special issue, *Philosophical Topics* 23, no. 2 (1995).

Hekman, Susan J. *Gender and Knowledge*. Boston: Northeastern University Press, 1990.

———. "Truth and Methods: Feminist Standpoint Revisited." *Signs* 22, no. 2 (1997): 341–65.

Jaggar, Alison M. *Feminist Politics and Human Nature*. Totowa, N.J.: Rowman and Littlefield, 1983.

Jaggar, Alison M., and Susan R. Bordo, eds. *Gender/Body/Knowledge*. New Brunswick. N.J.: Rutgers University Press, 1989.

Lennon, Kathleen, and Margaret Whitford, eds. *Knowing the Difference: Feminist Perspectives in Epistemology*. London: Routledge, 1994.

Lloyd, Genevieve. *The Man of Reason: "Male" and "Female" in Western Philosophy*. Minneapolis: University of Minnesota Press, 1984.

Narayan, Uma. "The Project of Feminist Epistemology: Perspectives from a Nonwestern Feminist." In *Gender/Body/Knowledge*, ed. Alison M. Jaggar and Susan R. Bordo. New Brunswick, N.J.: Rutgers University Press, 1989. 256–69.

Nelson, Lynn Hankinson. *Who Knows: From Quine to a Feminist Empiricism*. Philadelphia: Temple University Press, 1990.

Nicholson, Linda, ed. *Feminism/Postmodernism*. London: Routledge, 1990.

Rooney, Phyllis. "Gendered Reason: Sex Metaphor and Conceptions of Reason." *Hypatia* 6, no. 2 (1991): 77–103.

———. "Recent Work in Feminist Discussions of Reason." In *American Philosophical Quarterly* 31, no. 1 (1994): 1–21.

Scheman, Naomi. *Engenderings: Constructions of Knowledge, Authority, and Privilege*. Routledge, 1993.

Stanley, Liz, and Sue Wise. *Breaking Out Again: Feminist Ontology and Epistemology*. London: Routledge and Kegan Paul, 1983.

Whitford, Margaret. "Luce Irigaray's Critique of Rationality." In *Feminist Perspectives in Philosophy*, ed. Morwenna Griffiths and Margaret Whitford. Bloomington: Indiana University Press, 1988.

Ethics

Benhabib, Seyla. *Situating the Self: Gender, Community, and Postmodernism in Contemporary Ethics*. New York: Routledge, 1992.

Blum, Larry, Marcia Homiak, Judy Housman, and Naomi Scheman. "Altruism and Women's Oppression." *Philosophical Forum* 5, nos. 1–2 (1973–4): 196–221.

Cannon, Katie G. *Black Womanist Ethics*. Atlanta: Scholars Press, 1988.

Card, Claudia, ed. *Feminist Ethics*. Lawrence: University Press of Kansas, 1991.

———. *Adventures in Lesbian Philosophy*. Bloomington: Indiana University Press, 1994.

Christman, John. "Feminism and Autonomy." In *Nagging Questions: Feminist Ethics in Everyday Life*, ed. Dana E. Bushell. Lanham, Md.: Rowman and Littlefield, 1995. 17–39.

Collins, Patricia Hill. *Black Feminist Thought: Knowledge, Consciousness, and the Politics of Empowerment*. New York: Routledge, 2000.

Daly, Mary. *Gyn/ecology: The Metaethics of Radical Feminism*. Boston: Beacon Press, 1978.

Friedman, Marilyn. *What Are Friends For?* Ithaca, N.Y.: Cornell University Press, 1993.

———. "Impartiality." In *A Companion to Feminist Philosophy*, ed. Alison Jaggar and Iris Marion Young. Oxford: Blackwell, 1998. 393–401.

———. "Feminism in Ethics: Conceptions of Autonomy." In *The Cambridge Companion to Feminism in Philosophy*, ed. Miranda Fricker and Jennifer Hornsby. Cambridge: Cambridge University Press, 2000. 205–24.

Gilligan, Carol. *In a Different Voice: Psychological Theory and Women's Development*. Cambridge, Mass.: Harvard University Press, 1982.

Gilligan, Carol, Janie Victoria Ward, and Jill McLean Taylor, eds. *Mapping the Moral Domain*. Cambridge, Mass.: Harvard University Press, 1988.

Griffiths, Morwena. *Feminisms and the Self: The Web of Identity*. London: Routledge, 1995.

Grimshaw, Jean. *Philosophy and Feminist Thinking*. Minneapolis: University of Minnesota Press, 1986.

Hekman, Susan. *Moral Voices, Moral Selves: Carol Gilligan and Feminist Moral Theory*. University Park: Pennsylvania State University Press, 1995.

Held, Virginia. *Feminist Morality: Transforming Culture, Society, and Politics*. Chicago: Chicago University Press, 1993.

———, ed. *Justice and Care: Essential Readings in Feminist Ethics*. Boulder, Colo.: Westview Press, 1995.

Hill, Sharon Bishop. "Self-Determination and Autonomy." In *Today's Moral Problems*, 2nd ed., ed. Richard Wasserstrom. New York: Macmillan, 1979. 118–33.

Hoagland, Sarah Lucia. *Lesbian Ethics*. Palo Alto, Calif.: Institute of Lesbian Studies, 1988.

———. "Lesbian Ethics." In *A Companion to Feminist Philosophy*, ed. Alison Jaggar and Iris Marion Young. Oxford: Blackwell, 1998. 402–10.

Jaggar, Alison, ed. *Living with Contradictions: Controversies in Feminist Social Ethics*. Boulder, Colo.: Westview Press, 1994.

Kittay, Eva, and Diana Tietjens Meyers, eds. *Women and Moral Theory*. Savage, Md.: Rowman and Littlefield, 1987.

Larrabee, Mary Jeanne, ed. *An Ethic of Care: Feminist and Interdisciplinary Perspectives*. New York: Routledge, 1993.

Mackenzie, Catriona, and Natalie Stoljar, eds. *Relational Autonomy*. New York: Oxford University Press, 2000.

Meyers, Diana Tietjens. *Self, Society, and Personal Choice*. New York: Columbia University Press, 1989.

———. *Feminists Rethink the Self*. Boulder, Colo.: Westview Press, 1997.

———. "Agency." In *A Companion to Feminist Philosophy*, ed. Alison Jaggar and Iris Marion Young. Oxford: Blackwell, 1998. 372–82.

Noddings, Nel. *Caring: A Feminine Approach to Ethics and Moral Education*. Berkeley: University of California Press, 1984.

Ruddick, Sara. *Maternal Thinking: Towards a Politics of Peace*. New York: Beacon Press, 1989.

Shanner, Laura. "Procreation." In *A Companion to Feminist Philosophy*, ed. Alison Jaggar and Iris Marion Young. Oxford: Blackwell, 1998. 429–37.

Sherwin, Susan. "Abortion through a Feminist Ethics Lens." *Dialogue* 30 (1991): 327–42.

———. *No Longer Patient: Feminist Ethics and Health Care*. Philadelphia: Temple University Press, 1992.

———. "Health Care." In *A Companion to Feminist Philosophy*, ed. Alison Jaggar and Iris Marion Young. Oxford: Blackwell, 1998. 420–28.

Shildrick, Margrit. *Leaky Bodies and Boundaries: Feminism, Postmodernism and (Bio)ethics*. New York: Routledge, 1997.

Tong, Rosemarie. *Feminine and Feminist Ethics*. Belmont, Calif.: Wadsworth, 1993.

————.*Feminist Thought: A More Comprehensive Introduction.* Boulder, Colo.: Westview Press, 1998.

Tronto, Joan. *Moral Boundaries: A Political Argument for an Ethic of Care.* New York: Routledge, 1993.

Walker, Margaret. *Moral Understandings: A Feminist Study in Ethics.* New York Routledge, 1998.

Wolf, Susan, ed. *Feminism and Bioethics.* New York: Oxford University Press, 1996.

History of Philosophy

Atherton, Margaret, ed. *Women Philosophers of the Early Modern Period.* Indianapolis, Ind.: Hackett, 1994.

Bar On, Bat-Ami. *Modern Engendering: Critical Feminist Readings in Modern Western Philosophy.* Albany: State University of New York Press, 1994.

Clack, Beverley. *Misogyny in the Western Philosophical Tradition.* New York: Macmillan, 1999.

Conley, John J. *The Suspicion of Virtue: Women Philosophers in Neoclassical France.* Ithaca, N.Y.: Cornell University Press, 2002.

Deutscher, Penelope. *Yielding Gender: Feminism, Deconstruction, and the History of Philosophy.* London: Routledge, 1997.

Le Doeuff, Michèle. *The Philosophical Imaginary.* Trans. Colin Gordon. Stanford, Calif.: Stanford University Press, 1989.

Gardner, Catherine Villanueva. *Women Philosophers: Genre and the Boundaries of Philosophy.* Boulder, Colo.: Westview Press, 2004.

Grimshaw, Jean. *Feminist Philosophers: Women's Perspectives on Philosophical Traditions.* Brighton, U.K.: Wheatsheaf Books, 1986.

Kennedy, Ellen, and Susan Mendus, eds. *Women in Western Political Philosophy,* Brighton, U.K.: Wheatsheaf Books, 1987.

Lloyd, Genevieve. *The Man of Reason: "Male" and "Female" in Western Philosophy.* Minneapolis: University of Minnesota Press, 1984.

Ménage, Gilles. *The History of Women Philosophers* [1690]. Trans. B. Zedler. Lanham, Md.: University Press of America, 1984.

Okin, Susan Moller. *Women in Western Political Thought.* Princeton, N.J.: Princeton University Press, 1979.

Tougas, Cecile, and Sara Ebenreck, eds. *Presenting Women Philosophers.* Philadelphia: Temple University Press, 2000.

Tuana, Nancy. *Woman and the History of Philosophy.* St. Paul, Minn.: Paragon, 1992.

Waithe, Mary Ellen, ed. *A History of Women Philosophers.* 4 vols. Dordrecht: Kluwer, 1987–95.

Wider, Kathleen. "Women Philosophers in the Ancient Greek World: Donning the Mantle." *Hypatia* 1 (1986): 21–62.

Logic and Philosophy of Language

Bauer, Dale M., and Kelly Oliver, eds. Special issue on Philosophy and Language. *Hypatia* 7, no. 2 (1997).

Butler, Judith. *Bodies That Matter: On the Discursive Limits of "Sex."* New York: Routledge, 1993.

Cixous. Hélène. "The Laugh of the Medusa." Trans. K. Cohen and P. Cohen. *Signs* 1, no. 4 (1979): 875–93.

Daly, Mary. *Gyn/Ecology: The Metaethics of Radical Feminism.* Boston: Beacon Press, 1978.

Daly, Mary, and Jane Caputi. *Websters' First New Intergalactic Wickedary of the English Language.* Boston: Beacon Press, 1987.

Henderson, Mae Gwendolyn. "Speaking in Tongues: Dialogics, Dialectics, and the Black Woman Writer's Literary Tradition." In *Reading Black, Reading Feminist*, ed. Henry Louis Gates Jr. New York: Penguin Books, 1990. 116–42.

Irigaray, Luce. *This Sex Which Is Not One.* Trans. C. Porter and C. Burke. Ithaca, N.Y.: Cornell University Press, 1985.

MacKinnon, Catherine. *Only Words.* Cambridge, Mass.: Harvard University Press, 1993.

Moulton, Janice. "The Myth of the Neutral 'Man.' " In *Women, Knowledge, and Reality*, ed. Ann Garry and Marilyn Pearsall. Boston: Unwin Hyman, 1989. 219–32.

Nye, Andrea. "The Voice of the Serpent: French Feminism and Philosophy of Language." In *Women, Knowledge, and Reality*, ed. Ann Garry and Marilyn Pearsall. Boston: Unwin Hyman, 1989. 233–49.

———. *Words of Power.* New York: Routledge, 1990.

———. "Semantics." In *A Companion to Feminist Philosophy*, ed. Alison Jaggar and Iris Marion Young. Oxford: Blackwell, 1998. 153–61.

Tirrell, Lynne. "Language and Power." In *A Companion to Feminist Philosophy*, ed. Alison Jaggar and Iris Marion Young. Oxford: Blackwell, 1998. 139–52.

Vetterling-Braggin, Mary, ed. *Sexist Language: A Modern Philosophical Analysis.* Totowa, N.J.: Littlefield, Adams, 1981.

Metaphysics

Ferguson, Ann. "A Feminist Aspect Theory of the Self." In *Women, Knowledge, and Reality*, ed. Ann Garry and Marilyn Pearsall. Boston: Unwin Hyman, 1989. 93–107.

Flax, Jane. "Political Philosophy and the Patriarchal Unconscious: A Psychoanalytic Perspective on Epistemology and Metaphysics." In *Discovering Reality: Feminist Perspectives on Epistemology, Metaphysics, Methodology, and Philosophy of Science*, ed. Sandra Harding and Merrill B. Hintikka. Dordrecht: Reidel, 1983. 245–79.

Frye, Marilyn. "To See and Be Seen: The Politics of Reality." In *Women, Knowledge, and Reality*, ed. Ann Garry and Marilyn Pearsall. Boston: Unwin Hyman, 1989. 77–92.

Haslanger, Sally. "Feminism in Metaphysics: Negotiating the Natural." In *The Cambridge Companion to Feminism in Philosophy*, ed. Miranda Fricker and Jennifer Hornsby. Cambridge: Cambridge University Press, 2000. 107–26.

Witt, Charlotte. "Feminist Metaphysics." In *A Mind of One's Own: Feminist Essays on Reason and Objectivity*, ed. Louise Antony and Charlotte Witt. Boulder, Colo.: Westview Press, 1993. 302–18.

Whitbeck, Caroline. "A Different Reality: Feminist Ontology." In *Women, Knowledge, and Reality*, ed. Ann Garry and Marilyn Pearsall. Boston: Unwin Hyman, 1989. 51–76.

Methodology

Garry, Ann. "A Minimally Decent Philosophical Method? Analytic Philosophy and Feminism." *Hypatia* 10, no. 3 (1995): 7–30.

Moulton, Janice. "A Paradigm of Philosophy: The Adversary Method." In *Women, Knowledge, and Reality*, ed. Ann Garry and Marilyn Pearsall. Boston: Unwin Hyman, 1989. 5–20.

Sherwin, Susan. "Philosophical Methodology and Feminist Methodology: Are They Compatible?" In *Women, Knowledge, and Reality*, ed. Ann Garry and Marilyn Pearsall. Boston: Unwin Hyman, 1989. 21–36.

Trebilcot, Joyce. "Ethics of Method." In *Feminist Ethics*, ed. Claudia Card. Lawrence: University Press of Kansas, 1991. 45–51.

Philosophy of Mind

Butler, Judith. "Gendering the Body: Beauvoir's Philosophical Contribution." In *Women, Knowledge, and Reality*, ed. Ann Garry and Marilyn Pearsall. Boston: Unwin Hyman, 1989. 253–62.

James, Susan. "Feminism in Philosophy of Mind: The Question of Personal Identity." In *The Cambridge Companion to Feminism in Philosophy*, ed. Miranda Fricker and Jennifer Hornsby. Cambridge: Cambridge University Press, 2000. 29–48.

Lugones, Maria. "Playfulness, 'World'-Traveling, and Loving Perception." In *Women, Knowledge, and Reality*, ed. Ann Garry and Marilyn Pearsall. Boston: Unwin Hyman, 1989. 275–90.

Scheman, Naomi. "Feminism in Philosophy of Mind: Against Physicalism." In *The Cambridge Companion to Feminism in Philosophy*, ed. Miranda Fricker and Jennifer Hornsby. Cambridge: Cambridge University Press, 2000. 49–67.

Schott, Robin May. "Resurrecting Embodiment: Toward a Feminist Materialism."

In *A Mind of One's Own: Feminist Essays on Reason and Objectivity*, ed. Louise Antony and Charlotte Witt. Boulder, Colo.: Westview Press, 1993. 319–34.

Spelman, Elizabeth V. "Anger and Insubordination." In *Women, Knowledge, and Reality*, ed. Ann Garry and Marilyn Pearsall. Boston: Unwin Hyman, 1989. 263–73.

Philosophy of Religion

Adler, Rachel. *Engendering Judaism: Inclusive Ethics and Theology*. Philadelphia: Jewish Publication Society, 1997.

———. "Judaism." In *A Companion to Feminist Philosophy*, ed. Alison Jaggar and Iris Marion Young. Oxford: Blackwell, 1998. 245–52.

Daly, Mary. *Beyond God the Father: Toward a Theory of Women's Liberation*. Boston: Beacon Press, 1973.

Eugene, Toinette. "While Love Is Unfashionable: Ethical Implications of Black Spirituality and Sexuality." In *Women, Knowledge, and Reality*, ed. Ann Garry and Marilyn Pearsall. Boston: Unwin Hyman, 1989. 313–30.

Frankenberry, Nancy, and Marilyn Thie, eds. Special issue on Feminist Philosophy of Religion. *Hypatia* 9, no. 4 (1994).

Garry, Ann, and Marilyn Pearsall, eds. "Feminist Philosophy of Religion." In *Women, Knowledge, and Reality*. Boston: Unwin Hyman, 1989.

Pearsall, Marilyn, ed. *Women and Values*, chap. 6. Sacramento: California State Press, 1986.

Tayyab, Basharat. "Islam." In *A Companion to Feminist Philosophy*, ed. Alison Jaggar and Iris Marion Young. Oxford: Blackwell, 1998. 236–44.

Political and Social Philosophy

Allan, Anita. *Uneasy Access: Privacy for Women in a Free Society*. Totowa, N.J.: Rowman and Littlefield, 1998.

Appiah, Kwame Anthony. "Racisms." In *Anatomy of Racism*, ed. David Theo Goldberg. Minneapolis: University of Minnesota Press, 1990. 3–17.

Baier, Annette. "The Need for More than Justice." In *Science, Morality, and Feminist Theory*, ed. M. Hanen and K. Nielsen. Calgary, Canada: University of Calgary Press, 1987. 41–56.

Becker, M. "Prince Charming: Abstract Equality." *Supreme Court Review* (1988): 201–47.

Bordo, Susan. *Unbearable Weight: Feminism, Western Culture, and the Body*. Berkeley: California University Press, 1993.

Collins, Patricia Hill. *Black Feminist Thought: Knowledge, Consciousness, and the Politics of Empowerment*. New York: Routledge, 1990.

Cooke, M., and A. Woollacott, eds. *Gendering War Talk*. Princeton, N.J.: Princeton University Press, 1993.

Dwyer, Susan, ed. *The Problem of Pornography*. Belmont, Calif.: Wadsworth, 1995.

Elshtain, J. B., and S. Tobias, eds. *Women, Militarism, and War*. Totowa, N.J.: Rowman and Littlefield, 1990.

Engels, Friedrich. *The Origin of the Family, Private Property, and the State*, ed. E. Leacock. New York: International Publishers, 1972.

Ferguson, Ann. *Blood at the Root: Motherhood, Sexuality, and Male Domination*. London: Pandora, 1989.

Fraser, Nancy. *Unruly Practices: Power, Discourse, and Gender in Contemporary Social Theory*. Minneapolis: University of Minnesota Press, 1989.

———. "From Redistribution to Recognition? Dilemmas of Justice in a 'Post-Socialist' Age." *New Left Review* 212 (1995): 68–83.

Frye, Marilyn. *The Politics of Reality: Essays in Feminist Theory*. Freedom, Calif.: Crossing Press, 1983.

Grosz, Elizabeth, ed. Special issue on Feminism and the Body. *Hypatia* 6, no. 3 (1991).

Held, Virginia. "Rights." In *A Companion to Feminist Philosophy*, ed. Alison Jaggar and Iris Marion Young. Oxford: Blackwell, 1998. 500–10.

hooks, bell. *Feminist Theory from Margin to Center*. Boston: Southend Press, 1984.

Jaggar, Alison M. "Prostitution." In *Philosophy of Sex*, ed. Alan Soble. Lanham, Md.: Littlefield Adams, 1980. 348–68.

———. *Feminist Politics and Human Nature*. Totowa, N.J.: Rowman and Littlefield, 1983.

Kennedy, Ellen, and Susan Mendus. *Women in Western Political Philosophy: Kant to Nietzsche*. Hempstead, U.K.: Wheatsheaf Books, 1987.

Kittay, Eva, and Diana Tietjens Meyers, eds. *Feminist Morality: Transforming Culture, Society, and Politics*. Chicago: Chicago University Press, 1993.

Lugones, Maria, and Elizabeth Spelman. "Have We Got a Theory for You!" In *Women and Values*, ed. Marilyn Pearsall. Belmont, Calif.: Wadsworth, 1986. 19–31.

MacKinnon, Catherine. *The Sexual Harassment of Working Women*. New Haven, Conn.: Yale University Press, 1979.

———. *Feminism Unmodified: Discourses on Life and Law*. Cambridge, Mass.: Harvard University Press, 1987.

O' Brien, Mary. *The Politics of Reproduction*. Boston: Routledge and Kegan Paul, 1981.

Okin, Susan. *Women in Western Political Thought*. Princeton, N.J.: Princeton University Press, 1979.

———. *Justice, Gender, and the Family*. New York: Basic Books, 1989.

Pateman, Carole. *The Sexual Contract*. Cambridge, Mass.: Polity Press, 1988.

———, ed. *The Disorder of Women: Democracy, Feminism, and Political Theory*. Stanford, Calif.: Stanford University Press, 1989.

Pateman, Carole, and Elizabeth Gross, eds. *Feminist Challenges: Social and Political Theory.* Boston: Northeastern University Press, 1987.

Shanley, Mary Lyndon, and Uma Narayan, eds. *Reconstructing Political Theory: Feminist Perspectives.* University Park: Pennsylvania State University Press, 1997.

Shanley, Mary Lyndon, and Carole Pateman, eds. *Feminist Interpretations and Political Theory.* University Park: Pennsylvania State University Press, 1991.

Sherwin, Susan. "Abortion through a Feminist Ethics Lens." *Dialogue: Canadian Philosophical Review* 30, no. 3 (1991): 327–42.

Silvers, Anita. " 'Defective' Agents: Equality, Difference, and the Tyranny of the Normal." *Journal of Social Philosophy* 25 (June 1994): 154–75.

Superson, Anita M. "A Feminist Definition of Sexual Harassment." *Journal of Social Philosophy* 24, no. 1 (1993): 46–64.

Ruddick, Sara. *Maternal Thinking: Towards a Politics of Peace.* New York: Beacon Press, 1989.

———. "Notes on a Feminist Peace Politics." In *Gendering War Talk*, ed. M. Cooke and A. Woollacott. Princeton, N.J.: Princeton University Press, 1993.

Tronto, Joan. *Moral Boundaries: A Political Argument for an Ethic of Care.* New York: Routledge, 1993.

Warren, Karen J., and Duane L. Cady, eds. Special issue on Feminism and Peace. *Hypatia* 9, no. 2 (1994).

Wendell, Susan. "Toward a Feminist Theory of Disability." *Hypatia* 4, no. 2 (1989): 104–24.

Williams, Patricia J. *The Alchemy of Race and Rights.* Cambridge, Mass.: Harvard University Press, 1991.

"Women and Philosophy." Section 3, on Contemporary Social, Ethical, and Political Issues. Special issue, *Philosophical Forum* 5, nos. 1–2 (1973–1974).

Young, Iris. *Justice and the Politics of Difference.* Princeton, N.J.: Princeton University Press, 1990.

Zack, Naomi. "Philosophy and Racial Paradigms." *Journal of Value Inquiry* 33 (1999): 299–317.

INDIVIDUAL PHILOSOPHERS

Aquinas, Thomas

Allen, Prudence. *The Concept of Woman: The Aristotelian Revolution 750 BC–AD 1250.* Montreal: Eden Press, 1985.

Hartel, Joseph. "The Integral Feminism of St. Thomas Aquinas." *Gregorianum* 77, no. 3 (1996): 527–47.

McLaughlin, Eleanor. "Equality of Souls, Inequality of Sexes: Woman in Medieval

Theology." In *Religion and Sexism*, ed. Rosemary Reuther. New York: Simon and Schuster, 1974. 213–66.

Nolan, Michael. "The Aristotelian Background to Aquinas's Denial That 'Woman Is a Defective Male.' " *Thomist* 64 (2000): 21–69.

Traina, Cristina. *Feminist Ethics and Natural Law: The End of the Anathemas.* Washington, D.C.: Georgetown University Press, 1999.

Arendt, Hannah

Allen, Amy. "Solidarity after Identity Politics: Hannah Arendt and the Power of Feminist Theory." *Philosophy and Social Criticism* 25, no. 1 (1999): 97–118.

Benhabib, Seyla. "Feminist Theory and Hannah Arendt's Concept of Public Space." *History of the Human Sciences* 6, no. 2 (1993): 97–114.

Disch, Lisa J. *Hannah Arendt and the Limits of Philosophy.* Ithaca, N.Y.: Cornell University Press, 1994.

Honig, Bonnie, ed. *Feminist Interpretations of Hannah Arendt.* University Park: Pennsylvania State University Press, 1995.

May, Larry, ed. *Hannah Arendt: Twenty Years Later.* Cambridge, Mass.: MIT Press, 1996.

Minnich, Elizabeth K. "Thinking with Hannah Arendt: An Introduction." *International Journal of Philosophical Studies* 10, no. 2 (2002): 123–30.

Moynagh, Patricia. "A Politics of Enlarged Mentality: Hannah Arendt, Citizenship Responsibility, and Feminism." *Hypatia* 12, no. 4 (1997): 27–53.

Rich, Adrienne. *On Lies, Secrets, and Silence: Selected Prose 1966–1978.* New York: Norton, 1979.

Stone-Mediatore, Shari. "Hannah Arendt and Susan Griffin: Toward a Feminist Metahistory." In *Presenting Women Philosophers*, ed. Cecile Tougas and Sara Ebenreck. Philadelphia: Temple University Press, 2000. 280–300.

Waithe, Mary Ellen, ed. *A History of Women Philosophers.* Vol. 4. Dordrecht: Kluwer, 1995.

Aristotle

Allen, Christine Garside. "Can a Woman Be Good in the Same Way as a Man?" *Dialogue* 10 (1971): 534–44.

Bar On, Bat-Ami, ed. *Engendering Origins.* Albany: State University of New York Press, 1994.

Fememias, Maria Luisa. "Women and Natural Hierarchy in Aristotle." *Hypatia* 9, no. 1 (1994): 164–72.

Freeland, Cynthia A., ed. *Feminist Interpretations of Aristotle.* University Park: Pennsylvania State University Press, 1998.

Green, Judith. "Aristotle on Necessary Verticality, Body Heat, and Gendered Proper Places in the Polis: A Feminist Critique." *Hypatia* 7, no. 1 (1992): 70–96.

Horowitz, Maryanne Cline. "Aristotle and Women." *Journal of the History of Biology* 9 (1976): 183–213.

Kotzin, Rhoda Hadassah. "Ancient Greek Philosophy." In *A Companion to Feminist Philosophy*, ed. Alison Jaggar and Iris Marion Young. Oxford: Blackwell, 1998. 9–20.

Lange, Lynda. "Woman Is Not a Rational Animal: On Aristotle's Biology of Reproduction." In *Discovering Reality: Feminist Perspectives on Epistemology, Metaphysics, Methodology, and Philosophy of Science*, ed. Sandra Harding and Merrill B. Hintikka. Dordrecht: Reidel, 1983. 1–15.

Lovibond, Sabina. "Feminism in Ancient Philosophy: The Feminine Stake in Greek Rationalism." In *The Cambridge Companion to Feminism in Philosophy*, ed. Miranda Fricker and Jennifer Hornsby. Cambridge: Cambridge University Press, 2000. 10–28.

Matthews, Gareth B. "Gender and Essence in Aristotle." *Australasian Journal of Philosophy* Supp. 64 (1986): 16–25.

Morsink, Johannes. "Was Aristotle's Biology Sexist?" *Journal of the History of Biology* 12, no. 1 (1979): 83–112.

Mulgan, Richard. "Aristotle and the Political Role of Women." *History of Political Thought* 15, no. 2 (1994): 179–202.

Sakezles, Priscilla K. "Feminism and Aristotle." *Apeiron* 32, no. 1 (1999): 67–74.

Spelman, Elizabeth V. "Aristotle and the Politicization of the Soul." In *Discovering Reality: Feminist Perspectives on Epistemology, Metaphysics, Methodology, and Philosophy of Science*, ed. Sandra Harding and Merrill B. Hintikka. Dordrecht: Reidel, 1983. 17–30.

Stiehm, Judith Hicks. "The Unit of Political Analysis: Our Aristotelian Hangover." In *Discovering Reality: Feminist Perspectives on Epistemology, Metaphysics, Methodology, and Philosophy of Science*, ed. Sandra Harding and Merrill B. Hintikka. Dordrecht: Reidel, 1983. 31–43.

Thom, P. "Stiff Cheese for Women." *Philosophical Forum* 8, no. 1 (1976): 94–107.

Tress, Daryl McGowan. "The Metaphysical Science of Aristotle's 'Generation of Animals,' and Its Feminist Critics." *Review of Metaphysics* 46, no. 2 (1992): 307–41.

Tumulty, Peter. "Aristotle, Feminism, and Natural Law Theory." *New Scholars* 55 (1981): 450–64.

Ward, Julia K. ed. *Feminism and Ancient Philosophy*. New York: Routledge, 1996.

Astell, Mary

Bryson, Cynthia B. "Mary Astell: Defender of the 'Disembodied Mind.' " *Hypatia* 13, no. 4 (1998): 40–62.

Duran, Jane. "Mary Astell: A Pre-Humean Christian Empiricist and Feminist." Chap. 14 in *Presenting Women Philosophers*, ed. Cecile Tougas and Sara Ebenreck. Philadelphia: Temple University Press, 2000.

McCrystal, John. "Revolting Women: The Use of Revolutionary Discourse in Mary Astell and Mary Wollstonecraft Compared." *History of Political Thought* 14, no. 2 (1993): 189–203.

Waithe, Mary Ellen, ed. *A History of Women Philosophers*. Vol. 3. Dordrecht: Kluwer, 1991.

Augustine

Borrensen, Kari Elisabeth. "Patristic 'Feminism': The Case of Augustine." *Augustinian Studies* 25 (1994): 139–52.

Blazquez, Niceto. "Feminismo Augustiniano." *Augustinus* 27 (January–March 1982): 3–54.

Duval, Shannon. "Augustine's Radiant Confessional—Theatre of Prophecy." *Contemporary Philosophy* 15, no. 2 (1993): 1–4.

Reuther, Rosemary. "Misogynism and Virginal Feminism in the Fathers of the Church." In *Religion and Sexism*, ed. Rosemary Reuther. New York: Simon and Schuster, 1974. 150–83.

Weaver, F. Ellen, and Jean Laporte. "Augustine and Women: Relationships and Teachings." *Augustinian Studies* 12 (1981): 115–32.

Barre, François Poullain de la

Amorós, Celia. "Cartesianism and Feminism: What Reason Has Forgotten; Reasons for Forgetting." *Hypatia* 9, no. 1 (1994): 147–63.

Fraisse, Geneviève. *Poulain de la Barre ou le proces de prejuges*. Paris: Fayard, 1985.

Bacon, Francis

Keller, Evelyn Fox. "Baconian Science: A Hermaphroditic Birth." *Hypatia* 11, no. 3 (1988): 299–308.

Merchant, Carolyn. *The Death of Nature: Women, Ecology, and the Scientific Revolution*. San Francisco: Harper and Row, 1980.

Beauvoir, Simone de

Bergoffen, Debra B. "The Look as Bad Faith." *Philosophy Today* 36, no. 3 (1992): 221–27.

———. *The Philosophy of Simone de Beauvoir: Gendered Phenomenologies, Erotic Generosities.* Albany: State University of New York Press, 1997.

Bordo, Susan. "The Feminist as Other." *Metaphilosophy* 27, nos. 1–2 (1996): 10–27.

Farrell Smith, Janet. "Possessive Power." *Hypatia* 1 (1986): 103–20.

Hatcher, Donald L. "Existential Ethics and Why It's Immoral to Be a Housewife." *Journal of Values Inquiry* 23 (1989): 59–68.

Hollywood, Amy M. "Beauvoir, Irigaray, and the Mystical." *Hypatia* 9, no. 4 (1994): 158–85.

Langer, Monika. "A Philosophical Retrieval of Simone de Beauvoir's 'Pour Une Morale de l'amiguite.' " *Philosophy Today* 38, no. 2 (1994): 181–90.

Morgan, Kathryn Pauly. "Romantic Love, Altrusim, and Self-Respect." *Hypatia* 1, no. 1 (1986): 117–48.

Schutte, Ofelia. "A Critique of Normative Heterosexuality: Identity, Embodiment, and Sexual Difference in Beauvoir and Irigaray." *Hypatia* 12, no. 1 (1997): 40–62.

Seigfried, Charlene Haddock. " 'Second Sex': Second Thoughts." *Hypatia* in Women's Studies International Forum 3 (1985): 219–29.

Simons, Margaret A. "Two Interviews with Simone de Beauvoir." *Hypatia* 3 (1989): 11–27.

———. ed. *Feminist Interpretations of Simone de Beauvoir.* University Park: Pennsylvania State University Press, 1995.

Singer, Linda. "Interpretation and Retrieval: Rereading Beauvoir." *Hypatia* in Women's Studies International Forum 3 (1985): 231–38.

Tirrell, Lynne. "Definition and Power: Toward Authority without Privilege." *Hypatia* 8, no. 4 (1993): 1–34.

Blackwell, Antoinette Brown

Cazden, Elizabeth. *Antoinette Brown Blackwell.* New York: Feminist Press, 1983.

Deutscher, Penelope. "The Descent of Man and the Evolution of Woman." *Hypatia* 19, no. 2 (2004): 35–55.

Waithe, Mary Ellen, ed. *A History of Women Philosophers.* Vol. 3. Dordrecht: Kluwer, 1991.

Cavendish, Margaret

Merchant, Carolyn. *The Death of Nature: Women, Ecology, and the Scientific Revolution.* San Francisco: Harper and Row, 1980.

Schiebinger, Londa. *The Mind Has No Sex? Women in the Origins of Modern Science.* Cambridge, Mass.: Harvard University Press, 1989.

Thomas, Keith. *Man and the Natural World: A History of the Modern Sensibility.* New York: Pantheon Books, 1983.
Waithe, Mary Ellen, ed. *A History of Women Philosophers.* Vol. 3. Dordrecht: Kluwer, 1991.

Pizan, Christine de

Brabant, Margaret, ed. *Politics, Gender, and Genre: The Political Thought of Christine de Pizan.* Boulder, Colo.: Westview Press, 1992.
Green, Karen. "Christine de Pisan and Thomas Hobbes." In *Hypatia's Daughters,* ed. Linda Lopez McAlister. Indianapolis: Indiana University Press, 1996. 48–67.
Waithe, Mary Ellen, ed. *A History of Women Philosophers.* Vol. 2. Dordrecht: Kluwer, 1989.
Willard, Charity Cannon. *Christine de Pizan: Her Life and Works.* New York: Persea Books, 1984.

Coignet, Clarisse

Waithe, Mary Ellen, ed. *A History of Women Philosophers.* Vol. 3. Dordrecht: Kluwer, 1991.

Conway, Anne Finch

Duran, Jane. "Anne Viscountess Conway: A Seventeenth-Century Rationalist." In *Hypatia's Daughters,* ed. Linda Lopez McAlister. Indianapolis: Indiana University Press, 1996. 92–107.
Merchant, Carolyn. *The Death of Nature: Women, Ecology, and the Scientific Revolution.* San Francisco: Harper and Row, 1980.
Waithe, Mary Ellen, ed. *A History of Women Philosophers.* Vol. 3. Dordrecht: Kluwer, 1991.

Cooper, Anna Julia

Bailey, Cathryn. "Anna Julia Cooper: "Dedicated in the Name of My Slave Mother to the Education of Colored Working People." *Hypatia* 19, no. 2 (2004): 56–73.
May, Vivian M. "Thinking from the Margins, Acting at the Intersections: Anna Julia Cooper's *A Voice from the South.*" *Hypatia* 19, no. 2 (2004): 74–91.
Washington, Mary Helen. "An Introduction to *A Voice from the South.*" Chap. 2 in *Presenting Women Philosophers,* ed. Cecile Tougas and Sara Ebenreck. Philadelphia: Temple University Press, 2000.

Cruz, Sor Juana Inés de la

Beggs, Donald. "Sor Juana's Feminism from Aristotle to Irigaray. In *Hypatia's Daughters*, ed. Linda Lopez McAlister. Indianapolis: Indiana University Press, 1996. 108–27.

Paz, Octavio. *Sor Juana: Or, the Traps of Faith*. Cambridge, Mass.: Harvard University Press, 1988.

Waithe, Mary Ellen, ed. *A History of Women Philosophers*. Vol. 3. Dordrecht: Kluwer, 1991.

Daly, Mary

Frye, Marilyn, and Sarah Lucia Hoagland, eds. *Feminist Interpretations of Mary Daly*. University Park: Pennsylvania State University Press, 2000.

Derrida, Jacques

Armour, Ellen T. "Questions of Proximity: Woman's Place in Derrida and Irigaray." *Hypatia* 12, no. 1 (1997): 63–78.

Feder, Ellen K., et al., eds. *Derrida and Feminism: Recasting the Question of Woman*. New York: Routledge, 1997.

Holland, Nancy J., ed. *Feminist Interpretations of Jacques Derrida*. University Park: Pennsylvania State University Press, 1997.

Descartes, René

Amaros, Celia. "Cartesianism and Feminism: What Reason Has Forgotten; Reasons for Forgetting." *Hypatia* 9, no. 1 (1994): 147–63.

Atherton, Margaret. "Cartesian Reason and Gendered Reason." In *A Mind of One's Own: Feminist Essays on Reason and Objectivity*, ed. Louise Antony and Charlotte Witt. Boulder, Colo.: Westview Press, 1993. 21–37.

Bordo, Susan. *The Flight to Objectivity*. Albany: State University of New York Press, 1987.

———, ed. *Feminist Interpretations of René Descartes*. University Park: Pennsylvania State University Press, 1999.

Cantrell, Carol H. "Analogy as Destiny: Cartesian Man and the Woman Reader." *Hypatia* 5, no. 2 (1990): 7–19.

David, Anthony. "Le Doeuff and Irigaray on Descartes." *Philosophy Today* 41, nos. 3–4 (1997): 367–82.

Gatens, Moira. "Modern Rationalism." In *A Companion to Feminist Philosophy*, ed. Alison Jaggar and Iris Marion Young. Oxford: Blackwell, 1998. 21–29.

Hodge, Joanna. "Subject, Body, and the Exclusion of Women from Philosophy."

In *Feminist Perspectives in Philosophy*, ed. Morwenna Griffiths and Margaret Whitford. Bloomington: Indiana University Press, 1988. 152–68.

Scheman, Naomi. *Engenderings: Constructions of Knowledge, Authority, and Privilege.* New York: Routledge, 1993.

Thompson, J. "Women and the High Priests of Reason." *Radical Philosophy* 34 (Summer 1983): 10–13.

Elisabeth of Bohemia, Princess Palatine

Nye, Andrea. "Polity and Prudence: The Ethics of Elisabeth, Princess Palatine." In *Hypatia's Daughters*, ed. Linda Lopez McAlister. Indianapolis: Indiana University Press, 1996. 68–91.

———, ed. *The Princess and the Philosopher: Letters of Elisabeth of the Palatine to René Descartes.* Totowa, N.J.: Rowman and Littlefield, 1999.

Waithe, Mary Ellen, ed. *A History of Women Philosophers.* Vol. 3. Dordrecht: Kluwer, 1991.

Foucault, Michel

Butler, Judith. *Gender Trouble: Feminism and the Subversion of Identity.* New York: Routledge, 1990.

———. *Bodies That Matter: On the Discursive Limits of "Sex."* New York: Routledge, 1993.

Hekman, Susan J. *Feminist Interpretations of Michel Foucault.* University Park: Pennsylvania State University Press, 1996.

Gilman, Charlotte Perkins

Egan, Margaret L. "Evolutionary Theory in the Social Philosophy of Charlotte Perkins Gilman." In *Hypatia's Daughters*, ed. Linda Lopez McAlister. Indianapolis: Indiana University Press, 1996. 248–66.

Waithe, Mary Ellen, ed. *A History of Women Philosophers.* Vol. 4. Dordrecht: Kluwer, 1995.

Goldman, Emma

Solomon, Martha. *Emma Goldman.* Boston: Twayne Publishers, 1987.

Waithe, Mary Ellen, ed. *A History of Women Philosophers.* Vol. 4. Dordrecht: Kluwer, 1995.

Gouges, Olympe de

Groult, Benoite, ed. *Olympe de Gouges, Ouevres*. Paris: Mercure de France 1986.
Waithe, Mary Ellen, ed. *A History of Women Philosophers*. Vol. 3. Dordrecht: Kluwer, 1991.

Gournay, Marie le Jars de

Ilsley, Marjorie Henry. *A Daughter of the Renaissance*. The Hague, Neth.: Mouton, 1963.
Waithe, Mary Ellen, ed. *A History of Women Philosophers*. Vol. 2. Dordrecht: Kluwer, 1989.

Hildegard of Bingen

Allen, Prudence. *The Concept of Woman: The Aristotelian Revolution 750 BC–AD 1250*. Montreal, Eden Press, 1985.
John, Helen J. "Hildegard of Bingen: A New Medieval Philosopher?" *Hypatia* 7, no. 1 (1992): 115–123.
Waithe, Mary Ellen, ed. *A History of Women Philosophers*. Vol. 2. Dordrecht: Kluwer, 1989.

Hume, David

Baier, Annette. Good Men's Women: Hume on Chastity and Trust. *Hume Studies* 5 (April 1979): 1–19.
———. "Hume, the Women's Moral Theorist." In *Women and Moral Theory*, ed. Eva Kittay and Diana Tietjens Meyers. Savage, Md.: Rowman and Littlefield, 1987. 37–55.
———. *Moral Prejudices*. Cambridge, Mass.: Harvard University Press, 1994.
Bar On, Bat-Ami. "Could There Be a Humean Sex-Neutral General Idea of Man?" *Philosophy Research Archives* 13 (1987–1988): 367–77.
Battersby, Christine. "An Enquiry Concerning the Humean Woman." *Philosophy* 56 (July 1981): 303–12.
Burns, Steven. "The Humean Female." *Dialogue* 15 (1976): 415–24.
Immewahr, John. "David Hume, Sexism, and Sociobiology." *Southern Journal of Philosophy* 22 (Fall 1983): 359–70.
Jacobson, Anne Jaap, ed. *Feminist Interpretations of David Hume*. University Park: Pennsylvania State University Press, 2000.
Korsmeyer, Carolyn. "Hume and the Foundations of Taste." *Journal of Aesthetics and Art Criticism* 35 (Winter 1976): 201–15.

Levey, Ann. "Under Constraint: Chastity and Modesty in Hume." *Hume Studies* 23 (November 1997): 213–26.

Marcil-Lacoste, Louise. "The Consistency of Hume's Position on Women." *Dialogue* 15 (1976): 425–40.

Sapp, Vicki J. "The Philosopher's Seduction: Hume and the Fair Sex." *Philosophy and Literature* 19 (April 1995): 1–15.

Irigaray, Luce

Grosz, Elizabeth. *Sexual Subversions: Three French Feminists*. Sydney: Allen and Unwin, 1989.

Whitford, Margaret. *Luce Irigaray: Philosophy in the Feminine*. New York: Routledge, 1991.

Kant, Immanuel

Blum, Lawrence. "Kant's and Hegel's Moral Rationalism: A Feminist Perspective." *Canadian Journal of Philosophy* 2, no. 2 (1982): 95–110.

Dillon, Robin. "Toward a Feminist Conception of Self-Respect." *Hypatia* 7, no. 1 (1992): 52–69.

Gowans, Christopher W. "After Kant: Ventures in Morality Without Respect for Persons." *Social Theory and Practice* 22, no. 1 (1996): 105–29.

Herman, Barbara. "Could It Be Worth Thinking About Kant on Sex and Marriage?" In *A Mind of One's Own: Feminist Essays on Reason and Objectivity*, ed. Louise Antony and Charlotte Witt. Boulder, Colo.: Westview Press, 1993. 53–72.

Holland, Nancy. *The Madwoman's Dream: The Concept of the Appropriate in Ethical Thought*. University Park: Pennsylvania State University Press, 1998.

Hutchings, Kimberly. *Kant, Critique, and Politics*. New York: Routledge, 1996.

Jauch, Ursula Pia. *Immanuel Kant zur Geschlechterdifferenz*. Vienna: Passagen, 1989.

Kneller, Jane. "Discipline and Silence: Women and Imagination in Kant's Theory of Taste." In *Aesthetics in Feminist Perspective*, ed. Hilde Hein. Bloomington: Indiana University Press, 1993. 179–92.

Kofman, Sarah. "The Economy of Respect: Kant and Respect for Women." *Social Research* 49, no. 2 (1982): 383–404.

Moscovici, Claudia. *From Sex Objects to Sexual Subjects*. New York: Routledge, 1996.

Okin, Susan Moller. "Reason and Feeling in Thinking about Justice." *Ethics* 99 (1989): 229–49.

Piper, Adrian M. S. "Xenophobia and Kantian Rationalism." *Philosophical Forum* 24, nos. 1–3 (1992–1993): 188–232.

Schott, Robin May. *A Feminist Critique of the Kantian Paradigm*. University Park: Pennsylvania State University Press, 1993.

―――, ed. *Feminist Interpretations of Immanuel Kant*. University Park: Pennsylvania State University Press, 1997.

Sedgwick, Sally. "Can Kant's Ethics Survive the Feminist Critique?" *Pacific Philosophical Quarterly* 71, no. 1 (1990): 60–79.

Wiseman, Mary Bittner. "Beautiful Exiles in Aesthetics." In *Aesthetics in Feminist Perspective*, ed. Hilde Hein. Bloomington: Indiana University Press, 1993. 169–78.

Zweig, Arnulf. "Kant and the Family." In *Kindred Matters*, ed. Diana Tietjens Meyers. Ithaca, N.Y.: Cornell University, Press, 1993. 289–305.

Gottfried Wilhelm, Leibniz

Gatens, Moira. "Modern Rationalism." In *A Companion to Feminist Philosophy*, ed. Alison Jaggar and Iris Marion Young. Oxford: Blackwell, 1998. 21–29.

Merchant, Carolyn. *The Death of Nature: Women, Ecology, and the Scientific Revolution*. San Francisco: Harper and Row, 1980.

Macaulay, Catharine

Gardner, Catherine. "Catharine Macaulay's 'Letters on Education': Odd but Equal." *Hypatia* 13, no. 1 (1998): 118–37.

Hill, Bridget. *The Republican Virago: The Life and Times of Catharine Macaulay, Historian*. Oxford: Clarendon Press, 1992.

Waithe, Mary Ellen, ed. *A History of Women Philosophers*. Vol. 3. Dordrecht: Kluwer, 1991.

Makin, Bathsua Pell

Waithe, Mary Ellen, ed. *A History of Women Philosophers*. Vol. 3. Dordrecht: Kluwer, 1991.

Masham, Damaris Cudworth

Frankel, Lois. "Damaris Dudworth Masham: A Seventeenth Century Feminist Philosopher." *Hypatia* 4 (1989): 80–90.

Waithe, Mary Ellen, ed. *A History of Women Philosophers*. Vol. 3. Dordrecht: Kluwer, 1991.

Mill, John Stuart

Annas, Julia. "Mill and the Subjection of Women." *Philosophy* 52 (1977): 179–94.

Burgess Jackson, Keith. "John Stuart Mill, Radical Feminist." *Social Theory and Practice* 21, no. 3 (1995): 389–96.

Donner, Wendy. "John Stuart Mill's Liberal Feminism." *Philosophical Studies* 69, nos. 2–3 (1993): 155–66.

Goldstein, Leslie. "Mill, Marx, and Women's Liberation." *Journal of the History of Philosophy* 18, no. 3 (July 1980): 319–34.

Himmelfarb, Gertrude. *On Liberty and Liberalism: The Case of John Stuart Mill.* New York: Knopf, 1974.

Howes, John. "Mill on Women and Human Development." *Australasian Journal of Philosophy* Supp. 64 (1986): 66–74.

Knight, Jamie K. "With Liberty and Justice for Some." *International Journal of Applied Philosophy* 2 (1984): 85–90.

Mahowald, Mary B. "Against Paternalism: A Developmental View." *Philosophy Research Archives* 6, no. 1386 (1980).

———. "Freedom versus Happiness, and 'Women's Lib,' " *Journal of Social Philosophy* 6 (1975): 10–13.

Mendus, Susan. "John Stuart Mill and Harriet Taylor on Women and Marriage." *Utilitas* 6, no. 2 (1994): 287–99.

Morales, Maria H. *Perfect Equality: John Stuart Mill on Well-Constituted Communities.* Lanham, Md.: Rowman and Littlefield, 1996.

Okin, Susan. *Women in Western Political Thought.* Princeton, N.J.: Princeton University Press, 1979.

Pyle, Andrew, ed. *"The Subjection of Women": Contemporary Responses to John Stuart Mill.* Bristol, U.K.: Thoemmes Press, 1995.

Ring, Jennifer. "Mill's *The Subjection of Women*: The Methodological Limits of Liberal Feminism." *Review of Politics* 47, no. 1 (1985): 27–44.

Rossi, Alice, ed. *Essays on Sex Equality.* Chicago: University of Chicago Press, 1970.

Shanley, Mary L. "Marital Slavery and Friendship: John Stuart Mill's *The Subjection of Women*." *Political Theory* 9, no. 2 (1981): 229–47.

Tulloch, Gail. "Mill's Epistemology in Practice in his Liberal Feminism." *Educational Philosophy and Theory* 21, no. 2 (1989): 32–39.

Nietzsche, Friedrich

Ainley, Alison. "Ideal Selfishness: Nietzsche's Metaphor of Maternity." In *Exceedingly Nietzsche*, ed. David Farrell Krell. London: Routledge, 1988. 116–30.

Bergoffen, Debra B. "Nietzsche Was No Feminist." *International Studies in Philosophy* 26, no. 3 (1994): 23–31.

———. "On the Advantage and Disadvantage of Nietzsche for Women." In *The*

Question of the Other, ed. Arleen B. Dallery. Albany: State University of New York Press, 1989. 77–88.

Booth, David. "Nietzsche's 'Woman' Rhetoric." *History of Philosophy Quarterly* 8, no. 3 (1991): 311–25.

Diprose, Rosalyn. "Nietzsche, Ethics, and Sexual Difference." *Radical Philosophy* 52 (1989): 27–33.

Graybeal, Jean. *Language and "the Feminine" in Nietzsche and Heidegger.* Bloomington: Indiana University Press, 1990.

Higgins, Kathleen Marie. "Gender in *The Gay Science*." *Philosophy and Literature* 19, no. 2 (1995): 227–47.

Irigaray, Luce. *Marine Lover of Friedrich Nietzsche.* Trans. Gillian C. Gill. New York: Columbia University Press, 1991.

Johnson, Pauline. "Nietzsche's Reception Today." *Radical Philosophy* 80 (1996): 24–33.

Lorraine, Tamsin. "Nietzsche and Feminism: Transvaluing Women in *Thus Spoke Zarathustra*." *International Studies in Philosophy* 26, no. 3 (1994): 13–21.

Oliver, Kelly, and Marilyn Pearsall, eds. *Feminist Interpretations of Friedrich Nietzsche.* University Park: Pennsylvania State University Press, 1998.

Pasons, Katherine Pyne. "Nietzsche and Moral Change." *Feminist Studies* 2 (1974): 57–76.

Schutte, Ofelia. *Beyond Nihilism: Nietzsche without Masks.* Chicago: University of Chicago Press, 1984.

Plato

Allen, Christine Garside. "Plato on Women." *Feminist Studies* 2, nos. 2–3 (1975): 131–38.

Annas, Julia. "Plato's *Republic* and Feminism." *Philosophy* 51 (1976): 307–21.

Bluestone, Natalie Harris. *Women and the Ideal Society: Plato's* Republic *and Modern Myths of Gender.* Amherst: University of Massachusetts Press, 1987.

Bowery, Anne-Marie. "Diotima Tells a Story: A Narrative Analysis of Plato's *Symposium*." In *Feminist and Ancient Philosophy*, ed. Julie K. Ward. New York: Routledge, 1996.

Dickason, Anne. "Anatomy and Destiny: The Role of Biology in Plato's Views of Women." *Philosophical Forum* 5, nos. 1–2 (1973–1974): 45–53.

Freeman, Barbara. "(Re)writing Patriarchal Texts: *The Symposium*." In *Postmodernism and Continental Philosophy*, ed. Hugh J. Silverman and D. Welton. Albany: State University of New York Press, 1988.

Gardner, Catherine. "The Remnants of the Family: The Role of Women and Eugenics in *Republic V.*" *History of Philosophy Quarterly* 17, no. 3 (July 2000): 217–35.

Genova, Judith. "Feminist Dialectics: Plato and Dualism." In *Engendering Origins*, ed. Bat-Ami Bar On. Albany: State University of New York Press, 1994.

Hawthorne, Susan. "Diotima Speaks through the Body." In *Engendering Origins*, ed. Bat-Ami Bar On. Albany: State University of New York Press, 1994.

Joo, Maria. "The Platonic 'Eros' and Its Feminist Interpretations." *Magyar Filozófiai Szemle* 1, nos. 2–3 (1996): 1–30.

Lange, Lynda. "The Function of Equal Education in Plato's *Republic* and *Laws*." In *The Sexism of Social and Political Theory*, ed. L. Clark and L. Lange. Toronto: University of Toronto Press, 1979.

Levin, Susan B. "Women's Nature and Role in the Ideal Polis: *Republic V* Revisited." In *Feminist and Ancient Philosophy*, ed. Julie K. Ward. New York: Routledge, 1996.

Lovibond, Sabina. "An Ancient Theory of Gender: Plato and the Pythagorean Table." In *Women in Ancient Societies*, ed. Archer, Fischler, and Wyke. London, Routledge, 1994.

Okin, Susan Moller. "Philosopher Queens and Private Wives: Plato on Women and the Family." *Philosophy and Public Affairs* 6 (1977): 345–69.

———. *Women in Western Political Thought*. Princeton, N.J.: Princeton University Press, 1979.

Osbourne, Martha Lee. "Plato's Unchanging View of Woman: A Denial That Anatomy Spells Destiny." *Philosophical Forum* 6 (Summer 1975): 447–52.

Pierce, Christine. "Equality: *Republic V*." *Monist* 57 (January 1973): 1–11.

———. "Eros and Epistemology." In *Engendering Origins*, ed. Bat-Ami Bar On. Albany: State University of New York Press, 1994.

Pomeroy, Sarah. "Feminism in Book V of Plato's *Republic*." *Apeiron* 8, no. 1 (1974): 33–35.

Saxenhouse, Arlene W. "Eros and the Female in Greek Political Thought: An Interpretation of Plato's *Symposium*." *Political Theory* 12 (1984): 5–27.

Smith, Nicholas. "The Logic of Plato's Feminism." *Journal of Social Philosophy* 11 (1980): 5–11.

Tress, Daryl McGowan. "Relations in Plato's *Timaeus*." *Journal of Neoplatonic Studies* 3 (1994): 93–139.

Tuana, Nancy ed. *Feminist Interpretations of Plato*. University Park: Pennsylvania State University Press, 1994.

Rand, Ayn

Goldstein, Mimi Reisel, and Chris Matthews Sciabarra, eds. *Feminist Interpretations of Ayn Rand*. University Park: Pennsylvania State University Press, 1991.

Waithe, Mary Ellen, ed. *A History of Women Philosophers*. Vol. 4. Dordrecht: Kluwer, 1995.

Rousseau, Jean-Jacques

Bloch, M., and J. H. Bloch. "Women and the Dialectics of Nature in Eighteenth Century French Thought." In *Nature, Culture, and Gender*, ed. C. MacCormack and M. Strathern. Cambridge: Cambridge University Press, 1980. 25–41.

Fernon, Nicole. *Domesticating Passions: Rousseau, Women, and Nation.* Hanover, N.H.: University Press of New England, 1997.

Gatens, Moira. "Rousseau and Wollstonecraft: Nature vs. Reason." *Australasian Journal of Philosophy* Supp. 64 (1986): 1–15.

Green, Karen. "Rousseau's Women." *International Journal of Philosophical Studies* 4, no. 1 (1996): 87–109.

Kofman, Sarah. *Le respect des femmes: (Kant et Rousseau).* Paris: Editions Galilee, 1982.

Lange, Lynda. "Rousseau: Women and the General Will." In *The Sexism of Social and Political Theory*, ed. Lorenne Clark and Lynda Lange. Toronto: Toronto University Press, 1979. 41–52.

———, ed. *Feminist Interpretations of Jean-Jacques Rousseau.* University Park: Pennsylvania State University Press, 2002.

Lloyd, Genevieve. "Rousseau on Reason, Nature, and Women." *Metaphilosophy* 14, nos. 3–4 (1983): 308–26.

Martin, Jane. "Sophie and Emile: A Case Study of Sex Bias in the History of Educational Thought." *Harvard Educational Review* 51, no. 3 (1981): 357–71.

Pateman, Carole. " 'The Disorder of Women': Women, Love, and the Sense of Justice." *Ethics* 91 (1980): 20–31.

Rapaport, Elizabeth. "On the Future of Love: Rousseau and the Radical Feminists." *Philosophical Forum* 5, nos. 1–2 (1973–1974): 185–205.

Schwartz, Joel. *The Sexual Politics of Jean-Jacques Rousseau.* Chicago: University of Chicago Press, 1984.

Weiss, Penny A. "Rousseau, Antifeminism, and Women's Nature." *Political Theory* 15, no. 1 (1987): 81–98.

———. *Gendered Community: Rousseau, Sex, and Politics.* New York: New York University Press, 1993.

Zerilli, Linda. *Signifying Woman: Culture and Chaos in Rousseau, Burke, and Mill.* Ithaca, N.Y.: Cornell University Press, 1994.

Sartre, Jean-Paul

Barnes, Hazel E. "Sartre and Sexism." *Philosophy and Literature* (1990): 340–47.

Bergoffen, Debra B. "The Look as Bad Faith." *Philosophy Today* 36, no. 3 (1992): 221–27.

Collins, Margery, and Christine Pierce. "Holes and Slime: Sexism in Sartre's Psychoanalysis." In *Women and Philosophy: Toward a Theory of Liberation*, ed. Carol Gould and Marx X. Wartofsky. New York: G. P. Putnam's Sons, 1976. 112–27.

Fullbrook, Kate, and Edward Fullbrook. "Sartre's Secret Key." In *Feminist Interpretations of Simone de Beauvoir*, ed. Margaret A. Simons. University Park: Pennsylvania State University Press, 1995. 97–111.

Kruks, Sonia. "Simone de Beauvoir: Teaching Sartre about Freedom." In *Sartre Alive*, ed. R. Aronsen and A. van den Hoven. Detroit: Wayne State Press, 1991. 285–300.

Mui, Constance. "Sartre's Sexism Reconsidered." *Auslegung* 16, no. 1 (1990): 31–41.

Murphy, Julien S. "The Look in Sartre and Rich." *Hypatia* 2 (1987): 113–24.

———, ed. *Feminist Interpretations of Jean-Paul Sartre*. University Park: Pennsylvania State University Press, 1999.

Schurman, Anna Maria Van

Waithe, Mary Ellen, ed. *A History of Women Philosophers*. Vol. 3. Dordrecht: Kluwer, 1991.

Sophia

Waithe, Mary Ellen, ed. *A History of Women Philosophers*. Vol. 3. Dordrecht: Kluwer, 1991.

Benedict (Baruch) de Spinoza

Gatens, Moira. "Feminism as 'Password': Rethinking the 'Possible' with Spinoza and Deleuze." *Hypatia* 15, no. 2 (2000): 59–75.

James, Susan. "The Power of Spinoza: Feminist Conjunctions." Interview with Genevieve Lloyd and Moira Gatens. *Hypatia* 15, no. 2 (2000): 40–58.

Taylor Mill, Harriet

Jacobs, Jo Ellen. "Harriet Taylor Mill's Collaboration with John Stuart Mill." In *Presenting Women Philosophers*, ed. Cecile Tougas and Sara Ebenreck. Philadelphia: Temple University Press, 2000. 155–66.

Mendus, Susan. "John Stuart Mill and Harriet Taylor on Women and Marriage." *Utilitas* 6, no. 2 (1994): 287–99.

Pappe, H. O. *John Stuart Mill and the Harriet Taylor Myth*. New York: Cambridge University Press, 1962.

Rossi, Alice, ed. *Essays on Sex Equality*. Chicago: University of Chicago Press, 1970.

Waithe, Mary Ellen, ed. *A History of Women Philosophers*. Vol. 3. Dordrecht: Kluwer, 1991.

Wheeler, Anna Doyle

McFadden, Margaret. "Anna Doyle Wheeler (1785–1848): Philosopher, Socialist, Feminist." In *Hypatia's Daughters*, ed. Linda Lopez McAlister. Indianapolis: Indiana University Press, 1996. 204–14.

Waithe, Mary Ellen, ed. *A History of Women Philosophers*. Vol. 3. Dordrecht: Kluwer, 1991.

Wittgenstein, Ludwig

Davidson, Joyce, and Mick Smith. "Wittgenstein and Irigaray: Gender and Philosophy in a Language (Game) of Difference." *Hypatia* 14, no. 2 (1999): 72–96.

Lampshire, Wendy Lee. "History as Genealogy: Wittgenstein and the Feminist Deconstruction of Objectivity." *Philosophy and Theology* (1991): 313–31.

———. "Decisions of Identity: Feminist Subjects and Grammars of Sexuality." *Hypatia* 10, no. 4 (1995): 32–45.

———. "Women—Animals—Machines: A Grammar for a Wittgensteinian Ecofeminism." *Journal of Value Inquiry* 29, no. 1 (1995): 89–101.

Martin, Bill. "*To the Lighthouse* and the Feminist Path to Postmodernity." *Philosophy and Literature* 13 (1989): 307–15.

Orr, Deborah. "On Logic and Moral Voice." *Informal Logic* 17, no. 3 (1995): 347–63.

Scheman, Naomi, and Peg O'Connor, eds. *Feminist Interpretations of Wittgenstein*. University Park: Pennsylvania State University Press, 2002.

Wollstonecraft, Mary

Barker-Benfield, G. J. "Mary Wollstonecraft: Eighteenth-Century Commonwealthwoman." *Journal of the History of Ideas* 50 (1989): 95–115.

Brody, Miriam. "Mary Wollstonecraft: Sexuality and Women's Rights." In *Feminist Theories*, ed. Dale Spender. London: Women's Press, 1983.

Disch, Lisa. "Claire Loves Julie: Reading the Story of Women's Friendship in *La Nouvelle Heloise*." *Hypatia* 9, no. 3 (1994): 19–45.

Falco, Maria J., ed. *Feminist Interpretations of Mary Wollstonecraft*. University Park: Pennsylvania State University Press, 1996.

Gatens, Moira. "Rousseau and Wollstonecraft: Nature vs. Reason." *Australasian Journal of Philosophy* Supp. 64 (1986): 1–15.

Grimshaw, Jean. "Mary Wollstonecraft and the Tensions in Feminist Philosophy." *Radical Philosophy* 52 (1989): 11–17.

Gubar, Susan. "Feminist Misogyny: Mary Wollstonecraft and the Paradox of 'It Takes One to Know One.'" *Feminist Studies* 20, no. 3 (1994): 453–73.

Larson, Elizabeth. "Mary Wollstonecraft and Women's Rights." *Free Inquiry* 12, no. 2 (1992): 45–48.

Mackenzie, Catriona. "Reason and Sensibility: The Ideal of Women's Self-Governance in the Writings of M. Wollstonecraft." In *Hypatia's Daughters*, ed. Linda Lopez McAlister. Bloomington: Indiana University Press, 1996. 181–203.

McCrystal, John. "Revolting Women: The Use of Revolutionary Discourse in Mary Astell and Mary Wollstonecraft Compared." *History of Political Thought* 14, no. 2 (1993): 189–203.

Sabrosky, Judith A. *From Rationality to Liberation.* Westport, Conn.: Greenwood Press, 1979.

Sapiro, Virginia. *A Vindication of Political Virtue.* Chicago: University of Chicago Press, 1992.

Waithe, Mary Ellen, ed. *A History of Women Philosophers.* Vol. 3. Dordrecht: Kluwer, 1991.

About the Author

Catherine Villanueva Gardner studied as an undergraduate at the University of Leicester in the United Kingdom and earned an M.A. at the University College of Swansea in Wales. She received her Ph.D. from the University of Virginia and is an associate professor in philosophy at the University of Massachusetts, Dartmouth, where she teaches for the Department of Philosophy and for the Women's Studies program. A member of the board of the Society for the Study of Women Philosophers, she has served as a newsletter editor for the society. Her publications include *Women Philosophers: Genre and the Boundaries of Philosophy* (2003), an examination of forgotten women philosophers and the reasons for their disappearance. She has published various articles on ecofeminism and feminist history of philosophy, including "Heaven Appointed Educators of Mind: Catharine Beecher and the Moral Power of Women" and "The Remnants of the Family: The Role of Women and Eugenics in *Republic V*" on canon revision; and "An Ecofeminist Perspective on the Urban Environment" on feminist theory. She is currently writing a book on feminist history of philosophy.